S0-FJW-614

DEATH, GRIEF AND BEREAVEMENT II

A Bibliography
1975-1980

DEATH, GRIEF AND BEREAVEMENT II

A Bibliography
1975-1980

Compiled by
ROBERT FULTON

in collaboration with
MARGARET R. REED

with the assistance of
JOYCE H. THIELEN

ARNO PRESS

A New York Times Company
New York • 1981

25.00 Net

First Publication 1981 by Arno Press Inc.

Manufactured in the United States of America

Library of Congress Cataloging in Publication Data

Fulton, Robert Lester.
A bibliography on death, grief, and bereavement II, 1975-1980.

Continues: Death, grief, and bereavement.
1. Death--Bibliography. 2. Grief--Bibliography. 3. Bereavement--Bibliography. I. Reed, Margaret R. II. Thielen, Joyce H. III. Fulton, Robert Lester. Death, grief, and bereavement. IV. Title.
Z5725.F854 [BD444] 016.128'5 81-1368
ISBN 0-405-14212-9 AACR2

INTRODUCTION

The publication of this first supplement to the bibliography Death, Grief and Bereavement 1845-1975 spans the years 1975 to 1980 and reflects by its size the ever increasing interest in the field of Thanatology. The present volume contains more than 2300 items. The initial bibliography, covering a period of over 125 years, listed 3856 entries. Table 1 illustrates this dramatic growth.

The increase in the publication of books and articles on death-related topics has been accompanied by a comparable rise in courses on thanatology related topics in high schools, colleges and universities across the country. Within the preceeding five years, moreover, three new journals, devoted specifically to the field of death and dying, have made their appearance. "Death Education" under the editorship of Hannelore Wass, Center for Gerontological Programs and Studies, University of Florida; "Essence" under the editorship of Stephen Flemming and Richard Lonetto, Departments of Psychology, York University and University of Guelph, Ontario, Canada, respectively; and "Thanatos" under the editorship of Noranel Neely of the Florida Consumer Information Bureau of St. Petersburg.

The journals together with the increasingly active associations such as the "Foundation of Thanatology", the "Forum for Death Education and Research", the "National Hospice Organization", and the "International Work Group on Death, Grief and Bereavement",to name a few, now provide a more solid basis for research, communication as well as therapeutic intervention in this burgeoning field.

In keeping with the goal of the bibliography to facilitate research and communication, I am pleased to include in the supplement Dr. Joseph Santora's "Guide to Doctoral Dissertations on Death and Dying, 1970-1978". I would like to take this opportunity to thank him for permission to include his bibliography in this publication.

Dr. Santora's bibliography provides us with a valuable reference and guide to the academic work that has been done in the field of Thanatology during the 1970's. It provides us, also, with some unexpected insights. A content analysis of his bibliography shows not only that well-recognized and traditional concerns are addressed, such as suicide, but it shows us also that some glaring gaps still remain in our efforts to study sensitive and salient issues. It is important to note, for example, that while Dr. Santora lists 80 dissertations on suicide, there is thus far no research reported on the hospice movement, and only two studies listed on widowhood.

It is of some sociological interest also to observe that despite the concerns that the American public as well as the Federal Trade Commission have expressed regarding contemporary funeral practices over the past decade, no scholar has seen fit to look objectively and systematically into our contemporary funeral customs. Present day funeral practices represent an important area of study that is of concern to us all; it is hoped that the light of academic scholarship will soon be brought to bear on this cloudy and contentious issue as well.

The main body of the supplement also shows certain tendencies and developments in the literature that, while not of any statistical merit, do provide some indication as to the direction the field of Thanatology may be taking. There will be found in this issue of the bibliography, for instance, an unprecedented number of articles and books on the hospice movement, reflecting the rapid acceptance of this program of terminal care throughout the country. The reader will also find increasing interest in the topics of euthanasia, disaster, abortion, and capital punishment as well as greater attention to the topics of immortality, parapsychology and survival-after-death. On the other hand, a decrease can be observed in the number of publications dealing with funerals, mourning customs, pastoral care, religion, terminal care ethics and existentialism.

It will be interesting to see what the next five years will bring to the field.

As before, no special effort has been made to include foreign references. Books and articles, however, that have come to my attention or are available in translation have generally been included.

In an ongoing project such as this, errors of omission and commission will and do occur. I appreciate those friends and colleagues who have and will bring such errors to my attention.

I would like to thank Karl Krohn, Mardag Fellow, Center for Death Education and Research, and Cindy Medina, graduate student, Department of Sociology, for their cooperation, and Chris Papesh for her secretarial assistance in the preparation of this edition of the bibliography.

Robert Fulton
Center for Death Education and Research
University of Minnesota

October 14, 1980

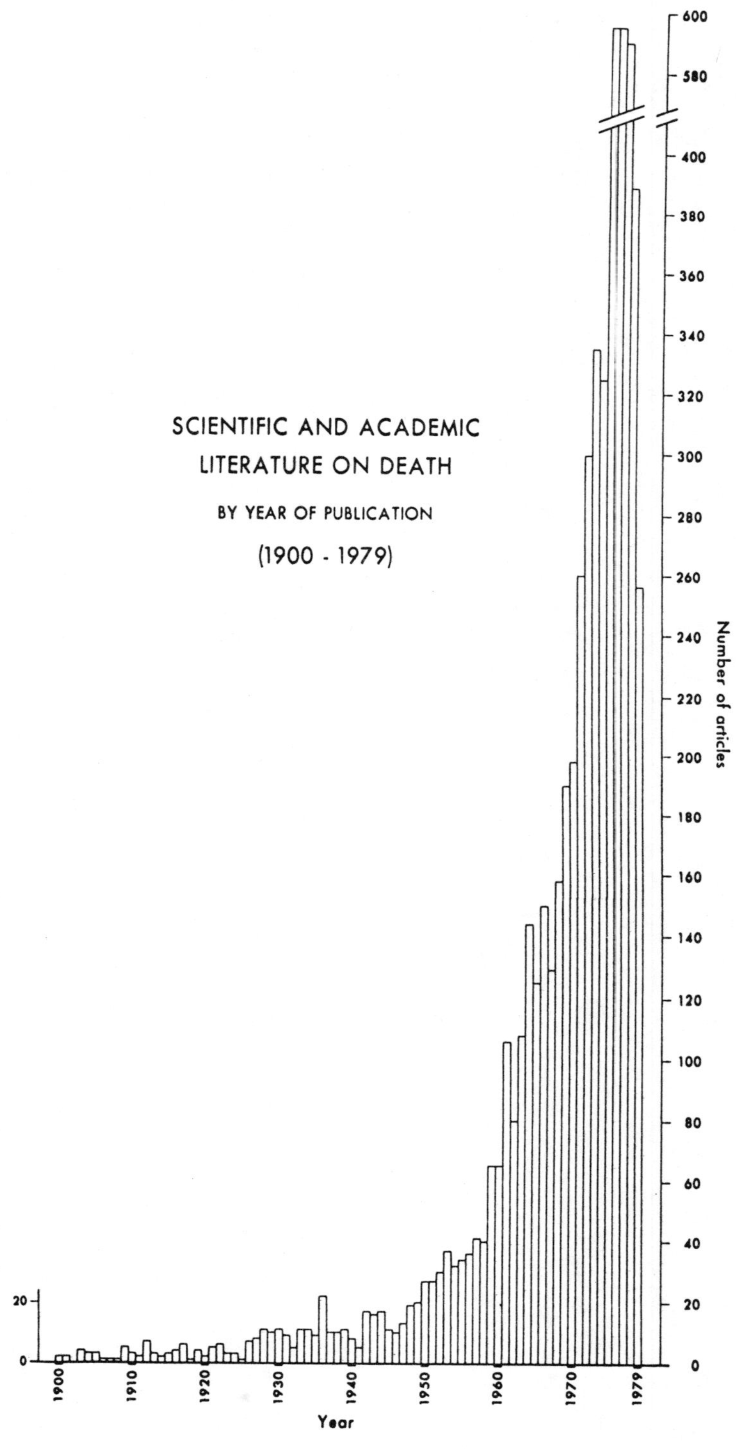

SCIENTIFIC AND ACADEMIC
LITERATURE ON DEATH
BY YEAR OF PUBLICATION
(1900 - 1979)
Number of articles
Year
0
20
40
60
80
100
120
140
160
180
200
220
240
260
280
300
320
340
360
380
400
580
600
1900
1910
1920
1930
1940
1950
1960
1970
1979

3857. Abrahamson, H. The Origin of Death: Studies in African Mythology. New York: Arno Press, 1976. (Orig. Pub. 1951).

3858. Abram, H.S. "Death and Denial in Conrad's 'The Nigger of the Narcissus'," Omega, 7:2 (1976), 125-135.

3859. _______. "Death and Dying in Camus' The Plague," Suicide and Life Threatening Behavior, 3 (Fall, 1973), 184-190.

3860. _______. "Death Psychology, Science Fiction and the Writings of Stanley G. Weinbaum," Suicide and Life Threatening Behavior, 5:2 (Summer, 1975),

3861. Abramson, J. "Facing the Other Fact of Life: Death in Recent Children's Fiction," School Library Journal, 21:4 (December, 1974), 31-33.

3862. Abramson, R. "A Dying Patient: The Question of Euthanasia," International Journal of Psychiatry and Medicine, 6:3 (1975), 431-454.

3863. Achte, K. "Death and Ancient Finnish Culture," Omega, 7:3 (1976), 249-259.

3864. Ackerman, A. "The Death of Frank," Occupational Health Nursing, 25:10 (October, 1977), 24-25.

3865. Ackerman, T.F. "Death With Dignity, Legislation in South Carolina: An Appraisal," Journal of South Carolina Medical Association, 73:8 (August, 1977), 364-366.

3866. Adamchak, D.J. "Trends in the Relationship Between Infant Mortality and Socioeconomic Status: 1950-1970," Sociological Focus, 11 (January, 1978), 47-52.

3867. Adamek, R.J. "It Has Happened Here," Human Life Review, 3 (Fall, 1977), 74-85.

3868. Adams, G.R. et al. "Contemporary Views of Euthanasia: A Regional Assessment: Social Biology, 25 (Spring, 1978), 62-68.

3869. Adams, J.R., D.R. Mader. Autopsy. London: Lloyd-Luke, 1976.

3870. Adams, J.R. The Sting of Death: Background for Reading for a Study Course on Death and Bereavement. New York: Seaburn Press, 1971.

3871. Adams, R. et al. "Informing the Individual of Impending Death - Yes or No," New Zealand Nursing Journal, 71 (October, 1978), 12-15.

3872. Adatto, I.J. "The Ethics of Caring for the Dying," Sh'ma, 7 (January, 1977), 51-52.

3873. Adler, C.S. et al, (eds). We Are But a Moment's Sunlight: Understanding Death. New York: Pocket Books, 1976.

3874. Adler, N.E. "Abortion - Social Psychological Perspective," Journal of Social Issues, 35 (1979), 100-119.

3875. Adrian, L.L., W.C. Fuller. "Grief: A Case Report," South Dakota Journal of Medicine, 30:4 (April, 1977), 81-83.

3876. Agate, J. "Let Me Go In Peace," Documentation in Medical Ethics, 5 (1975), 5.

3877. Agich, G.J. The Concepts of Death and Embodiment," Ethics in Science and Medicine, 3:2 (July, 1976), 95-105.

3878. __________. "The Ethics of Terminal Care," Death Education, 2 (Spring-Summer, 1978), 163-170.

3879. Agnew, L.R. "Of Grasshoppers, Figs and Death," British Medical Journal, 1 (April, 1979), 1053-1055.

3880. __________. "Therapy Through a Death Ritual," Social Work, 21:1 (June, 1976), 49-54.

3881. Aimard, G. et al. "Death or Absence of Father. Its Role in the Genesis of Psychotic Process Happening Between 15 and 25 years." Nouvelle Presse Medicale (Paris), 5 (28 August - 4 September, 1976), 1739-1742.

3882. Aires, P. et al. Death in America. Philadelphia: University of Pennsylvania Press, 1975.

3883. Alden, H.M. A Study of Death. Saint Clair Shores, MI: Scholarly Press, 1976.

3884. Alden, T. A Collection of American Epitaphs and Inscriptions With Occasional Notes. New York: Arno Press, 1976. (Orig. Pub. 1814)

3885. Alderson, M. "Relationship Between Month of Birth and Month of Death in the Elderly," British Journal of Preventive and Social Medicine, 29:3 (September, 1975), 151-156.

3886. Aldwinckle, R.F. Death in the Secular City. London: Allen and Unwin, 1972.

3887. Alexander, C.S. "Sudden Infant Death, Long Q-T Interval and Long Q.Y. Syndrome Letter," American Journal of Medicine, 62:1 (January, 1977), 164.

3888. Alexander, P., M.D. "A Psychotherapist's Reaction to His Patient's Death," Suicide and Life-Threatening Behavior, 7:4 (Winter, 1977), 203-210.

3889. Allen, S.S., R.V. Heckel. "Death Fantasies and Future Time Perspective," Journal of Clinical Psychology, 34:2 (April, 1978), 419-420.

3890. Allentuck, Andrew. The Cost of Age. Toronto: Fitzhenry & Whiteside, 1977.

3891. Almansi, R.J. "Fear of Death, Acting Out and The Psychology of Action," Psychoanalytic Quarterly, 48 (1979), 360-361.

3892. Alsofrom, J. "The Hospice Way of Dying - At Home With Friends and Family," American Medical News, 20 (1977), 7-9.

3893. Amado, A. et al. "Cost of Terminal Care: Home Hospice vs. Hospital," Nursing Outlook, (August, 1979), 522-526.

3894. Amelsvoort, V.V. "Thanatomania in an Asmat Community. A Report of Successful 'Western' Treatment," Tropical and Geographical Medicine, 28:3 (September, 1976), 244-248.

3895. Ammon, G. "The National Institute for the Care of the Seriously Ill and Dying," Fortschritte Medicine, 95:9 (March 3, 1977), 529-530.

3896. Ammon, G., F. Nicholas. "Death and Identity," The Human Context, 7 (Spring 1979), 94-102.

3897. Amulree, L. et al. On Dying Well: An Anglican Contribution to the Debate on Euthanasia. London. Church Information Office, 1975.

3898. Amundsen, D.W. "The Physician's Obligation to Prolong Life: A Medical Duty Without Classical Roots," Hastings Center Report, 8 (August, 1978), 23-30.

3899. Anders, R.I. "Death and Dying- Its The Coming Thing," Journal of Continuing Education for Nurses, 5:5 (September-October, 1974), 45-48.

3900. Andersen, R.S. "Operation Honecoming: Psychological Observations of Repatriated Vietnam Prisoners of War," Psychiatry, 38:1 (February, 1975), 65-74.

3901. Anderson, N. Issues of Life and Death: Abortion, Birth Control, Capital Punishment and Euthanasia. Downers Grove: InterVarsity Press, 1977.

3902. ________. "The Prolongation of Life, Transplant Surgery, Euthanasia and Suicide," in: Issues of Life and Death: Abortion, Birth Control, Capital Punishment and Euthanasia. Downers Grove: InterVarsity Press, 1977. 85-107.

3903. Angeli, N. "The Dark Side of Nursing: Special Skills for Special Patients," Nursing Mirror, 148 (April, 1979), 17-18.

3904. Angelica, D.M. "A Comparative Study of Attitudes Toward and Denial of Their Own Death of Episcopal Clergymen and Laymen in Connecticut," Dissertation Abstracts International, 37 (March, 1977), 4661.

3905. Anger, D., D.W. Anger. "Dialysis Ambivalence: A Matter of Life and Death," American Journal of Nursing, 76:2 (February, 1976), 276-277.

3906. Annas, G.J. "After Saikewicz: No-Fault Death," Hastings Center Report, 8 (June, 1978), 16-18.

3907. ________. "The Incompetent's Right to Die: The Case of Joseph Saikewicz," Hastings Center Report, 8 (February, 1978), 21-23.

3908. Anspaugh, D.J. "The Hospice: Advocate For the Dying," Health Education, 9 (November-December, 1978), 3-4.

3909. Anthony, S. "Intervention in the Development of the Concept of Death," Bulletin of the British Psychological Society, 32 (April, 1979), 148.

3910. Apostel, L. "Tragic Action, Tragedy and Action Logic," Communication and Cognition, 76 (1976), 11-33.

3911. Appleton, W.S. "The Blame of Dying Young," American Journal of Psychoanalysis, 35:4 (Winter, 1975), 377-381.

3912. Aradine, C.R. "Books for Children About Death," Pediatrics, 57:3 (March, 1976), 372-378.

3913. Arafat, I., D. Allan. "Attitudes on Abortion: Legality vs. Religious and Personal Morality," Free Inquiry, 3 (May, 1975), 1-15.

3914. Archer, H.G. The Burial Service: Musical Setting. Philadelphia: General Council Publication Board, 1912.

3915. Arenhart-Treichel, J. "Teaching Doctors How to Care for the Dying," Science News, 107:11 (March, 1975), 176-177.

3916. Aires, P. Western Attitudes Toward Death: From the Middle Ages to the Present. Baltimore: Johns Hopkins University Press, 1974.

3917. Arling, Greg. "The Elderly Widow and Her Family, Neighbors and Friends," Journal of Marriage and the Family, 38:4 (November, 1976), 757-767.

3918. Armstrong, H.G. The American Way of Dying. Hicksville, New York: Exposition Press, 1978.

3919. ________. The Emerging Death Mistique: The Challenge and the Promise. Hicksville, New York: Exposition Press, 1978.

3920. Arney, W.R., W.H. Trescher. "Trends in Attitudes Toward Abortion, 1972-1975," Family Planning Perspectives, 8 (May-June, 1976), 117-124.

3921. Arnstein, R.L. "The Threat of Death as a Factor in Psychological Reaction to Illness," Journal of the American College Health Association, 23:2 (December, 1974), 154-156.

3922. Arseni, C. et al. "Criteria for Assessing Brain Death," Revista De Medicina Interna, Neurologie, Psihiatrie, Neurochirugie, Dermato-Venerologie (Bucharest), 22:1 (January-March, 1977), 45-52.

3923. Artiss, K.L., A.S. Levine. "Doctor-Patient Relation in Severe Illness," The New England Journal of Medicine, 288 (June, 1973), 45-52.

3924. Aslin, A.L. "Counseling 'Single Again' (Divorced and Widowed) Women," Counseling Psychologist, 76:6 (1976), 37-41.

3925. Astrachan, M. "Management of a Staff Death in a Children's Institution," Child Welfare, 56 (June, 1977), 380-385.

3926. Atchley, R.C. "Dimensions of Widowhood in Later Life," Gerontologist, 15:2 (April, 1975), 176-178.

3927. Austin, M. Experiences Facing Death. New York: Arno Press, 1976. (Orig. Publ. 1931).

3928. Autton, N. The Pastoral Care of the Bereaved. London: Society for Promoting Christian Knowledge, 1967.

3929. Avdeev, M.I. "Classifications of Causes and Circumstances of Death," (Author's Translation), Zeitschrift Fur Rechtsmedizin. (Journal of Legal Medicine - Berlin), 78 (1976), 321-324.

3930. Bacon, F. The Historie of Life and Death With Observations Naturall and Experimentall for the Prolonging of Life. New York: Arno Press, 1976. (Orig. Pub. 1638)

3931. Bahr, H.M., C.D. Harvey. "Correlates of Loneliness Among Widows Bereaved in a Mining Disaster," Psychological Reports, 44 (1979), 367-385.

3932. Baider, L. "The Silent Message: Communication in a Family With a Dying Patient," Journal of Marriage & Family Counseling, 3 (July, 1977), 23-28.

3933. Baier, K. "The Ethics of Passive Euthanasia," Critical Care Medicine, 4 (November-December, 1976), 317-319.

3934. Baile, W.F., J.A. Brinker. "Sudden Death Letter," Psychosomatic Medicine, 39:3 (May-June, 1977), 198-201.

3935. Bailey, L.R., Sr. Biblical Perspectives on Death. Philadelphia, Pennsylvania: Fortress Press, 1978.

3936. Bailey, M.C. "Attitudes Toward Death and Dying in Nursing Students," Dissertation Abstracts International, 38 (July, 1977), 139.

3937. Bailey, R.W. The Minister and Grief. New York: Hawthorn Books, 1976.

3938. Bailey, W.C. "Murder and Capital Punishment: Some Further Evidence," American Journal of Orthopsychiatry, 45:4 (July, 1975), 669-688.

3939. Bailey, W.C., D. Glaser. "Use of the Death Penalty vs. Outrage at Murder: Some Additional Evidence and Considerations," Crime and Delinquency, 22 (January, 1976), 31-39.

3940. Bailis, L.A. "Death in Children's Literature: A Conceptual Analysis," Omega, 8 (1977-1978), 295-303.

3941. Bailis, L., R.W. Kennedy. "Effects of A Death Education Program Upon Secondary School Students," Journal of Educational Research, 71 (November-December, 1977), 63-66.

3942. Baird, R.M. "Existentialism, Death and Caring," Journal of Religion and Health, 15:2 (April, 1976), 108-115.

3943. Balkin, E. et al. "Attitudes Toward Classroom Discussions of Death and Dying Among Urban and Suburban Children," Omega, 7:2 (1976), 183-189.

3944. Ball, J.F. "Widow's Grief: The Impact of Age and Mode of Death," Omega, 7:4 (1976), 307-333.

3945. Ball, M. Death. New York: Oxford Press, 1976.

3946. Bandman, E.L., B. Bandman. "The Nurse's Role in Protecting the Patient's Right to Live or Die," Advances in Nursing Science, 1 (April, 1979), 21-35.

3947. Bandman, E.L. "The Dilema of Life and Death: Should We Let Them Die," Nursing Forum, 17 (1978), 118-132.

3948. Bane, J.D., A.H. Kutscher. Death & The Ministry. New York: Schocken, 1975.

3949. Banker, J.R. "Mourning a Son: Childhood and Paternal Life in the Consolateria of Giannozzo Manetti," Journal of Psychohistory, 3:3 (Winter, 1976), 351-362.

3950. Bankowsky, L.H. et al. "The Medical and Legal Determination of Death--Its Effect on Cadaveric Organ Procurement," Journal of Legal Medicine, 2:6 (November-December, 1974), 44-48.

3951. Baqui, M.A. "Muslin Teaching Concerning Death," Nursing Times, 75 (April, 1979), 43-44.

3952. Barckley, V. "Grief, a Part of Living," Ohio's Health, 20 (1968), 34-38.

3953. Bardis, P.D. "Abortion Attitudes Among Catholic College Students," Adolescence, 10:39 (Fall, 1975), 433-441.

3954. Barinbaum, L. "Death of Young Sons and Husbands," Omega, 7:2 (1976), 171-175.

3955. Barlow, J.M. "Loss and Mourning: Some Implications for Psychotherapy," Journal of Tennessee Medical Association, 67:10 (October, 1974), 834-836.

3956. Barnes, R.N., J.M. Martt. "Sudden Death Syndrome," Texas Medicine, 72:10 (October, 1976), 49-57.

3957. Baron, C.H. "Assuring 'Detached but Passionate Investigation and Decision': The Role of Guardians ad Litem in Saikewitcz-Type Cases," American Journal of Law and Medicine, 4 (Summer, 1978), 111-130.

3958. Baron, L. "Surviving the Holocaust," Journal of Psychology and Judaism, 1 (Spring, 1977), 25-37.

3959. Barraclough, B.M. "Reliability of Violent Death Certification in One Coroner's District," British Journal of Psychiatry, 132 (January, 1978), 39-41.

3960. Barraclough, B.M., D.M. Shepherd. "Public Interest: Private Grief," British Journal of Psychiatry, 129 (August, 1976), 109-113.

3961. ________. "The Immediate and Enduring Effects of the Inquest on Relatives of Suicides," British Journal of Psychiatry, 131 (October, 1977), 400-404.

3962. Barrett, C.J. "Effectiveness of Widows' Change Groups in Facilitating Change," Journal Consulting Clinical Psychology, 46:1 (February, 1978) 20-31.

3963. Barrett, P.G. et al. Willingness to Discuss Death: The Influence of Organizational Setting and Personal Exposure. Georgia Southern College, Statesboro, 1977.

3964. Barry, J.R. "Counseling and Death," Catalogue of Selected Documents in Psychology, 774 (August, 1976).

3965. Barth, K. The Resurrection of the Dead. New York: Arno Press, 1976. (Orig. Pub. 1933.)

3966. Barton, D. et al. "Psychological Death: An Adaptive Response to a Life-Threatening Illness," Psychiatry Medicine, 3:3 (July, 1972), 227-236.

3967. Barton, D. (ed). Dying and Death: A Clinical Guide for Caretakers. Baltimore: Williams & Wilkins, 1977.

3968. Bartrom, A. Tombstone Lettering in the British Isles. United Kingdom: Lund Humphries, 1978.

3969. Bartrop, R.W. et al. "Depressed Lymphocyte Function after Bereavement," Lancet, 1:8016 (April, 1977), 834-836.

3970. Bascue, L.O. et al. "Death Attitudes and Experiences of Rehabilitation Counselors," Suicide and Life-Threatening Behavior, 8 (Spring, 1978), 14-17.

3971. ________. "Counselor Experiences With Client Death Concerns," Rehabilitation Counseling Bulletin, 21 (September, 1977), 36-38.

3972. Bassett, S.D. "Death, Dying and Grief: A Personal View," Texas Reports Biology and Medicine, 32:1 (Spring, 1974), 347-350.

3973. Bauer, D.H. "Aging and Dying: Implications for Community Mental Health,: Journal of Community Psychology, 5 (January, 1977), 28-36.

3974. Bauer, W. "The Adolescent Who Has Lost a Significant Other," Illinois Journal of Medicine, 148:6 (December, 1975), 614-615.

3975. Bayless, R. Apparitions and Survival of Death. Secaucus, New Jersey: University Books.

3976. Bayly, J. The Last Thing We Talk About. (rev. ed.) Elgin, Illinois: Cook Publishing Company, 1973.

3977. Beardsley, R.S. et al. "The Pharmacist's Interaction With The Dying Patient," Journal of the American Pharmacy Association, 17:12 (December, 1977), 750-752.

3978. Bean, D.W., C.M. Roberts. "Widows and Widowhood," South Dakota Journal of Medicine, 32 (April, 1979), 9-11.

3979. Beattie, J. "The Right to Life," New Zealand Law Journal 1975 , (August, 1975), 501-528.

3980. Beaucamp, T.L. "A Reply to Rachels on Active and Passive Euthanasia," in: Beaucamp, T.L., S. Perlin (eds). Ethical Issues in Death and Dying. Englewood Cliffs, New Jersey: Prentice Hall, 1978, 246-258.

3981. ________. Ethical Issues in Death and Dying. Englewood Cliffs, New Jersey: Prentice Hall, 1978.

3982. Beaucamp, T.L., et al, (eds). Contemporary Issues in Bioethics. Encino, California: Dickenson Publishing Company, 1978.

3983. Beauchamp, J.M. "Euthanasia and the Nurse Practitioner," Nursing Forum, 14:1 (1975), 56-73.

3984. Becker, D. et al. "The Legal Aspects of the Right to Die: Before & After the Quinlan Decision," Kentucky Law Journal, 65 (1977), 823-879.

3985. Becker, E. The Denial of Death. New York: The Free Press (Macmillan), 1973.

3986. ________. Escape From Evil. New York: Free Press (Macmillan), 1975.

3987. Beckley, J.S. "Problems Which Pertain to the Welfare Aspect of Sudden Death in Infancy," Public Health, 89:4 (May, 1975), 147-151.

3988. Beckwith, J.B. "Sudden Infant Death Syndrome: A New Theory," Pediatrics, 55:5 (May, 1975), 583-584.

3989. Bedau, H.A. "The Right to Die by Firing Squad," Inquiry, 7:1 (February, 1977), 5-7.

3990. Bedau, H.A., M. Zeik. "Condemned Mans Last Wish - Organ Donation and a Meaningful Death," Hastings Center Report, 9 (1979), 16-17.

3991. Beilin, R.L. Managing Relations in Terminality: The Social Intelligibility of Denial of Death. University of California, Los Angeles, 1977.

3992. Beineke, J.A. "An Analysis of Attitudes Toward Death of Secondary School Students," Dissertation Abstracts International, 38 (April, 1978), 6048.

3993. ________ Death and the Secondary School Student. Washington, D.C.: University Press of America, 1979.

3994. Bell, B.D. The Effectiveness of Primary Relational Support Structures Under Disaster Induced Conditions of Stress. University of Nebraska, Omaha, 1977.

3995. Bell, T.J. et al. "The Status of Sudden Infant Death Syndrome (1974), and SIDS in Charleston County, South Carolina," Journal of the South Carolina Medical Association, 71:10 (October, 1975), 312-315.

3996. Bellah, R.N. "To Kill and Survive or to Die and Become: The Active Life and The Contemplative Life as Ways of Being Adult," Daedalus, 105:2 (Spring, 1976), 57-76.

3996a. Bender, D.L. (ed). Problems of Death: Opposing Viewpoints. Minneapolis, Minnesota: Greenhaven Press, 1974.

3997. Bendit, L.J. The Mirror of Life and Death. Wheaton, Illinois: Theosophical Publishing House, 1967.

3998. Benefield, D.G. et al. "Grief Response of Parents After Referral of The Critically Ill Newborn to a Regional Center," New England Journal of Medicine, 294:18 (April, 1976), 975-978.

3999. Bengston, G.O. "Terminal Care and Treatment of Cancer Patients," Sykepleien, 64:3 (February, 1978), 154-155.

4000. Bengston, V.L. et al. "Stratum Contrasts and Similarities in Attitudes Toward Death," Journal of Gerontology, 32 (January, 1977), 76-88.

4001. Benjamin, M. "Distinguishing the Social from the Pathological. Death, Where is Thy Cause?," Hastings Center Report, 6:3 (June, 1976), 15-16.

4002. Benoliel, J.Q. "Social Characteristics of Death as a Recorded Hospital Event," Communicating Nursing Research, 8 (March, 1977), 245-267.

4003. ________. "Conceptual Precision and Research About Human Dying," Communicating Nursing Research, 9 (April, 1977), 237-243.

4004. ________. "The Changing Social Context For Life and Death Decisions," Essence, 2 (1978), 65-72.

4005. ________. "A Holistic Approach to Terminal Illness," Cancer Nursing, 1:2 (April, 1978), 143-149.

4006. Bensley, L.B., Jr. "Death Education as a Learning Experience," National Institute of Education, Washington, D.C., Scrip No. 3, (November, 1975), 24 pp.

4007. Berdes, C. Social Services for the Aged, Dying and Bereaved. International Federation on Aging, 1900 K. Street N.W., Washington, D.C., 1978.

4008. Berg, C.D. "Helping Children Accept Death and Dying Through Group Counseling," Personnel and Guidance Journal, 57 (November, 1978), 169-172.

4009. Berg, D.L. "The Right to Die Dilemma. Where Do You Fit In?" RN, 40:8 (August, 1977), 48-54.

4010. Bergman, A.B. "Sudden Infant Death Syndrome: An Approach to Management," Primary Care, 3:1 (March, 1976), 1-8.

4011. ________. "Editorial: Sudden Infant Death Syndrome: Current Status of the Problem," Southern Medical Journal, 69:1 (January, 1976), 1-3.

4012. Berman, D.B. "The Facilitation of Mourning: A Preventive Mental Health Approach," Dissertation Abstracts International, 39 (July, 1978), 190-191.

4013. Berkman, M. "The Aged, The Hospice and Death," Revista Interamerica De Radiologia, 27:6 (June 1977), 499-502.

4014. Berman, A.L. "Dyadic Death-Murder-Suicide," Suicide and Life-Threatening Behavior, 9 (1979), 15-23.

4015. Berman, L.E. "Sibling Loss as an Organizer of Unconscious Guilt: A Case Study," Psychoanalytic Quarterly, 47 (1978), 568-587.

4016. Bermensolo, P., S. Groenwald. "Are We Death and Dying Our Patients to Death," Oncology Nursing Forum, 5 (October, 1978), 8-10.

4017. Bernstein, A.H. "The Law of the Dead," Hospitals, 48:19 (October, 1974), 162&175.

4018. Bernstein, B. "Lawyer and Counselor as an Interdisciplinary Team Serving the Terminally Ill," Death Education, 3 (Spring, 1979), 11-19.

4019. Bernstein, J.E. Helping Children Cope With Death & Separation Resources for Children. Urbana, Illinois: CBD, 1976.

4020. ________. When People Die. New York: Dutton, 1976.

4021. ________. Books to Help Children Cope With Separation and Loss. New York: Bowker, 1977.

4022. Berry, R. "Is Death Our Failure?" Journal of Practical Nursing, 24:11 (November, 1974), 30&37.

4023. Beshai, J.A. "Mourning the Suicide of a Patient," Essence, 1:2 (1976), 99-105.

4024. ________. "American and Egyptian Attitudes Toward Death," Essence, 2 (1978), 155-158.

4025. Best, K. Write Your Own Will. Tadworth, Surrey, England: Elliot Right Way Books, 1978.

4026. Beverly, E.V. "Understanding and Helping Dying Patients and Their Families," Geriatrics, 31:3 (March, 1976), 121-122.

4027. Bichat, X. Physiological Researches on Life and Death. New York: Arno Press, 1976. (Orig. Pub. 1827)

4028. Bierner, J. "Death--Unacceptable Problem or Acceptable Fact?" International Journal of Social Psychiatry, 21:1 (Winter-Spring, 1974-1975), 1-3.

4029. Biggers, T.A. "Death By Murder - A Study of Women Murderers," Death Education, 3 (1979), 1-9.

4030. Binik, Y.M. et al. "Sudden Death in the Laboratory Rat: Cardiac Function, Sensory and Experimental Factors in Swimming Deaths," Psychosomatic Medicine, 39 (March-April, 1977), 82-91.

4031. Biorck, G. "Some Personal Reflections about Terminal Care Nursing," Lakartidningen, 76:32 (August, 1976), 2624-2627.

4032. Birtchnell, J. "Early Parental Death and The Clinical Scales of the MMPI," British Journal of Psychiatry, 132 (June, 1978), 574-579.

4033. Bitensky, R. "Death: The Psychotherapeutic Cure for Cancer," Journal of Health, Politics, Policy and Law, 4 (Spring, 1979), 5-10.

4034. Bixler, F. "Euthanasia: The Painful Need for Reasonable Standards," Glendale Law Review, 1 (1976), 244-254.

4035. Black, C.R., L.A. Platt. Attitudes Toward Death and Dying: A Survey of Workers With The Elderly. Georgia Southern College, Statesboro, 1978.

4036. Black, D. "What Happens to Bereaved Children?," Proceedings of the Royal Society of Medicine, 69:11 (November, 1976), 842-844.

4037. ________. "The Bereaved Child," Journal of Child Psychology and and Psychiatry, 19:3 (July, 1978), 287-292.

4038. Black, P.M. "Criteria of Brain Death: Review and Comparison," Postgraduate Medicine, 57:2 (February, 1975), 69-74.

4039. ________. "Three Definitions of Death," Monist, 60 (January, 1977), 136-146.

4040. ________. "Focusing on Some of the Ethical Problems Associated With Death and Dying," Geriatrics, 31:1 (January, 1976), 138-141.

4041. Blackwell, R.D. Living With Death. Old Tappan, New Jersey: Revell, 1978.

4042. Blain, M. "The Role of Death in Political Conflict," Psychoanalytic Review, 63:2 (Summer, 1976), 249-265.

4043. Blanchard, D.G. et al. "The Young Widow: Depressive Symptomatology Throughout The Grief Process," Psychiatry, 39:4 (November, 1976), 394-399.

4044. Blank, H. "Crisis Consultation," International Journal of Social Psychiatry, 21:3 (Autumn, 1975), 179-189.

4045. Blatt, B. "Bandwagons Also Go To Funerals," Journal of Learning Disabilities, 12 (1979), 222-224.

4046. Blau, D. "On Widowhood, Discussion," Journal of Geriatric Psychiatry, 8:1 (1975), 29-40.

4047. Blazer, J.A. "The Concept of Death as a Factor in Mental Health," Psychology, 15 (February, 1978), 68-77.

4048. Bleeker, J.A. "Brief Psychotherapy With Lung Cancer Patients," Psychotherapy and Psychosomatics, 29 (1978), 1-4 & 282-287.

4049. Bleeker, J.A., H.B. Pomerantz. "The Influence of a Lecture Course in Loss and Grief On Medical Students: An Empirical Study of Attitude Formation," Medical Education, 13 (March, 1979), 117-128.

4050. Blewett, L.J. "To Die at Home," American Journal of Nursing, 70 (1970), 2602-2604.

4051. Bliss, V.J. "Sharing Another's Death," Nursing (Jenkintown), 6:4 (April, 1976), 30.

4052. Bloch, S. "A Clinical Course on Death and Dying for Medical Students," Journal of Medical Education, 50:6 (June, 1975), 630-632.

4053. Blom-Cooper, L., G. Drewry. "The Sanctity of Human Life," in: Blom-Cooper, L., G. Drewry (eds). Law and Morality. London: Gerald Duckworth, 1976.

4054. Bluestein, V. "Notes and Observations on Teaching 'The Psychology of Death'," Teaching of Psychology, 3:3 (October, 1976), 115-118.

4055. ________. "Loss of Loved Ones and the Drawing of Dead or Broken Branches on The HTP," Psychology in the Schools, 15 (July, 1978), 365-366.

4056. Blum, A.H. "Children's Conceptions of Death and An After-Life," Dissertation Abstracts International, 36:10-B (April, 1976), 5248.

4057. Blumenfield, M. et al. "The Wish to be Informed of a Fatal Illness," Omega, 9 (1978-1979), 323-326.

4058. Blumenfield, M. et al. "Do Patients Want to Be Told," Letter. New England Journal of Medicine, 299 (November, 1978), 1138.

4059. Boccuzzi, N.K. "Humanistic Supervision for Terminal Care," Supervisor Nurse, 8 (August 1977), 26-27.

4060. Bohart, J.B., B.W. Berglund. "Impact of Death and Dying Counseling Groups on Death Anxiety in College Students," Death Education, 2 (1979), 381-391.

4061. Bok, S. "Personal Directions for Care at The End of Life," New England Journal of Medicine, 295 (August, 1976), 367-369.

4062. Bojanovsky, J. "Morbidity and Mortality of Widowed Persons," Fortschritte Medicine, 95:9 (March 3, 1977), 593-596.

4063. ________. "Psychological Reactions Due to Death of Spouse," Fortschritte Medicine, 95:6 (February 10, 1977), 327-330.

4064. Bolt, M. "Purpose in Life and Death Concern," Journal of Genetic Psychology, 132 (March, 1978), 159-160.

4065. Bongartz, E.B. et al. "Definition and Determination of Brain Death," Anaesthesiologische Und Intensivmedizinische Praxis, 13 (Feb, 1977), 59-67.

4066. Bortoluzzi, E. et al. "Brain Death," Minerva Medicine, 68 (January, 1977), 277-284.

4067. Borup, J. et al. "Relocation and Its Effects on Mortality," Gerontologist, 19 (April, 1979), 135-140.

4068. Boshes, B. "A Definition of Cerebral Death," Annual Review Medicine, 26 (1975), 465-470.

4069. ________. "Death: Historical Evolution and Implication of the Concept," Annals of the New York Academy of Sciences, 315 (November 17, 1978), 11- 18.

4070. Bourne, S. "Stillbirth, Grief and Medical Education Letter," British Medical Journal, 1:6069 (April, 1977), 1157.

4071. Botwinick, J. et al. "Predicting Death and Behavioral Test Performance," Journal of Gerontology, 33 (September, 1978), 755-762.

4072. Bowlby, J. Separation: Anxiety and Anger. New York: Basic Books, 1977.

4073. Boyd, K. "Attitudes to Death: Some Historical Notes," Journal of Medical Ethics, 3:3 (September, 1977), 124-128.

4074. Boyle, J.M. "On Killing and Letting Die," New Scholasticism, 94 (July, 1977), 48.

4075. Brace, S.M. " Psychological Study of the Aged in the Last Stages of of Terminal Illness," Dissertation Abstracts International, 38 (February, 1978), 4671.

4076. Brady, E.M."Telling the Story: Ethics and Dying," Hospital Progress, 60 (March, 1979), 57-62.

4077. Brain, J.L. et al. "Sex, Incest & Death: Initiation Rites Reconsidered," Current Anthropology, 18 (June, 1977), 191-198.

4078. Braito, R., D. Anderson. Singles and Aging: Implications for Needed Research. University of Denver, 1978.

4079. Branson, H.K. "Grieving and Growing," Journal of Practical Nursing, 26 (December, 1976), 34.

4080. Brantner, J. "Life Threatening Disease as a Manageable Crisis,' Seminars in Oncology, 1:2 (June, 1974), 153-157.

4081. ________. "Positive Approaches to Dying," Death Education, 1 (Fall, 1977), 293-304.

4082. Braun, O.H. "The Dying Child and Its Psychological Problems," Deutsche Zahnaerztliche Zeitschrift, 29:11 (November, 1976), 631-635.

4083. Bred, D.L. "Nuclear Scare Tests Hospitals Disaster Plan," Hospitals Journal of the American Hospital Association, 53 (1979), 33-36.

4084. Breindel, C.L., R.M. Boyle. "Implementing a Multiphases Hospice Program," Hospital Progress, 60 (March, 1979), 42-45 & 76.

4085. Brenner, C. "The Concept and Phenomenology of Depression With Special Reference to the Aged," Journal of Geriatric Psychiatry, 7:1 (1974), 6-20.

4086. Brenner, G. "Euthanasia and The Human Right to Live. Medico-Legal Questions on Death With Dignity," Medizinische Welt, 28:14 (April 8, 1977), 690-694.

4087. Brent, S.B. "Puns, Metaphors, and Misunderstandings in a Two-Year Old's Conception of Death," Omega, 8 (1977-1978), 285-293.

4088. Brimblecombe, F. "Discussion of Papers on the Inner London Survey on Sudden Death in Infancy," Public Health, 89:4 (May, 1975), 163.

4089. Briscoe, C.W., J.B. Smith. "Depression in Bereavement and Divorce, Relationship to Primary Depressive Illness: A Study of 128 Subjects," Archives of General Psychiatry, 32:4 (April, 1975), 439-443.

4090. Brock, A.M. et al. "Demythologizing the Issues," Journal of Gerontology Nursing, 4 (November, December, 1978), 26-32.

4091. Brodie, H. Ethical Decisions in Medicine. Boston: Little Brown & Co., 1976.

4092. Brodsky, G.M. "A Pragmatic Discussion of the Norms of Dying," Connecticut Medicine, 42:7 (July, 1978), 457-461.

4093. Brody, E.B. "Research in Reincarnation and Editorial Responsibility," Journal of Nervous and Mental Disease, 165:3 (September, 1977), 151.

4094. Brody, E.M. et al. "Survival and Death in the Mentally-Impaired Aged," Journal of Chronic Disease, 28:7-8 (August, 1975), 389-399.

4095. Brody, E.M. Long-Term Care of Older People: A Practical Guide. New York: Human Sciences Press, 1977.

4096. Brody, H. et al. "The Complexities of Dying," New England Journal of Medicine, 296, (May, 1977), 1237-1240.

4097. Brook, R. "Un-Natural Death Letter," Hastings Center Report, 6:6 (December, 1976), 4&40.

4098. Bromberg, W. "Death Fantasies as an Escape Mechanism," American Journal of Psychiatry, 133:11, (November, 1976), 1348-1349.

4099. Bron, B. "The Problem of Death in Current Medicine," Confina Psychiatrica, 19:4 (1976), 222-235.

4100. Broughton, J. "The Cognitive Developmental Approach to Mortality: A Reply to Kurtines and Grief," Journal of Moral Education, 7 (January, 1978), 81-96.

4101. Brown, A., T.K. Marshall. "Body Temperature as a Means of Estimating Time of Death," Forensic Science, 4:2 (October, 1974), 125-133.

4102 . Brown, G.W. et al. "Depression and Loss," British Journal of Psychiatry, 130 (January, 1977), 1-18.

4103 . Brown, H.O. Death Before Birth. Nashville: Thomas Nelson, 1977.

4104 . Brown, N.K. et al. "Decision Making for the Terminally Ill Patient," Cancer: The Behavioral Dimensions, New York: Raven Press, 1976, 319-329.

4105 . Brown, R.H., R.B. Truitt. "Euthanasia and the Right to Die," Ohio Northern University Law Review, 3 (1976), 615-642.

4106 . Brown, S.M. et al. "Natural Death: Clarifying the Definition," Hastings Center Report, 4 (December, 1977), 39-40.

4107 . Browne, T. Hydrotaphia, Urne-Buriall. New York: Arno Press, 1976. (Orig. Pub. 1658)

4108 . Bruce, M. "The Family and the Bereaved," Nursing Times, 74 (June, 1978), 71-72.

4109 . Brunson, M. Death, Dying and Grief. Independence, Missouri: Herald House, 1978.

4110. Bryant, C.D., D.J. Shoemaker. Death and the Dead for Fun and Profit: Thanatological Entertainment as Popular Culture. Virginia Polytechnic Institute & State University, Blacksburg, Virginia, 1977.

4111. Bryant, E.H. "Teacher in Crisis: A Classmate is Dying," Elementary School Journal, 78 (March, 1978), 233-241.

4112 . Bryer, K.B. "Amish Way of Death - Study in Family Support Systems," American Psychologist, 34 (1979), 255-261.

4113 . Brzecki, A. "Guidelines for Early Diagnosis of Brain Death," Neurologia 1 Neurochiarurgia Polska, 11:4 (July-August, 1977), 465-571.

4114 . Buckingham, R.W., S. Lack. Hospice. First American Hospice: Three Years of Home Care. New Haven, Connecticut: Hospice, 1978.

4115 . Buckingham, R.W., J. Kron. The Hospice Concept. New York: Health Sciences Publishing Company, 1977.

4116. Buckingham, R.W. et al. "Living With the Dying: Use of the Technique of Participant Observation," Canadian Medical Association Journal, 115:12 (December, 1976), 1211-1215.

4117. Buckingham, R.W. III, S.H. Foley. "A Guide to Evaluation Research in Terminal Care Programs," Death Education, 2 (Spring-Summer, 1978), 127-140.

4118. Buehler, J.S. "What Contributes to Hope in the Cancer Patient," American Journal of Nursing, 73 (1973), 1588-1591.

4119. Bugen, L.A. "Human Grief: A Model for Prediction and Intervention," American Journal of Orthopsychiatry, 47 (April, 1977), 196-206.

4120. ________. "Effects of Death Education on Stability of Concern About Death," Psychological Reports, 43 (December, 1978), 1086.

4121. ________. Death and Dying: Theory, Research and Practice. Dubuque, Iowa: William C. Brown Company, 1979.

4122. Bunch, B., D. Zahra. "Dealing With Death. The Unlearned Role." American Journal of Nursing, 76:9 (September, 1976), 1486-1488.

4123. Burgess, A.W., A. Lazare. "The Bereaved" in Community Mental Health Target Populations. New Jersey: Prentice Hall, 1976, 93-103.

4124. Burgess, J., W.K. Kohn. The Widower. Boston: Beacon Press, 1978.

4125. Burgess, K.E. "The Influence of Will on Life and Death," Nursing Forum, 15:3 (1976), 238-258.

4126. Burkhalter, P.K. "Fostering Staff Sensitivity to the Dying Patient," Supervisor Nurse, 6 (April 1975) 55-59.

4127. Burkhardt, M. "Death: A Developmental Viewpoint," Arizona Nurse, 28:2 (March-April, 1975), 12-13.

4128. Burnet, M. "A Time To Die," Sciences, 18 (May-June, 1978), 20-23.

4129. Burnett, G.B. "Editorials: Management of Death and Dying," Texas Medicine, 71:12 (December, 1975), 132-133.

4130. Burnight, R.G., B. Leoprapai. "Attitudes of Rural Thai Women Toward Induced Abortions," Journal of Biosocial Science, 9 (January, 1977), 61-72.

4131. Burns, J.M., J.S. Hamlon. "Minnesota Brain Death Legislation - Step Forward, or Backward," Minnesota Medicine, 62 (1979), 273-277.

4132. Bursztajn, H. "The Role of A Training Protocol in Formulating Patient Instructions as to Terminal Care Choices," Journal of Medical Education, 54:2 (April, 1977), 347-348.

4133. Burt, R.A. "Authorizing Death for Anomalous Newborns," in: Milunsky, A., G.J. Annas (eds). Genetics and The Law. New York: Plenum Press, 1976.

4134. Burton, A. "Attitudes Toward Death of Scientific Minorities on Death," Psychoanalytic Review, 65 (Fall, 1978), 415-432.

4135. Bush, E.D. et al. Euthanasia and Its Decision-Making Variable. Southwest Texas State University, San Marcos, 1978.

4136. Butler, A.F. "Scratchy Is Dead," Teacher, 95 (February, 1978), 67-68.

4137. Buxton, M.J., R.R. West. "Letter: The Cost of Death," Lancet, 2:7923, (July, 1975), 38.

4138. Byrne, P.A. "On Death," Modern Medicine, 75:6 (June, 1978), 256-258.

4139. Byrne, P.M., M.J. Stogre. "Agathansia and the Care of the Dying," Canadian Medical Association Journal, 112:12 (June, 1975), 1396-1397.

4140. Caddell, J.L. "Hepatic Trace Elements in the Sudden Infant Death Syndrome Letter," Journal of Pediatrics, 90:6 (June, 1977), 1039.

4141. Cahill, L.G. Euthanasia: A Catholic and a Protestant Perspective. University of Chicago, 1976.

4142. _______. "A 'Natural Law' Reconsideration of Euthanasia," Linacre Quarterly, 44 (February, 1977), 47-63.

4143. _______. "Comment on Euthanasia," Linacre Quarterly, 44 (November, 1977), 299-300.

4144. Cain, L.P. "Social Workers Role in Teenage Abortions," Social Work, 24 (1979), 52-55.

4145. Caine, L. Life-Lines, New York: Doubleday, 1977.

4146. Calderaro, P. "Ethics: A Time to Die," American Journal of Nursing, 77:5 (May, 1977), 861.

4147. Calhoun, L. et al. Dealing With Crisis. New York: Prentice Hall/ Spectrum, 1976.

4148. Callahan, D. "On Defining 'Natural Death'," Hastings Center Report, 7:3 (June, 1977), 32-37.

4149. Callan, J.P. "The Hospice Movement Editorial," Journal of the American Medical Association, 241 (February 9, 1979), 600. (June 15, 1979), 2600.

4150. Calvert, P. et al. "Death in a Country Area and its Effects on the Health of Relatives," Medical Journal of Australia, 2:19 (November, 1977), 635-638.

4151. Cameron, J.M. "Sudden Death in Infancy," Public Health, 89:4 (May, 1975), 161-162.

4152. Cameron, P., J.C. Tichenor. "The Swedish 'Children Born to Women Denied Abortion' Study: A Radical Criticism," Psychological Reports, 39:2 (October, 1976), 391-394.

4153. Campbell, L.P. "Abortion: A Problem-Solving Approach," Social Studies, 68:3 (May-June, 1977), 120-123.

4154. Campbell, R.R. "Death Fear in Relation to Futurity and Ego Development," Dissertation Abstracts International, 38 (January, 1978), 3385.

4155. Cannon, M. "To Sharon, With Love," American Journal of Nursing, 79 (April, 1979), 642-645.

4156. Cannons, R. "Waiting for Our Patients to Die," Nursing Mirror, 140:11 (March, 1975), 57.

4157. Cantarow, E. "Abortion and Feminism in Italy: Women Against Church and State," Radical America, 10 (November-December, 1976), 8-27.

4158. Cantor, N.L. "Quinlan, Privacy, and the Handling of Incompetent Dying Patients," Rutgers Law Review, 30 (Winter, 1977), 243-266.

4159. Cantor, R.C. And a Time to Life: Toward Emotional Well-Being During The Crisis of Cancer. New York: Harper & Row, 1976.

4160. Caplan, G.,M. Killilea (eds) Support Systems and Mutual Help. New York: Grune & Stratton, 1976.

4161. Cappon, D. "Attitudes of the Aging Toward Death," Essence, 2 (1978), 139-147.

4162. Cardarelle, J.A. "A Group for Children with Deceased Parents," Social Work, 20:4 (July, 1975), 328-329.

4163. Carey, R.G. "The Widowed: A Year Later," Journal of Counseling Psychology, 24:2 (March, 1977), 125-131.

4164. ________. "Emotional Adjustment in Terminal Patients: A Quantitative Approach," Journal of Counseling Psychology, 21:5, (September, 1974), 433-439.

4165. ________. "Counseling the Terminally Ill," Personnel and Guidance Journal, 55:3 (November, 1976), 124-126.

4166. Carey, R., E. Pasovac. "Attitudes of Physicians on Disclosing Information to and Maintaining Life for Terminal Patients," Omega, 9 (1978-1979), 67-77.

4167. Carey, W.B. "Commentary: Sudden Infant Death Syndrome and Temperment," Journal of Pediatrics, 88:3 (March, 1976), 516-517.

4168. Carhart, R.L. "Death-Agnst: A Synthesis in Developmental Perspective," Dissertation Abstracts International, 38 (October, 1977), 1885.

4169. Carpenter, R.G., J.L. Emery. "Final Results of Study of Infants at Risk of Sudden Death," Nature, 268 (August, 1977), 5622.

4170. Carpenter, R.G. et al. "Multistage Scoring System for Identifying Infants at Risk of Unexpected Death," Archives of Diseases of Children, 52:8 (August, 1977), 606-612.

4171. Carr, S., B. Schoenberg. Grief: Selected Readings. New York: Health Sciences Publishing Company, 1975.

4172. Carrick, C. The Accident. New York: Seabury, 1976.

4173. Carrington, H. Death: Its Causes and Phenomena With Special Reference to Immortality. New York: Arno Press, 1976. (Orig. Pub. 1921).

4174. Carse, J.P. "The Social Effects of Changing Attitudes Toward Death," Annals of the New York Academy of Sciences, (November 17, 1978), 322-328.

4175. ________. Death and Human Existence: A Conceptual History of Human Mortality. New York: Wiley, 1980.

4176. Carse, J.P., A.B. Dallery (eds). Death and Society: A Book of Readings and Sources. New York: Harcourt, Brace & Jovanovich, 1977.

4177. Carson, R.A. "The Death of One's Own," Postgraduate Medicine, 65 (January, 1979), 197-201 & 202-203.

4178. Carter, R. "Letter: Sudden Death in Infancy Syndrome--The Fatal Burp," Medical Journal of Australia, 01:15 (April, 1975), 483.

4179. Cassem, N.H., R.S. Stewart. "Management and Care of the Dying Patient," International Journal of Psychiatry and Medicine, 6 (1975), 293-304.

4180. Cassidy, R.C. "Euthanasia: Passive or Active?" St. Luke's Journal of Theology, 20 (December, 1976), 6-13.

4181. Castles, M. Dying in An Institution. New York: Appleton-Century-Crofts, 1979.

4182. Caughill, R.E. (ed). The Dying Patient: A Supportive Approach. Boston: Little, Brown & Company, 1976.

4183. Cauthorne, C.V. "Coping With Death in the Emergency Department," Journal of Emergency Nursing, 1 (November-December, 1975), 24-26.

4184. Cavenar, J.O. Jr., et al. "Grief: Normal or Abnormal?," North Carolina Medical Journal, 39 (January, 1978), 31-34.

4185. ________. "Child's Reaction to Mother's Abortion," Military Medicine, 144 (1979), 412-413.

4186. Cerny, L.J. "Death Perspectives and Religious Orientation as a Function of Christian Faith with Specific Reference to Being 'Born Again'," Dissertation Abstracts International, vol 38 (October 1977), 1872.

4187. Chapman, C. "Care of the Terminal Patient. What Can I Say? (A Christian Nurse's View of Dying), " Nursing Times, 75 (March, 1979), 487-488.

4188. Charmaz, K.C. "The Coroner's Strategies for Announcing Death," Urban Life, 4 (October, 1975), 296-316.

4189. Charron, W.C. "Death: A Philosophical Perspective on the Legal Definitions," Washington University Law Quarterly, 1975 (1975), 979-1008.

4190. Chellam, G. "Awareness of Death and Self-Engagement in Later Life: The Engagement Continuum," International Journal of Aging and Human Development, 8:2 (1977-1978), 111-127.

4191. Cherico, D.J. et al (eds). Thanatology Course Outlines, General. Edison, NJ: MSS Information Corporation, 1978.

4192. ____________. Thanatology Course Outlines: Religion, Philosophy. Edison, NJ: MSS Information Corporation, 1978.

4193. Cherkofsky, N. "Should You Tell Your Patient the Truth," Nursing Care, 11 (December, 1978), 18.

4194. Chiappetta, W. et al. "Sex Differences in Coping With Death Anxiety," Psychological Reports, 39 (December, 1976), 945-946.

4195. Choi, S.Y. "Death in Young Alcoholics," Journal of Studies on Alcohol. 36 (September, 1975), 1224-1229.

4196. Christopherson, L.K. "Cardiac Transplant: Preparation for Dying or for Living," Health and Social Work, 1 (February, 1976), 58-72.

4197. Christoffers, C. "Management Program for Sudden Infant Death," Nursing News, 50 (June, 1977), 1&3.

4198. Cicirelli, V.G. "The Relationship of Task Reinforcement to Personal Loss Themes Revealed in Earliest Memories of Elderly Subjects," Experimental Aging Research, 2 (September, 1976), 435-447.

4199. Ciompi, L., J. Medvecka. "Comparative Study of Long-Term Mortality in Mental Illness," Schweizer Archiv Fur Neurologie, Neurochirugie Und Psychiatrie, vol. 76; 118:1 (1976), 111-135.

4200. Ciuca, R. et al. "When a Disaster Happens: How Do You Meet Emotional Needs?," American Journal of Nursing, 77 (March, 1977), 454-456.

4201. Clark, J. et al. "Care of the Dying," Nursing Mirror, 143 suppl: I-IV (August, 1976).

4202. Clarke, M., A.J. Williams. "Depression in Women After Perinatal Death," Lancet, 1 (1979), 916-917.

4203. Clarkson, L. Death, Disease and Famine in Pre-Industrial England. Dublin: Gill & Macmillan, 1975.

4204. Clay, V.S. "Children Deal With Death," School Counselor, 23 (January, 1976), 175-183.

4205. Clayton, P.J. "The Effects of Living Alone on Bereavement Symptoms," American Journal of Psychiatry, 132 (Febauary, 1975), 133-137.

4206. ________. "Epidemiological Review of the Mortality of Bereavement (letter)," Psychosomatic Medicine, 40 (August, 1978), 435-438.

4207. Cleary, F.X. "On Death and Afterlife: A Biblical and Theological Interpretation," <u>Hospital Progress</u>, 56 (December, 1975), 40-44.

4208. Clemens, N.A. "An Intensive Course for Clergy on Death, Dying and Loss," <u>Journal of Religion and Health</u>, 15 (October, 1976), 223-229.

4209. Cleveland, A.P. "Sudden Infant Death Syndrome (SIDS): A Burgeoning Medicolegal Problem," <u>American Journal of Law and Medicine</u>, 1 (March, 1975), 55-69.

4210. Cleveland, W.P., D.T. Gianturco. "Remarriage Probability After Widowhood: A Retrospective Method," <u>Journal of Gerontology</u>, 31 (January, 1976), 99-103.

4211. Codden, P. "The Meaning of Death for Parents and the Child," <u>Maternal-Child Nursing Journal</u>, 6 (Spring, 1977), 9-16.

4212. Coddington, M.N. "A Mother Struggles to Cope with her Child's Deteriorating Illness," <u>Maternal-Child Nursing Journal</u>, 5 (Spring, 1976), 39-44.

4213. Coffin, M.M. <u>Death in Early America</u>. New York: Thomas Nelson, 1976.

4214. Coggan, D. "On Dying and Dying Well: Extracts from the Edwin Stevens Lecture," <u>Journal of Medical Ethics</u>, 3 (June, 1977), 57-60.

4215. Cohen, A.I. "The Impact of the Death of a Group Member on a Therapy Group," <u>International Journal of Group Psychotherapy</u>, 26 (April, 1976), 203-212.

4216. Cohen, F.S. "Removal of the Dead: From Room to Morgue," <u>Journal of Nursing Education</u>, 17 (March, 1978), 36-41.

4217. Cohen, K.P. <u>Hospice Care: Prescriptions for Terminal Care</u>. Germantown, Maryland: Aspen Systems, 1979.

4218. Cohen, L. et al. "Perinatal Mortality: Assisting Parental Affirmation," <u>American Journal Orthopsychiatry</u>, 48 (October, 1978), 727-731.

4219. Cohen, R.J. "Is Dying Being Worked to Death?," <u>American Journal of Psychiatry</u>, 133 (May, 1976), 575-577.

4220. Cohler, R.J. "Some Problems in the Study of Aging and Death," Human Development, 20 (1977), 210-216.

4221. Colbert, J.G. "Euthanasia and Natural Law," Linacre Quarterly, 45 (May, 1978), 187-198.

4222. Cole, M.A. "Sex and Marital Status Differences in Death Anxiety," Omega, 9 (1979), 139-148.

4223. Coleman, S.B., M.D. Stanton. "The Role of Death in the Addict Family," Journal of Marriage and Family Counseling, 4 (January, 1978), 79-91.

4224. Colen, B.D. "The 'Right to Die' Lobbyist Heartened," Washington Post, (12 December, 1976), A2.

4225. ________. Karen Ann Quinlan: Dying in the Age of Eternal Life. New York: Nash Publishing Corportion, 1976.

4226. Collester, D.G. "Death, Dying and the Law: A Prosecutorial View of the Quinlan Case," Rutgers Law Review, 30 (Winter, 1977), 304-328.

4227. Collison, B.B. "The Mrs. Lincoln Response," Personnel and Guidance Journal, 57 (December, 1978), 180-182.

4228. Collomb, H. "Death as a Determinant of Psychosomatic Syndromes in Africa," Journal of American Academy of Psychoanalysis, 4 (April, 1976), 227-236.

4229. Colman, H. Hanging On. New York: Atheneum, 1977.

4230. Combs, D.C. "The Role of Death Education in Increasing and Decreasing Death Anxiety and Increasing Death Acceptance," Dissertation Abstracts International, 39 (September, 1978), 1334.

4231. Comiskey, R.J. "From Opposition to Dialog: New Dimensions in Catholic Thought Toward the Legalization of Voluntary Euthanasia," Ann Arbor: University Microfilms International, 1977, 228 pages.

4232. Comper, F.M.M. (ed). The Book of the Craft of Dying and Other Early English Tracts Concerning Death. New York: Arno Press, 1976. (Orig. Pub. 1917)

4233. Coombs, R.H., P.S. Powers. "Socialization for Death: The Physician's Role," Urban Life, 4 (October, 1975), 250-271.

4234. Congdon, H. The Pursuit of Death. Nashville: Abingdon, 1977.

4235. ________. "Toward a Definition of Death," in: The Pursuit of Death. Nashville: Abingdon, 1977. 29-39.

4236. Conroy, R.C. "Widows and Widowhood," New York State Journal of Medicine, 77 (March, 1977), 357-360.

4237. Cook, F.J. Julia's Story: The Tragedy of an Unnecessary Death. New York: Hold, Rinehart & Winston, 1976.

4238. Cope, G. (ed). Dying, Death and Disposal. London: Society for the Promotion of Christian Knowledge, 1970.

4239. Corbett, K.A.,R.M. Raciti. "Withholding Life-Prolonging Medical Treatment from the Institutionalized Person--Who Decides?," New England Journal of Prison Law, 3 (1976), 47-83.

4240. Corbett, T.L., D.M. Hai. "Searching for Euthanatos: The Hospice Alternative," Hospital Progress, 60 (March, 1979), 38-41 & 76.

4241. Cornwell, J. et al. "Family Response to Loss of a Child by Sudden Infant Death Syndrome," Medical Journal of Australia, 1 (April, 1977), 656-658.

4242. Corr, C.A. "A Model Syllabus for Death and Dying Courses," Death Education, 1 (Winter, 1978), 433 457.

4243. Corroned, M., B.R. Kasner. "A Study of Abortion and Problems in Decision Making," Journal of Marriage and Family Counseling, 3 (January, 1977), 69-76.

4244. Coutant, H. First Snow. New York: Alfred Knopf, 1974.

4245. Coute, L. Conversations With a Dying Friend. Los Angeles, California: Pacific Perception, 1977.

4246. Cox, G.R. "An Analysis of Factors Influencing Attitudes Toward Death," Dissertation Abstracts International, 37 (July, 1976), 638.

4247. Coyne, A.B. "A Conceptual Framework for Death Education for Nurses," Dissertation Abstracts International, 38 (October, 1977), 1916.

4248. Craig, Y. "The Bereavement of Parents and Their Search for Meaning," British Journal of Social Work, 7 (Spring, 1977), 41-54.

4249. Crane, D. The Sanctity of Social Life: Physicians' Treatment of Critically Ill Patients. New Brunswick, New Jersey: Transaction Books, 1977.

4250. Crary, W.G. et al. "Bereavement: A Working Paper," Catalog of Selected Documents in Psychology, 8 (May, 1978), 37-38.

4251. Crase, D. "The Need to Assess the Impact of Death Education," Death Education, 1 (Winter, 1978), 423-431.

4252. Crase, D.R., D. Crase. "Helping Children Understand Death," Young Children, 32 (November, 1976), 2025.

4253. ________. "Life Issues Surrounding Death Education," Comprehensive Nursing Quarterly, 10 (August, 1975), 81-86.

4254. ________. "Attitudes Toward Death Education for Young Children," Death Education, 3 (1979), 31-40.

4255. Creighton, H. "Law for the Nurse Supervisor: Terminating Life Support," Supervisor Nurse, 9 (October, 1978), 68-75.

4256. Crichton, I. The Art of Dying. New York: Humanities Press, 1976.

4257. Cristofer, M. The Shadow Box (A Play). New York: Drama Book Specialists, 1977.

4258. Crook, T., A. Raskin. "Association of Childhood Parental Loss with Attempted Suicide and Depression," Journal of Consulting and Clinical Psychology, 43 (April, 1975), 277.

4259. Croskery, B.F. Death Education: Attitudes of Teachers, School Board Members and Clergy. Palo Alto, California: R&E Research Associates, Incorporated, 1979.

4260. Crouch, B.M. "The Occupation of Funeral Director: A Research Note on Work Orientations," Journal of Vocational Behavior, 6 (June, 1975), 365-372.

4261. Crowder, J.E. et al. "Training Registered Nurses as Bereavement Counselors in an Occupational Health Service," Hospital and Community Psychiatry, 27 (December, 1976), 851-852.

4262. Cullen, J.W. et al (eds). Cancer: The Behavioral Dimensions. New York: Raven Press, 1976.

4263. Culliton, B.J. "Helping the Dying Die: Two Harvard Hospitals Go Public with Policies," Science, 193 (17 September, 1976), 1105-1106.

4264. Cunningham, A.S. "Letter: Infant Feeding and SIDS," Pediatrics, 58 (September, 1976), 467-468.

4265. Cunningham, R.M. Jr. "When Enough is Enough," Hospitals, 53 (1 July, 1979), 63-65.

4266. Curl, J.S. The Victorial Celebration of Death. Detroit: Partridge Press, 1972.

4267. Curlin, G.T. et al. "Demographic Crisis: The Impact of the Bangladesh Civil War (1971) on Births and Deaths in a Rural Area of Bangladesh," Population Studies, 30 (March, 1976), 87-105.

4268. Curran, C.E. "An Overview of Medical Ethics," New Catholic World, 219 (September-October, 1976), 227-232.

4269. Curran, W.J. "Law-Medicine Notes - Guyana Mass Suicide - Medico-legal Re-evaluation," New England Journal of Medicine, 300 (1979), 1321.

4270. Curtain, L. The Mask of Euthanasia. Cincinnati: Nurses Concerned for Life, 1976.

4271. __________. "Euthanasia: A Clarification," Update on Ethics, 1 (May, 1977), 1-10.

4272. Damiani, P., M. Aubenque. "Model of Transition Between Causes of Death," International Journal of Epidemiology, 4 (June, 1975), 113-117.

4273. Daniels, J. "Our Baby is Dead," Training, 12 (April, 1975), 63-64.

4274. Daniels, J. "The Victory," Nursing (Jenkintown), 6 (May, 1976), 39.

4275. Danto, B.L. et al. "Crisis Intervention in the Classroom Regarding the Homicide of a Teacher," School Counselor, 26 (November, 1978), 69-102.

4276. Datan, N. "The Life Cycle, Aging and Death: Dialectical Perspectives," Human Development, 20 (1977), 185-216.

4277. Datan, N., L. Ginsberg (eds). Life-Span Developmental Psychology (Normative Life Crises). New York: Academic Press, 1975.

4278. David, C.J. "Grief, Mourning and Pathological Mourning," Primary Care, 2 (March, 1975), 81-92.

4279. Davidson, C.S. When You Are a Widow. St. Louis: Concordia Publishing House, 1968.

4280. Davidson, G.P. "Coming To Terms With Cancer," New Zealand Nursing Journal, 71 (June, 1978), 4-6.

4281. Davidson, G.W. "In Search of Models of Care," Death Education, 2 (Spring-Summer, 1978), 145-160.

4282. ________. "Death of the Wished-For Child: A Case Study," Death Education, 1 (Fall, 1977), 265-275.

4283. Davidson, H.R. The Road to Hel; A Study of the Conception of the Dead in Old Norse Literature. New York: Greenwood Press, 1968.

4284. Davies, J. "Sudden Death in Infancy," Public Health, 89 (May, 1975), 143.

4285. Davies, L.J. "Attitudes Toward Old Age and Aging As Shown By Humor," Gerontologist, 17 (June, 1977), 220-226.

4286. Davis, D.M. "Editorial: SIDS: An Opportunity for Primary Prevention," American Journal of Psychiatry, 132 (June, 1975), 648-649.

4287. Davis, J.J. Mummies, Men and Madness. Grand Rapids, Michigan: Baker Book House, 1972.

4288. Davis, S.F. et al. "Relationship of Fear and Death and Level of Self-Esteem in College Students," Psychological Reports, 42 (April, 1978), 419-422.

4289. Davis, T.M. "The Effect of the Death Education Film 'In My Memory' On Elementary School Students in La Crosse, Wisconsin Public Schools," Dissertation Abstracts International, 36(12-A) (June, 1976), 7945-7946.

4290. Davis-Cambridge, J. "Parapsychology: A New Perspective on Dying," Suicide and Life-Threatening Behavior, 6 (Fall, 1976), 179-188.

4291. Dawson, A. "Survey: Sids Research and Counseling," American Journal of Nursing, 76 (October, 1976), 1602-1603.

4292. Deboer, C. "The Polls: Abortion," The Public Opinion Quarterly, 4 (Winter, 1977-1978), 553-564.

4293. Decker, D.J. "Grief: In the Valley of the Shadow," American Journal Nursing, (March, 1978), 416-417.

4294. Deckla, W.D. "A Time to Die," Life Sciences, 16 (January, 1975), 31-44.

4295. Deeble, K.A. "A Chance to Care," Nursing Mirror, 140 (April, 1975), 59-61.

4296. Defrasne, J.P. "Struggle for Life or Right to Die," Soins, 22 (June, 1977), 49-51.

4297. Degner, L.F. "Death in Disaster: Implications for Bereavement," Essence, 1 (1976), 69-75.

4298. DeGraves, D. "The Widow's Consultation Centre: Development of a Service in Grief Intervention," Canadian Journal of Psychiatric Nursing, 18 (November-December, 1977), 9-11.

4299. Dehejia, V. Living and Dying: An Inquiry Into the Enigma of Death and After-Life. Chicago: Advent Books, Inc. 1979.

4300. Delisle, R.G., A.S. Woods. "Death and Dying in Children's Literature: An Analysis of Three Selected Works," *Language Arts*, 53 (September, 1976), 683-688.

4301. Demi, A.S. "Adjustment to Widowhood After a Sudden Death: Suicide and Nonsuicide Survivors Compared," *Communicating Nursing Research*, 11 (1978), 20-23.

4302. Dempsey, D.R. *The Way We Die: An Investigation of Death and Dying in America Today*. New York: MacMillan, 1975. McGraw, 1977.

4303. Denbeau, M.S. "The Process of Coming to Terms With Death as a Psychic Energy Release," *Dissertation Abstracts International*, 37 (February, 1977), 4135.

4304. Denes, M. *In Necessity and Sorrow: Life and Death in an Abortion Hospital*. New York: Basic Books, 1976. Penquin Books, 1977.

4305. Deni, L. "Death and Nursing Care," *Nursing Care*, 11 (September, 1978), 20-23.

4306. Denton, J.A., V.B. Jr. Winsenbaker. "Death Experience and Death Anxiety Among Nurses and Nursing Students," *Nursing Research*, 26 (January-February, 1977), 61-64.

4307. Des Pres, T. *The Survivor: An Anatomy of the Death Camps*. New York: Oxford University Press, 1976.

4308. Dettmer, C.M. "Hospice," *Ohio State Medical Journal*, 74 (September, 1978), 579-580.

4309. DeVaul, R.A., S. Zisook. "Psychiatry: Unresolved Grief. Clinical Considerations," *Postgraduate Medicine*, 59 (May, 1976), 267-271.

4310. DeVeber, L.L. "Letter: On Withholding Treatment," *Canadian Medical Association Journal*, 111 (December 7, 1974), 1183&1185.

4311. Devins, G.M., D.I. Templer. "Comment on 'The Time of Death of Psychologists," *Essence*, 1 (1977), 163-169.

4312. Devins, G.M. "Death Anxiety and Voluntary Passive Euthanasia - Influences of Proximity to Death and Experiences With Death in Important Other Persons," *Journal of Consulting and Clinical Psychology*, 47 (1979), 301-309.

4313. Dezso, L. "Euthanasia or the Crisis of Medical Ethics," Orvosi Hetilap, 117 (May 30, 1976), 1323-1328.

4314. D'Heurle, A., J.N. Feimer. "Lost Children: The Role of the Child in Psychological Plays of Henrik Ibsen," Psychoanalytic Review, 63 (Spring, 1976), 27-47.

4315. Dial, A.L. "Death in the Life of Native Americans," Indian Historian, 11 (Summer, 1978), 33-37.

4316. Diamond, B.L. "Murder and the Death Penalty: A Case Report," American Journal of Orthopsychiatry, 45 (July, 1975), 712-722.

4317. Diamond, R. "The Archetype of Death and Renewal in 'I Never Promised You a Rose Garden'," Perspectives of Psychiatric Care, 13 (January-March, 1975), 21-24.

4318. Dickinson, G.E. "Death Education in U.S. Medical Schools," Journal of Medical Education, 51 (February, 1976), 134-136.

4319. Dickinson, G.E., A.A. Pearson. "Death Education in Selected Medical Schools as Related to Physicians' Attitudes And Reactions Toward Dying Patients," Annual Conference of Research and Medical Education, 16 (1970), 31-36.

4320. _______. "Sex Differences of Physicians in Relating to Dying Patients," Journal of the American Medical Women's Association, 34, (January, 1979), 45-47.

4321. _______. "Differences in Attitudes Toward Terminal Patients Among Selected Medical Specialties of Physicians," Medical Care, 17 (June, 1979), 682-685.

4322. Dickstein, L.S. "Self-report and Fantasy Correlates of Death Concern," Psychological Reports, 37 (August, 1975), 147-158.

4323. _______. "Attitudes Toward Death, Anxiety and Social Desirability," Omega, 8 (1977-1978), 369-378.

4324. Dietrich, B.C. Death, Fate and the Gods: The Development of a Religious Idea in Greek Popular Belief and in Homer. London: Athlone Press, 1967.

4325. Dimsdale, J.E. "Emotional Causes of Sudden Death," American Journal of Psychiatry, 134 (December, 1977), 1361-1366.

4326. Dinsmore, J.S. (ed). Death and Dying: An Examination of Legislative and Policy Issues. Washington: Georgetown University, Health Policy Center, 1977.

4327. Dobbelaere, C.J. "A Teaching Strategy on Tragedy," Health Education, 8 (November-December, 1977), 11-12.

4328. Dobson, J. "Children, Death and the Media," Counseling and Values, 21 (April, 1977), 172-179.

4329. Doherty, G., J. Doherty. "Dying and the Conspiracy of Denial," Essence, 1 (1976), 34-38.

4330. Doka, K.J., E. Schwarz. "Assigning Blame - Restoration of Sentimental Order Following an Accidental Death," Omega, 9 (1979), 287-292.

4331. Dolan, J.P. "Euthanasia: A Historical Perspective" Journal of the South Carolina Medical Association, 75 (March, 1979), 115-118.

4332. Dondlinger, P. "Was Terry Dead?," Nursing (Jenkintown), 5 (April, 1975), 18.

4333. Donne, J. Biothanatos. New York: Arno Press, 1976. (Orig. Pub. 1930)

4334. Donner, G. "Death and Dying: A Personal Perspective," Canadian Nurse, 74 (November, 1978), 20-21.

4335. Donohue, W.R. "Student Death: What Do We Do?," National Association of Student Personnel Administrators Journal, 14 (Spring, 1977), 29-32.

4336. Donovan, D.M. "Some Thoughts on Being and Having," International Journal of Social Psychiatry, 21 (Winter-Spring, 1974-1975), 12-13.

4337. Donovan, M.I., S.G. Pierce. Cancer Care Nursing. New York: Appleton-Century-Crofts, 1976.

4338. Donovan, R.J. "Prescribe Home Care? Now I Can," Medical Economics, 54 (5 September, 1977), 145-153.

4339. ________. "Death and Dying: Some Observations," Maryland State Medical Journal, (March, 1977), 35-40.

4340. Dorf, I. "Quinlan Case Leaves Physicians With Life-Death Decisions," Hospitals, 50 (January, 1976), 83-85.

4341. Dornette, W.H. "Editorial: Death Decision," Journal of Legal Medicine, 3 (November-December, 1975), 10.

4342. Dorph, M.H. "Care of the Dying: Is Hospice Necessary? Editorial," Delaware Medical Journal, 51 (January, 1979), 38-39.

4343. Doty, W.L. Where is Your Victory? Death as a Dynamic Theme of Christian Spirituality. Peterson, New Jersey: St. Anthony Guild Press, 1970.

4344. Downie, P.A. "Symposium: Care of the Dying: A Personal Commentary on the Care of the Dying on the North American Continent," Nursing Mirror, 139 (October, 1974), 68-70.

4345. Doyle, J.T. "Mechanisms and Prevention of Sudden Death," Modern Concepts of Cardiovascular Disease, 45 (July, 1976), 111-116.

4346. Drabeck, T.E. et al. "The Impact of Disaster on Kin Relationships," Journal of Marriage and the Family, 37 (August, 1975), 481-492.

4347. Drabeck, T.E., W.H. Key. "The Impact of Disaster on Primary Group Linkages," Mass Emergencies, 1 (February, 1976), 89-105.

4348. Dracup, K.A., C.S. Brew. "Using Nursing Research Findings to Meet the Needs of Grieving Spouses," Nursing Research, 27 (July-August, 1978), 212-216.

4349. Drake, D.C. "One Must Die So That the Other Might Live," Nursing Forum, 16 (1977), 228-249.

4350. Draughton, M. "Step-Mother's Model of Identification in Relation to Mourning in the Child," Psychological Report, 36 (February, 1975), 183-189.

4351. Drazin, Y. How to Prepare for Death. New York: Hawthorn, 1976.

4352. DuBois, P. Hospices: A New Way to Die. New York: Human Services Press, 1979.

4353. Dudeck, S,A, Reflections on the Meaning of Twentieth Century Art Forms," Journal of Creative Behavior, 9 (4th Quarter, 1975), 277-282 & 295.

4354. Duff, R.S., A.G.M. Cambell. "On Deciding The Care of Severely Handicapped or Dying Persons: With Particular Reference to Infants," Pediatrics, 57 (April, 1976), 487-493.

4355. Duke, E.H. "Meaning in Life and Acceptance of Death in Terminally Ill Patients," Dissertation Abstracts International, 38 (February, 1978), 3874-3875.

4356. Duke, M. "I Need My Rest," Journal of Practical Nursing, 29 (May, 1979), 38.

4357. Dugan, M.N. "Fear of Death: The Effect of Parental Behavior and Personality Upon the Behavior and Personality of Their Children," Dissertation Abstracts International, 38 (September, 1977), 1318.

4358. Dugas, M., C. Gueriot. "Psychological and Psychopathological Consequences of Mourning in Children," Revue De Praticien (Paris) 25 (October, 1975), 3653-3654.

4359. Duncan, S., P. Rodney. "Hope: A Negative Force," Canadian Nurse, 74 (November, 1978), 22-23.

4360. Dunea, G. "Death With Dignity," British Medical Journal, 1 (April, 1976), 824-825.

4361. Dunlop, J.L. "Bereavement Reaction Following Stillbirth," Practitioner, 222 (January, 1979), 115-118.

4362. Dunstan, G.R. "Mercy Killing: Does the Law Really Need to Create a New Offense," Times (London), (30 November, 1976), 13.

4363. ________. "Euthanasia: Clarifying the Issues," Documentation in Medical Ethics, 5 (1975), 4.

4364. Durlack, J.A., J.A. Burchard. "Preliminary Evaluation of a Hospital-Based Continuing Education Workshop on Death and Dying," Journal of Medical Education, 52 (May, 1977), 423-424.

4365. Durlack, J.A. "Comparison Between Experiential and Didactic Methods of Death Education," Omega, 9 (1979), 57-66.

4366. Dyck, A.J. "Conflicting Views of Beneficence in Euthanasia Debate," in: On Human Care: An Introduction to Ethics. Nashville: Abingdon, 1977, 72-91.

4367. _______. On Human Care: An Introduction to Ethics. Nashville: Abingdon, 1977.

4368. Dynes, R.R. .Organized Behavior in Disaster, Columbus, Ohio: Ohio State University, 1976, VII, 235 pages.

4369. ________. "The Comparative Study of Disaster: A Social Organizational Approach," Mass Emergencies, 1 (October, 1975), 21-31.

4370. Earle, A.M. et al (eds). The Nurse as Caregiver for the Terminal Patient and his Family. New York: Columbia University Press, 1976.

4371. Easson, W.M. The Dying Child: The Management of the Child or Adolescent Who is Dying. Springfield, Illinois: Charles C. Thomas Publishers, 1971.

4372. Eastman, M. "Feelings are Facts in This House. Hospices Care for Those With no Cure," American Pharmacy, 18 (November, 1978) 18-22.

4373. Ebira, T., A. Shimizu. "Euthanasia and the Handicapped," Japan Journal of Nursing, 41 (August, 1977), 797-808.

4374. Ebon, M. The Evidence For Life After Death. New York: Signet, 1977.

4375. Eccles-Smith, C. "The Doctor and The Dying Patient," Australian Family Physician, 5 (October, 1976), 1262-1263 & 1265-1266.

4376. Eddy, D.C. Angel Whispers: or, The Echo of Spirit Voices (designed to comfort those who mourn). Boston: Wentworth and Company, 1856.

4377. Edmund-Davies. "Edwin Stevens Lecture. On Dying and Dying Well. Legal Aspects," Proceedings of the Royal Society of Medicine, 70 (February, 1977), 73-74.

4378. Edwards, D., M.J. Graves (ed). Death-The Doorway to the Future. LeVale, Maryland: Excelsior, 1977.

4379. Eels, J. "In The Time of Grief," Journal of Religion and Health, 16 (April, 1977), 116-118.

4380. Eger, M.J. "The Fear of Dying Editorial," Journal of American Optometric Association, 48 (October, 1977), 1219-1220.

4381. Ehrenwald, J. "Out of the Body Experiences and the Denial of Death," Journal of Nervous and Mental Disease, 159 (October, 1974) 227-233.

4382. Eisenstadt, J.M. "Parental Loss and Genius," American Psychologist, 33 (March, 1978), 211-233.

4383. Elfert, H. "The Nurse and the Grieving Patient," Canadian Nurse, 71 (February, 1975), 30-31.

4384. Eliot, S.V. "The Determinants of Psychological Response to Abortion," Dissertation Abstracts International, 36 (February, 1976), 4151.

4385. Elkind, D. "Life and Death: Concepts and Feelings in Children," Day Care and Early Education, 4 (January-February, 1977), 26-29 & 39.

4386. Elkowitz, E.B. "Death and the Elderly Patient," Journal of the American Geriatric Society, 26 (January, 1978), 36-38.

4387. Ellington, P.D. "The Right to Life: An Ethical Dilemma: A Physician's Viewpoint," Journal of the Medical Association of Georgia, 67 (February, 1978), 113-132.

4388. Elliott, B.A. "Neonatal Death: Reflections for Parents," Pediatrics, 62 (July, 1978), 100-102.

4389. Elliott, B.A., H.A. Hein. "Neonatal Death: Reflections for Physicians," Pediatrics, 62 (July, 1978), 96-100.

4390. Embry, C.R. "Love, Death and Liberal Education," Liberal Education , 62 (October, 1976), 444-456.

4391. Emde, R.N., C. Brown. "Adaptation to the Birth of a Down's Syndrome Infant: Grieving and Maternal Attachment," Journal of The American Academy of Child Psychiatry, 17 (Spring, 1978), 299-323.

4392. Emerson, P. "Covert Grief Reaction in Mentally Retarded Clients," Mentally Retarded, 15 (December, 1977), 46-47.

4393. Engel, G.L. "The Death of a Twin: Mourning and Anniversary Reactions," International Journal of Psychoanalysis, 56 (1975), 23-40.

4394. Engelhardt, H.T. "Treating Aging: Restructuring the Human Condition," in: Neugarten, B.L., R.J. Havighurst (eds). Extending the Human Life Span: Social Policy and Social Ethics. Washington: U.S. Government Printing Office, 1977.

4395. Engelhardt, H.T. et al. "Euthanasia in Texas: A Little Known Experiment," Hospital Physician, 12 (September, 1976), 30-31.

4396. Engelman, R.M., R.S. Smith. "Dealing with Death: An Exercise in Thematic Programming and Development of Community," National Association of Student Personnel Administrators Journal, 13 (Winter, 1976), 52-56.

4397. Epley, R.J., C.H. McCaughy. "The Stigma of Dying: Attitudes Toward the Terminally Ill," Omega, 8 (1977-1978), 379-393.

4398. Epstein, G. et al. "Research on Bereavement: A Selective and Critical Review," Comprehensive Psychiatry, 16 (November-December, 1975), 537-546.

4399. Epstein, G.M. et al. "Professionals Preferences for Support Systems for the Bereaved Family," Journal of Community Psychology, 4 (January, 1976), 69-73.

4400. Epstein, G. "Evaluating the Bereavement Process as it is Affected by Variation in the Time of Intervention," Dissertation Abstracts International, 38 (November, 1977), 2362.

4401. Epting, F.R. et al. "Construction of Death and Levels of Death Fear," Death Education, 3 (1979), 21-30.

4402. Erickson, K.T. "Loss of Communality at Buffalo Creek," American Journal of Psychiatry, 133 (March, 1976), 302-305.

4403. ________. Everything In Its Path. New York: Simon & Schuster, 1976.

4404. Erickson, P.E. et al. "Families in Disaster: Patterns of Recovery," Mass Emergencies, 1 (July, 1976), 203-216.

4405. Escoffier-Lambiotte. "The Physician Facing Death," Bruxelles-Medical (Brussels), 57 (September, 1977), 356-360.

4406. Etienne, R. "Ancient Medical Conscience and the Life of Children," Journal of Psychohistory, 4 (Fall, 1976), 131-161.

4407. Evans, F. "The Right to Die--A Basic Constitutional Right," Journal of Legal Medicine, 5 (August, 1977), 17-20.

4408. Evans, J.R. et al. "Teenagers: Fertility Control Behavior and Attitudes Before and After Abortion, Childbearing or Negative Pregnancy Test," Family Planning Perspectives, 8 (July-August, 1976), 192-200.

4409. Evans, N.S. "Mourning as a Family Secret," Journal of American Academy of Child Psychiatry, 15 (Summer, 1976), 502-509.

4410. Everett, M.G. "Helping Parents Teach About Death," Health Education, 7 (July-August, 1976), 27-29.

4411. Everson, R.B., J.F. Fraumeni, Jr. "Mortality Among Medical Students Young Physicians," Journal of Medical Education, 50 (August, 1975), 809-811.

4412. Eyer, J. "Prosperity as a Cause of Death," International Journal of Health Science, 7 (1977), 125-150.

4413. Faella, J.D. "Medico-Legal Aspects of the Concept of Brain Death: An Appraisal," Rhode Island Medical Journal, 59 (December, 1976), 560-561.

4414. Fairey, W.F. "A Definition of Death," Journal of the South Carolina Medical Association, 73 (January, 1977), 5-8.

4415. Fallon, M.R. "Fear of Death in Young Adolescents: A Study of the Relationships Between Fear of Death and Selected Anxiety, Personality and Intelligence Variables," Dissertation Abstracts International, 36 (March, 1976), 5941-5942.

4416. Fang, B., K.A. Howell. "Death Anxiety Among Graduate Students," Journal of American College Health Association, 25 (June, 1977), 310-313.

4417. Farley, C. The Garden is Doing Fine. New York: Atheneum, 1975.

4418. Faschingbauer, T.R. et al. "Development of the Texas Inventory of Grief," American Journal of Psychiatry, 134 (June, 1977), 696-698.

4419. Fassler, J. My Grandpa Died Today. New York: Behavioral Publications, 1971.

4420. Fast, N. "Visit to the New Venture Graveyard," Research Management, 22 (1979), 18-22.

4421. Fath, G. "Pastoral Care and the Hospice," Hospital Progress, 60 (March, 1979), 73-75.

4422. Fatteh, A. "Dead Woman Allowed to Die: A Unique Case in Florida," Journal of Legal Medicine, 5 (January, 1977), 24.

4423. Favorita, J. et al. "Apnea Monitoring to Prevent SIDS," American Journal of Nursing, 79 (1979), 101-104.

4424. Fechner, G.T. The Little Book of Life After Death. New York: Arno Press, 1976. (Orig. Pub. 1904)

4425. Feder, S.L. "Attitudes of Patients With Advanced Malignancy," in: Shneidman, E.S. (ed) Death: Current Perspectives. Palo Alto, California: Mayfield Publishing Company, 1976.

4426. Feifel, H. "Death and Dying in Modern America," Death Education, 1 (Spring, 1977), 5-14.

4427. ________. New Meanings of Death. New York: McGraw-Hill, 1977.

4428. Feigenberg, L. Terminal Ward. Lund: Liber Laromedel, 1977.

4429. Feinberg, J. "Voluntary Euthanasia and the Inalienable Right to Life," Philosophy and Public Affairs, 7 (Winter, 1978), 93-123.

4430. Feinleib, M. et al. "Prodromal Symptoms and Signs of Sudden Death," Circulation, 52 (December, 1975), 155-159.

4431. Feinleib, M., R. Fabsitz. "Do Bio-Rhythms Influence the Day of Death?" New England Journal of Medicine, 298 (18 May, 1978), 1153.

4432. Fell, J. "Grief Reactions in the Elderly Following the Death of a Spouse: The Role of Crisis Intervention in Nursing," Journal of Gerontological Nursing, 3 (November-December, 1977), 17-20.

4433. Felner, R.D. et al. "Crisis Events and School Mental Health Referral Patterns of Young Children," Journal of Consulting and Clinical Psychology, 43 (June, 1975), 305-310.

4434. Fenn, J., B. Fassel. "Research in Critical Care Education - Production of Videotapes for In-Hospital Use," Heart and Lung, 8 (1979), 311-317.

4435. Ferber, M. "Death, Dying and Bereavement - An Indepth Study. 'I Cried But Not for Irma'," Lamp, 35 (March, 1978), 4-5.

4436. Ficarra, B.J. "The Aged, The Dying, The Dead: Medical Legal Considerations,"Psychosomatics, 19 (January, 1978), 41-45.

4437. ________. "Legal Rights of Sepulcher," Legal Medical Annual, (1974) 137-146.

4438. Fine, M.R. "Psychological Considerations of the Child With a Progressive Terminal Condition in a Residential Setting," New Outlook For the Blind, 69 (March, 1975), 121-130.

4439. Fisch, D. "Is It My Turn to Die?" Union Medicale du Canada, 105 (November, 1976), 1695-1698.

4440. Fischer, E.H. "Student Nurses View an Abortion Client - Attitude and Context Effects," Journal of Population, 2 (1979), 33-46.

4441. Fischhoff, J., M. O'Brien. "After the Child Dies," Journal of Pediatrics, 88 (January, 1976), 140-146.

4442. Fjelstad, O.C. "The Funeral Service and the Funeral Address," Theological Forum, 6 (1934), 203-211.

4443. Flannery, E.J. "Statutory Recognition of the Right to Die," Boston University Law Review, 57 (January, 1977), 148-177.

4444. Flannery, R.B., Jr. "Behavior Modification and Geriatric Grief," International Journal of Aging and Human Development, 5 (Spring, 1974), 197-203.

4445. Fleming, S.J. "Nurses' Death Anxiety and Clinical Geriatric Training," Dissertation Abstracts International, 36 (April, 1976), 5254.

4446. ________. "Perceptual Defensiveness and Death Anxiety," Psychological Report, 41 (October, 1977), 391-396.

4447. Fleming, S., R. Lonetto. Children's Conceptions of Aging and Death. New York: Springer, 1978.

4448. Fleming, T., A.H. Kutscher (eds). Communicating Issues in Thanatology. New York: MSS Information Corportion, 1976.

4449. Fleshman, J.K., D.R. Peterson. "The Sudden Infant Death Syndrome Among Alaskan Natives," American Journal of Epidemology, 105 (June, 1977), 555-558.

4450. Fletcher, J. "Abortion, Euthanasia, and the Care of Defective New-borns," New England Journal of Medicine, 292 (January, 1975), 75-78.

4451. Flexner, J.M. "The Hospice Movement in North America--Is It Coming of Age," Southern Medical Journal, 72 (March, 1979), 248-250.

4452. Foelber, P.F. Bach's Treatment of the Subject of Death in His Choral Music. Washington: Catholic University of America Press, 1961.

4453. Folscher, C.W. "Determination of Brain Death," South African Nursing Journal, 42 (December, 1975), 10-11.

4454. Foot, P. "Euthanasia," Philosophy and Public Affairs, 6 (Winter, 1977), 85-112.

4455. Forbes, J.D. "Religious Freedom and The Protection of Native American Places of Worship and Cemeteries," Native American Studies, University of Californa at Davis, 1977.

4456. Ford, M. et al. On The Other Side. Plainfield, New Jersey: Logos, 1978.

4457. Fordyce, E.J. "Early Mortality Measures as Indicators of Socio-Economic Well-Being for Whites and Non-Whites: a Re-Appraisal," Sociology and Social Research, 61 (January, 1977), 125-137.

4458. Formby, J. "Christian Teaching Concerning Death," Nursing Times, 74 (May, 1978), suppl. 58-60.

4459. Formanek, R. "When Children Ask About Death," Elementary School Journal, 75 (November, 1974), 92-97.

4460. Forrester, A.C. "Brain Death and the Donation of Cadaver Kidneys," Health Bulletin (Edinberg), 34 (July, 1976), 199-204.

4461. Forsythe, D.M. "The Will to Live and the Right to Die," The Practitioner, 220 (March, 1978), 362-366.

4462. Fost, N. "Proxy Consent for Seriously Ill Newborns," in: Smith, D.H. (ed) No Rush to Judgement: Essays on Medical Ethics. Indiana University Poynter Center, Bloomington, Indiana, 1977, 1-17.

4463. Foster, H.J., Jr. "Time of Death," New York State Journal of Medicine, 76 (December, 1976), 2187-2197.

4464. Foster, J.R. "To Die Young, To Die Old," Journal of Geriatric Psychiatry, 8 (1975), 111-126.

4465. Foster, Z. "Standards for Hospice Care" Assumptions and Principles," Health Social Work, 4 (February, 1979), 117-128.

4466. Fowkes, F.G.R. et al. "Abortion and the NHS - 1st Decade," British Medical Journal, 1 (1979), 217-219.

4467. Fox, R.A. "Guidelines for the Cognitive Domain of Education for Death and Dying for Criminal Justice Majors at John Hay College of Criminal Justice," Dissertation Abstracts International, 37 (March, 1977), 5619.

4468. Fox, R.C. "Advanced Medical Technology--Social and Ethical Implications," in: Inkeles, A. et al (Eds) Annual Review of Sociology, 2, Annual Reviews, Palo Alto, California, 1976, 231-268.

4469. Fraikor, A.L. "Parental Snoring and SIDS: A Testable Hypothesis Letter," Pediatrics, 60 (September, 1977), 85-86.

4470. Franciosi, R.A. "Diagnosis of Sudden Infant Death Syndrome, SIDS Letter," Minnesota Medicine, 60 (January, 1977), 43.

4471. ________. "Sudden Infant Death and Adrenal Insufficiency Letter," Archives of Pathology and Laboratory Medicine, 101 (October, 1977), 555.

4472. ________. "Approaching the Problem of Sudden Infant Death Syndrome," Minnesota Medicine, 60 (February, 1977), 117-119.

4473. ________. "Editorial: Sudden Infant Death Syndrome," Minnesota Medicine, 58 (September, 1975), 683.

4474. Francome, C. "Abortion and Opinion," New Society, 47 (1979), 678.

4475. Frazer, J.G. The Fear of the Dead in Primitive Religion. New York: Arno Press, 1976. (Orig. Pub. 1933/1934/1936)

4476. Franzino, M.A. et al. "Group Discussion Among the Terminally Ill," International Journal of Group Psychotherapy, 26 (January, 1976), 43-48.

4477. Frederick, D.L., D. Frederick. Death Education and Counseling: A Training Manual. Berkeley, California: Pilgrimage, 1978.

4478. Fredrick, J.F. "Grief as a Disease Process," Omega, 7 (1976-1977), 297-305.

4479. Fredlund, D.J. "Children and Death from the School Setting Viewpoint," Journal of School Health, 47 (November, 1977), 533-537.

4480. Freeman, F. "Death is a Muffled Sound--An Empty Place," Journal of Americah Health Care Association, 3 (March, 1977), 21-22.

4481. Freeman, E.W. "Abortion: Beyond Rhetoric to Access," Social Work, 21 (November, 1976), 483-486.

4482. Freeman, J. "Death and Dying in Three Days," Phi Delta Kappan, 60 (October 1978).

4483. Freese, A.S. Help For Your Grief: Turning Emotional Loss Into Growth. New York: Schocken Books, 1977.

4484. Freihofer, P. et al. "Nursing Behaviors in Bereavement: An Exploratory Study,: Nursing Research, 25 (September-October, 1976), 332-337.

4485. Fremantle, F., C. Trungpa. The Tibetan Book of the Dead. (Transl.) New York: Random House, 1975.

4486. Freud, S. Civilization, War and Death. London: Hogarth Press, 1953.

4487. Friedlander, W.J. "Death: An Operational Definition," Nebraska Medical Journal, 62 (June, 1977), 181-184.

4488. Frigenberg, L. Terminal Care: Friendship Contracts With Dying Cancer Patients. New York: Brunner-Mazel, 1980.

4489. Froggatt, P. "A Cardiac Cause in Cot Death: A Discarded Hypothesis," Irish Medical Journal, 70 (September, 1977), 408-414.

4490. Frost, N.R., P.J. Clayton, "Bereavement and Psychiatric Hospitalization," Archives of General Psychiatry, 34 (October, 1977), 1172-1175.

4491. Fry, C. Death is a Kind of Love. Cranberry Isles, Maryland: The Tidal Press, 1979.

4492. Fulton, J.S. "Death and Dying," Ohio State Medical Journal, 74 (December, 1978), 769-771.

4493. Fulton, R. (ed), R. Bendiksen. Death and Identity. (rev. ed.) Bowie, Maryland: Charles Press, 1976.

4494. Fulton, R. Death, Grief and Bereavement: A Bibliography. 1845-1975. New York: Arno Press, 1977.

4495. Fulton, R. "Anticipatory Grief, Stress and the Surrogate Griever," in: Tache, J. et al (eds) Cancer, Stress and Death. New York: Plenum Publishing Company, 1979.

4496. ________. "The Sociology of Death," Death Education, 1 (Spring, 1977), 15-25.

4497. ________. "Death and the Funeral in Contemporary Society," in: Wass, H. (ed) Dying: Facing the Facts. New York: Hemisphere Publishing, 1979.

4498. ________, D.J. Gottesman. "Anticipatory Grief: A Psychosocial Concept Reconsidered," British Journal of Psychiatry. (July, 1980), 45-54.

4499. ________. et al. "SIDS: The Survivor as Victim," Omega, 8 (November, 1978), 227-234.

4500. ________. "Current Issues in Death and Dying," essay prepared for Courses by Newspaper. Reprinted in 450 newspapers throughout the United States and Canada and also in Newspaper Article Booklet, Death and Dying: Challenge and Change. Reading, Massachusetts: Addison-Wesley, 1979, 2-4.

4501. ________. "Death in Popular Culture" (with Eric Markusen), essay prepared for Courses by Newspaper. Reprinted in 450 newspapers throughout the United States and Canada and also in Newspaper Article Booklet, Death and Dying: Challenge and Change. Reading, Massachusetts: Addison-Wesley, 1979, 8-10.

4502. ________. "The Luo Way of Death: Rendezvous With Rebellion," (with Amos Odenyo and Sonja Fagenberg) Studia Africana, 1, 2 (Spring, 1978), 127-142.

4503. ________. "Death," in: World Book Encyclopedia. Chicago: Field Enterprises Education Corporation, 1978. Vol. 5, 52-53.

4504. ________. "Funeral Customs," in: World Book Encyclopedia. Chicago: Field Enterprises Educational Corporation 1978. Vol. 7, 482-483.

4505. ________. "Death and Dying in Sweden," (With Loma Feigenberg) Lakartidningen (Swedish Medical Journal, Stockholm), 73:23 (June 2, 1976), 2179-2258.

4506. ________. "Care of the Dying: A Swedish Perspective," (with Loma Feigenberg), Omega, 8:3 (1977), 215-228.

4508. Furlow, T.W., Jr. "Tyrrany of Technology: A Physician Looks at Euthanasia," The Humanist, 34 (July-August, 1974), 609.

4509. Furman, E. "Helping Children Cope With Death," Young Children, 33 (May, 1978), 25-32.

4510. Gable, P. "Freud's Death Instinct and Sartre's Fundamental Project," Psychoanalytic Review, 61 (Summer, 1974), 217-227.

4511. Gaffney, K.F. "Helping Grieving Parents," Journal of Emergency Nursing," 2 (July-August, 1976), 42-43.

4512. Fajdusek, R.E. "Death, Incest and the Triple Bond in the Later Plays of Shakespeare," American Imago, 31 (Summer, 1974), 109-158.

4513. Galbajgh, J.J. "A Study of Relationships Between Personality Categories and Death Concern in Selected Group of Nurses," Dissertation Abstracts International, 36 (February, 1976), 5069.

4514. Galton, V.A. "Cancer Nursing at St. Christopher's Hospice," Proceedings of the National Conference on Cancer Nursing. Chicago: American Cancer Society, 1973.

4515. Gummage, S.L. et al. "The Occupational Therapist and Terminal Illness: Learning to Cope With Death," American Journal of Occupational Therapy, 30 (May-June, 1976), 294-299.

4516. Gammeltoff, M., R.J. Sommers. "Abortion Views and Practices Among Danish Family Physicians," Journal of Biosocial Science, 8 (July, 1976), 287-292.

4517. Gandour, M. "Coping With Grief as 'Bearing Up' and 'Bearing Down': An Exchange on James Agee's 'A Death in the Family'," Suicide and Life Threatening Behavior, 8 (Spring, 1978), 60-65.

4518. Gandy, R.J. "Estimate of the Effect of Abortions on the Stillbirth Rate," Journal of Biosocial Science, 11 (1979), 173-178.

4519. Gardner, A., M. Pritchard. "Mourning, Mummification and Living With the Dead," British Journal of Psychiatry, 130 (January, 1978), 23-28.

4520. Gardner, A.E., L Acklen. "Does Death Education Belong in the Middle School Curriculum," National Association of Secondary School Principals, 62 (January, 1978), 134-137.

4521. Gardner, G.G. "Childhood, Death and Human Dignity: Hypnotherapy for David," International Journal of Clinical and Experimental Hypnosis, 24 (April, 1976), 122-139.

4522. Gardner, J. "Swandron Discusses Ethics of 'Dickering With Death'," Canadian Medical Association Journal, 120 (March, 1979), 718-722.

4523. Gardner, L.I. "Thanatopsis Revisited. The Family and The Dying Infant," American Journal of Diseases of Children, 130 (September, 1976), 921-922.

4524. Gardner, R.F. "A New Ethical Approach to Abortion and Its Implications for the Euthanasia Dispute," Journal of Medical Ethics, 1 (September, 1975), 127-131.

4525. Garfield, C.A. (Ed). Psychosocial Care of the Dying Patient. New York: McGraw-Hill, 1978.

4526. ________. Psychological Aspects of Terminal Patient Care. New York: McGraw-Hill, 1978.

4527. ________. "Support for the Dying, The Shanti Project," Voluntary Action Leadership, (Spring, 1979), 37-40.

4528. Garfield, C.A., R.O. Clark. "The Shanti Project: A Community Model," Death Education, 1 (Winter, 1978), 397-408.

4529. Gargaro, W.J., Jr. "Cancer Nursing and the Law: Cancer Nurses and 'No Code' Orders," Cancer Nursing, 2 (February, 1979), 62-63.

4530. Garland, M. "Politics, Legislation and Natural Death. The Right to Die in California," Hastings Center Report, 6 (October, 1976), 5-6.

4531. ________. "Views on the Ethics of Infant Euthanasia," in: Jonsen, A.R., M.J. Garland, Ethics of Newborn Intensive Care. San Francisco: University of California Health Policy Program, 1976, 126-141

4532. Garner, J. "Palliative Care: It's the Quality of Life Remaining That Matters," Canadian Medical Association Journal, 115 (July, 1976), 179-180.

4533. Garrison, W. Strange Facts About Death. Nashville: Abingdon, 1978.

4534. Garrity, T.F., J. Wyss. "Death, Funeral and Bereavement Practices in Appalachian and Non-Appalachian Kentucky," Omega, 76 (1976), 209-228.

4535. Gates, M.S., G.G. Mayer. "Are You Too Sure of Your Stand on the Right to Die," RN, 41 (December, 1978), 75-82.

4536. Gattegno, C. On Death. New York: Educational Solutions, Inc., 1978.

4537. Gaylin, N.L. "On the Quality of Life and Death," Family Coordinator, 24 (July, 1975), 247-255.

4538. Gaylin, W. et al. "Who Should Decide? The Case of Karen Quinlan," Christianity and Crisis, 35 (January, 1976), 322-331.

4539. Gayton, W.F. et al. "Comparison of the MMPI and the Mini-Mult with Women Who Request Abortion," Journal of Clinical Psychology, 32 (July, 1976), 648-650.

4540. Geelhoed, G.W., L.T. Bowles. "Fear of Dying: Introducing the Medical Student to the Stresses of the Dying Patient," Journal of the American Health Care Association, 3 (May, 1977), 45-49.

4541. Gelles, R.J., M.A. Straus. "Family Experience and Public Support of the Death Penalty," American Journal of Orthopsychiatry, 45 (July, 1975), 596-613.

4542. Gerber, I. et al. "Anticipatory Grief and Aged Widows and Widower," Journal of Gerontology, 30 (March, 1975), 225-229.

4543. Gerber, I. et al (eds). Perspectives on Bereavement. New York: MSS Information Corportion, 1978.

4544. Gerchick, E. (ed). The Role of the Community Hospital in the Care of the Dying Patient and the Bereaved. New York: MSS Information Corporation, 1976.

4545. Gergo, J. "Life and Death--A Parent's View," Social Education, 43 (April, 1979), 324-326.

4546. Germann, D. Too Young to Die. New York: Farnsworth Publishing, 1975.

4547. Getson, R.F., D.L. Benshoff. "Four Experiences of Death and How Death and How to Prepare to Meet Them," School Counselor, 24 (May, 1977), 310-314.

4548. Gibson, D.A. "Saying Goodbye," Canadian Nurse, 74 (November, 1978), 30-31.

4549. Gibson, G. "I Was Supposed to Die Two Years Ago," RN, 40 (October, 1977), 46-48.

4550. Gillespie, D.S. "The Black Death and the Peasant's Revolt: A Reassessment," Humboldt Journal of Social Relations, 2 (Spring-Summer, 1975), 4-13.

4551. Gillis, R.J. Children's Books For Times of Stress: An Annotated Bibliography. Bloomington, Indiana: Indiana University Press, 1978.

4552. Gilson, G.J. "Care of the Family Who Has Lost a Newborn," Post-graduate Medicine, 60 (December, 1976), 67-70.

4553. Gittelsohn, A., J. Senning. "Studies of the Reliability of Vital and Health Records: Comparison of Cause of Death and Hospital Record Diagnoses," American Journal of Public Health, 69 (1979), 680-689.

4554. Giudice, L. Alone Until Tomorrow. Atlanta: John Knox Press, 1974.

4555. Glaser, D. "A Response to Bailey: More Evidence on Capital Punishment as Correlate of Tolerance for Murder," Crime and Delinquency, (January, 1976), 40-43.

4556. ________. "Capital Punishment--Deterrent or Stimulus to Murder - Our Unexamined Deaths and Penalties," University of Toledo Law Review, 10 (1979), 317-333.

4557. ________. "The Use of the Death Penalty v. Outrage at Murder," Crime and Delinquency, 20 (October, 1974), 333-338.

4558. Glicken, M.D. "The Child's View of Death," Journal of Marriage and Family Counseling, 4 (April, 1978), 75-81.

4559. Glickman, L. "Letter: Dealing with Dying Patients," American Journal of Psychiatry, 132 (June, 1975), 670-671.

4560. Glover, J. Causing Death and Saving Lives. Harmondsworth: Pelican Original. Penquin Books, 1977.

4561. Golan, N. "Wife to Widow to Woman," Social Work, 20 (September, 1975), 369-373.

4562. Gold, P. et al. "The Impact of Normal Volunteers on a Psychiatric Research Unit," American Journal of Psychiatry, 136 (April, 1979), 401-405.

4563. Goldberg, J.H. "The Extraordinary Confusion Over 'The Right to Die'," Medical Economics, 54 (January, 1977), 121-122.

4564. Goldreich, G. "What is Death? The Answers in Children's Books," Hastings Center Report, 7 (June, 1977), 18-20.

4565. Gonda, T.A. "Coping With Dying and Death," Geriatrics, 32 (September, 1977), 71-73.

4566. Gonzales, M.A. "The Physician, Death and Dying," Gaceta Medica de Mexico, 113 (January, 1977), 5-10.

4567. Gonzales, R. "Understanding Life and Death From a Dialectical Perspective," Suicide, 6 (Winter, 1976), 243-249.

4568. Goodall, J. "Life and Death at Gombe," National Geographic, 155 (1979), 592-621.

4569. Goodfriend, M., E.A. Wolpert. "Death From Fright: Report of a Case and Literature Review," Psychosomatic Medicine, 38 (September-October, 1976), 348-356.

4570. Gordon, A.V. "Psychological Sequelae of Abortion," New Zealand Psychologist, 5 (April, 1976), 37-47.

4571. Gordon, A., D. Klass. "The Facts of Life--and Death: The Role of Schools in Teaching About Death and Dying," American Teacher, 60 (April, 1976), 8-10.

4572. ________. "Goals for Death Education," School Counselor, 24 (May, 1977), 343-347.

4573. Gordon, R.R. "Perinatal and Infant Mortality Letter," British Medical Journal, 2 (September, 1977), 705.

4574. Gordon, R. "Death and Creativity: A Jungian Approach," Journal of the Annals of Psychology, 22 (April, 1977), 106-124.

4575. Gordon, R.W. "Crystal-Balling Death," Baylor Law Review, 30 (1978), 35-64.

4576. Gorer, G. Death, Grief and Mourning. New York: Arno Press, 1976. (Orig. Pub. 1965)

4577. Gortmaker, S.L. "Poverty and Infant Mortality in the United States," American Sociological Review, 44 (1979), 280-297.

4578. Gosselin, J.Y. et al. "Attitude of Psychiatrists Toward Terminally Ill Patients," Psychiatric Journal of the University of Ottawa, 2 (September, 1977), 120-123.

4579. Gottsegen, M.G. "Management of Mourning of a Dead or Dying Parent," American Journal of Psychotherapy, 31 (January, 1977), 36-42.

4580. Gould, J. "Euthanasia," Catholic Medical Quarterly, 28 (August, 1976), 8-15.

4581. Gow, C.M., J.I. Williams. "Nurses' Attitudes Toward Death and Dying: A Causal Interpretation," Social Science and Medicine, 11 (February, 1977), 191-198.

4582. Grady, F.P. "A Case Study Approach to the Kubler-Ross Theory of the Five Stages of Dying," Dissertation Abstracts International, 37 (January, 1977), 3579-3580.

4583. Grady, M. "An Assessment of the Behavioral Scientist's Role with The Dying Patient and The Family," Military Medicine, 140 (November, 1975), 789-792.

4584. Graham, S. "Little Victims--7. Early Gathered," Nursing Times, 74 (September, 1977), 1450-1451.

4585. Granqvist, H.N. Muslin Death and Burial: Arab Customs and Traditions Studied in a Village in Jordan. Commentationes Humanarum Literarum (34), Helsinki, 1965.

4586. Grass, E.R. "Proceedings: The Joint Role of EEG with Other Clinical and Laboratory Studies in the Determination of Cerebral Death," Electroencephalogram and Clinical Neurophysiology, 39 (October, 1975), 435.

4587. Graves, J.S. "Differentiating Grief, Mourning and Bereavement," American Journal of Psychiatry, 135 (July, 1978), 874-875.

4588. Gray, A. "Dying at Home," Nursing Times, 73 (August 11, 1977), 9-10.

4589. Gray, R.H. "Letter: On Infant Mortality," American Journal of Public Health, 65 (October, 1975), 113-1114.

4590. Greely, A. Death and Beyond. Chicago: Thomas More Press, 1976.

4591. Greeley, J. Euthanasia: The Debate. Cincinnati: Pamphlet Publications, 1977.

4592. Green, J.S. et al. "Understanding the Problems of Death and Dying: A Health Professionals' Attitude Survey," Journal of Allied Health, 7 (Fall, 1978), 294-301.

4593. Green, M.L.J. "The Image of Death as Portrayed in Fiction for Children," University Microfilms, Box 1754, Ann Arbor, Michigan, 126 pp. Dissertation.

4594. Greenberg, B. "Motherdear --A Tribute of Love," Journal of Gerontology Nursing, 3 (May-June, 1977), 13-15.

4595. Greenblatt, G.M. "A Proposal: Some New, 'old' Terms and a Scoring System for Irreversible Coma," Arizona Medicine, 38 (August, 1976), 626-627.

4596. Greenblatt, M. "The Grieving Spouse," American Journal of Psychiatry, 135 (January, 1978), 43-47.

4597. Greene, J. "Killer Disease: Sudden Infant Death Syndrome," Nursing Care, 8 (April, 1975), 18-20.

4598. Greenhouse, K. "Death--Form of Life in Flanner O'Connor," Suicide and Life Threatening Behavior, 8 (Summer, 1978), 118-128.

4599. Greenstein, L.R. "Bioethics: Occupational Therapy Attitudes Toward the Prolongation of Life," American Journal of Occupational Therapy, 31 (February, 1977), 77-80.

4600. Griffen, B., D. Blazer. "Hospice in North Carolina: Background and Unanswered Questions," North Carolina Journal of Medicine, 40 (April, 1979), 208-211.

4601. Griffith, J.A. et al. "Three Medical Students Confront Death in a Pediatric Ward," Comprehensive Nursing Quarterly, 10 (August, 1975), 74-80.

4602. Griggs, S.A. "Annotated Bibliography of Books on Death, Dying, and Bereavement," School Counselor, 24 (May, 1977), 362-371.

4603. Grinsell, L.V. Barrow, Pyramid, and Tomb: Ancient Burial Customs in Egypt, The Mediterranean and the British Isles. London: Thames and Hudson, 1975.

4604. Grisez, G., J.M. Boyle. "An Alternative to 'Death With Dignity'," Human Life Review, 4 (Winter, 1978), 26-43.

4605. Grisez, G. "Suicide and Euthanasia," in: Horan, D.J., D. Mall (eds) Death, Dying and Euthanasia. Washington: University Publications of America, 1977.

4606. Grof, S., J. Halifax. The Human Encounter With Death. New York: E.P. Dutton, 1978.

4607. Grollman, E.A. "Explaining Death to Children," Journal of School Health, 47 (June, 1977), 336-339.

4608 ________. Talking About Death: A Dialogue Between Parent and Child. (Rev. Ed.) Boston: Beacon, 1976.

4609. ________. Living When a Loved One Has Died. Boston: Beacon Press, 1977.

4610. Groot, J.L. "Mourning in a 6 Year Old Girl," Psychoanalytic Study of Children, 31 (1976), 273-281.

4611. Gross, G. "Child Care Workers Response to the Death of a Child, Child Care Quarterly, 8 (1979), 59-66.

4612. Grossman, L. "Train Crash: Social Work and Disaster Services," Social Work, 18 (September, 1973), 38-44.

4613. Grosso, P. "Death, Dying and Decision Making," Imprint, 24 (December, 1977), 33-35.

4614. Grove, S. "I Am A Yellow Ship," American Journal of Nursing, (March, 1978), 414.

4615. Grubb, C.A. "Is the Baby Alive or Dead: Psychological Work of a Woman With an Interuterine Fetal Death," Maternal Child Nursing Journal, 5 (Spring, 1976), 25-37.

4616. Gruman, G.J. A History of Ideas About the Prolongation of Life. New York: Arno Press, 1976. (Orig, Pub. 1966)

4617. ________. "Ethics of Death and Dying, A Historical Perspective," Omega, 9 (1979), 203-237.

4618. Gsell, O. "General Directions for the Care of the Dying Patient by the Swiss Academy of Medical Sciences," (Author's Translation) Aktuelle Gerentologie (Stuttgart), 7 (September, 1977), 481-486.

4619. Gubrium, J.E. Living and Dying at Murray Manor. New York: St. Martins Press, 1976.

4620. Guerrero, R., O.I. Rojas. "Spontaneous Abortion and Aging of Human Ova and Spermatozoa," New England Journal of Medicine, 293 (September, 1975), 573-575.

4621. Guilleminalut, C., R. Ariagno. "Sudden Infant Death Syndrome," Bulletin European de Physiopathologie Respiratoire, 13 (September-October, 1977), 591-597.

4622. Guntheroth, W.C. "Sudden Infant Death Syndrome," American Heart Journal, 93 (June 1977), 784-793.

4623. Gupta, S. "Infant Mortality Editorial," Indian Pediatrics, 13 (June, 1976), 493-494.

4624. Guthman, R.F., Jr., S.K. Womack. Death, Dying and Grief: A Bibliography. Waco, Texas: Word Services, 1978.

4625. Gutman, G.M., C.P. Herbert. "Mortality Rates Among Relocated Extended-Care Patients," Journal of Gerontology, 31 (May, 1976), 352-357.

4626. Gyulay, J.E. "Care of the Dying Child," Nursing Clinics of North America, 11 (March, 1976), 95-107.

4627. ________. The Dying Child. New York: McGraw-Hill, 1978.

4628. Hacker, T.A. "Some Aspects of Transference and Countertransference in Therapy with Dying and Nondying Patients," Suicide and Life Threatening Behavior, 7 (Fall, 1977), 189-198.

4629. Hackett, T.P. "Psychological Assistance for the Dying Patient and His Family," Annual Review of Medicine, 76 (1976), 371-378.

4630. Hackley, J.A. "Financing and Accrediting Hospices," Hospital Progress, 60 (March, 1979), 51-53.

4631. Hafen, B.Q. "Death and Dying," Health Education, 8 (November-December, 1977), 4-7.

4632. Hagen, J.M. "Infant Death: Nursing Interaction and Intervention With Grieving Families," Nursing Forum, 13 (1974), 371-385.

4633. Hagglund, T.B. "Guarantee the Dying Psychological Help," Nord Medicine, 90 (January, 1975), 8.

4634. ________. Dying: A Psychoanalytical Study. Monographs of the Psychiatric Clinic of the Helsinki University Central Hospital, Helsinki, 1976.

4635. Haines, K.J. "Lorenzo in Wonderland: A Short Play Upon the Death of D.H. Lawrence," Suicide and Life Threatening Behavior, 8 (Winter, 1978), 250-256.

4636. Hajal, F. "Post-Suicide Grief Work in Family Therapy," Journal of Marriage and Family Counseling, 3 (April, 1977), 35-42.

4637. Halacki, S. "A Lesson You Won't Learn in Lectures," RN, 39 (May, 1976), 46-48.

4638. Hall, B.P. "The Developing Consciousness of Dying," Counseling and Values, 21 (April, 1977), 146-159.

4639. Hall, P.A., P.W. Landreth. "Assessing Some Long Term Consequences of a Natural Disaster," Mass Emergencies, 1 (October, 1975), 55-61.

4640. Hall, R.B. "The Use of Death Notices in Research: A Neglected Data Source," Milligan College, Tennessee, 1977.

4641. Halper, T. "On Death, Dying and Terminality: Today, Yesterday and Tomorrow," Journal of Health Political Policy Law, 4 (Spring, 1979), 11-20.

4642. Halporn, R. The Thanatology Library. New York: Highly specialized Promotions, 1976.

4643. Haltresht, M. "The Meaning of De Quincey's 'Dream-Fugue On...Sudden Death'," Literature and Psychology, 76 (1976), 31-36.

4644. Hamera, E.K. "Positive and Negative Effects of Life Threatening Illness," Dissertation Abstracts International, 38 (January, 1978), 3469-3470.

4645. Hamilton, J.W. "Some Comments About Freud's Conceptualization of the Death Instinct," International Review of Psycho-Analysis, 76 (1976), 151-164.

4646. ________. "The Significant Other of Object Loss in Individual Response to Accidental Truama," Comprehensive Psychiatry, 18 (March-April, 1977), 189-199.

4647. Hamlon, J.S., J.M. Burns. "Minnesota Brain Death Legislation - Step Forward - or Backward," Minnesota Medicine, 62 (1979), 363.

4648. Hammell, M.I., C.E. Trinca. "Patient Needs Come First at Hillhaven Hospice. Pharmacy Services Essential for Pain Control," American Pharmacist, 18 (November, 1978), 15-17.

4649. Hammett, E.B. et al. "Atypical Grief - Anniversary Reactions," Military Medicine, 144 (1979), 320-321.

4650. Hampe, J.C. To Die Is Gain: The Experience of One's Own Death. Atlanta: John Knox Press, 1979.

4651. Hampe. S.O. "Needs of the Grieving Spouse in a Hospital Setting," Nursing Research, 24 (March-April, 1975), 113-120.

4652. Hampton, C. Transition Called Death. Wheaton, Illinois: Theosophical Publishing House, 1979.

4653. Hampton, M.W. Once There Were Three. Chicago, Illinois: Moody Press, 1977.

4654. Hanawalt, B.A. "Violent Death in Fourteenth and Early Fifteenth Century England," Comparative Studies in Society and History, 18 (July, 1976), 297-320.

4655. Handke, P. A Sorrow Beyond Dreams. A Life Story. New York: Farrar, Strauss & Giroux, 1974.

4656. Hankoff, L.D. "Adolescence and the Crisis of Dying," Adolescence, 10 (Fall, 1975), 373-389.

4657. Hanlan, A.J. Autobiography of Dying. New York: Doubleday, 1979.

4658. Hanley, E. Life After Death. New York: Norton Publications, Leisure Books, 1977.

4659. Hannam, C. "What Shall We Tell Our Children," Times Educational Supplement (London), 3286 (June 30, 1978), 16-17.

4660. Hanson, S. et al. "Natural Disaster Long Range Impact on Human Response to Future Disaster Threats," Environment and Behavior, 11 (1979), 268-284.

4661. Hanson, W. "Grief Counseling With Native Americans," White Cloud Journal, 1 (Fall, 1978), 19-21.

4662. Harbin, R.K. "Death, Euthanasia & Parental Consent," Pediatric Nursing, 2 (July-August, 1976), 26-28.

4663. Hardman, M.L., C.J. Drew. "Life Management Practices With the Profoundly Retarded: Issues of Euthanasia and Withholding Treatment," Mentally Retarded, 16 (December, 1978), 390-396.

4664. Hardt, D.V. "Development of an Investigatory Instrument to Measure Attitudes Toward Death," Journal of School Health, 45 (February, 1975), 96-99.

4665. ________. "Investigation of States of Bereavement," Omega, 9 (1979), 279-285.

4666. ________. Death: The Final Frontier. Englewood Cliffs, New Jersey: Prentice Hall, 1979.

4667. Haremlstin, R.T. "Family Therapy Following the Death of a Child," Journal of Marital and Family Therapy, 5 (1979), 51-59.

4668. Hargreaves, A. et al. "Blizzard of 1978 - Dealing With Disaster," American Journal of Nursing, 79 (1979), 268-271.

4669. Harkness, G.E. _The Dark Night of the Soul_. New York: Abingdon-Cokesbury,

4670. Harmer, R.M. _A Consumer Bibliography on Funerals_. Burnsville, North Carolina: Celo Press, 1977.

4671. Harmon, N.B. _The Pastor's Ideal Funeral Manual_. New York, Nashville: Abingdon-Cokesbury Press, 1942.

4672. Harper, B.C. _Death: The Coping Mechanism of the Health Professional_. Greenville, South Carolina: Southeastern University Press, 1977.

4673. Harrell, G.F. "Some Moral Aspects of Health Care," _Maryland State Medical Journal_, 26 (December, 1977), 66-69.

4674. Harris, W.H. "Some Reflections Concerning Approaches to Death Education," _Journal of School Health_, 48 (March, 1978), 162-165.

4675. Harrison, C.E., Jr. et al. "Survey of Sudden Death in the Offices of Atlanta Physicians and Dentists," _Southern Medical Journal_, 69 (November, 1976), 1476.

4676. Hart, E.J. "Philosophical Views of Death," _Health Education_, 8 (November-December, 1977), 2-3.

4677. ________. "Death Education and Mental Health," _Journal of School Health_, 46 (September, 1976), 407-412.

4678. ________. "Effects of Death Anxiety and Mode of Case Study Presentation on Shifts of Attitude Toward Euthanasia," _Omega_, 9 (1979), 239-244.

4679. Hartel, K.D. _The Curse of the Pharaohs_. Philadelphia: Lippincott, 1975.

4680. Hartfield, V.J. "Dying in the Hospital," _New Zealand Nursing Journal_, 71 (January, 1978), 7-10.

4681. Harton, S. _Doors of Eternity_. New York: Morehouse-Barlow, 1965.

4682. Hartveit, F. "Clinical and Post-Mortem Assessment of the Cause of Death," _Journal of Pathology_, 123 (December, 1977), 193-210.

4683. Hasselmeyer, E.G., J.C. Hunter. "The Sudden Infant Death Syndrome," Obstetrics and Gynecology Annual, 4 (1975), 213-236.

4684. Hauerwas, S., R. Bondi. "Memory, Community and The Reasons for Living," Journal of the American Academy of Religion, 44 (1976), 439.

4685. Haug, M.R. "Aging and the Right to Terminate Medical Treatment," Journal of Gerontology, 33 (July, 1978), 586-591.

4686. Haun, D.L. "Perceptions of the Bereaved, Clergy and Funeral Directors Concerning Bereavement," Dissertation Abstracts International, 37 (April, 1977), 6791.

4687. Hause, K. "Outdoor Education and Death," Independent School, 36 (February, 1977), 43-44.

4688. Hauser, M.J., D.R. Feinberg. "An Operational Approach to the Delayed Grief and Mourning Process," Journal of Psychiatric Nursing, 14 (July, 1976), 29-35.

4689. Hawkinson, J.R. "Teaching About Death," Today's Education, 65 (September-October, 1976), 41-42.

4690. Hayes, D.M. Between Doctor and Patient. Valley Forge: Judson Press, 1977.

4691. Hays, D.R. "Perceived Needs for Support of Women Who Participate in a Red Cross Widow's Program," Dissertation Abstracts International, 38 (January, 1978), 3129.

4692. Hecht, P.K., P. Cutright. "Racial Differences in Infant Mortality Rates - United States, 1969," Social Forces, 57 (1979), 1180-1193.

4693. Hecker, J.A. et al. "Changing Trend of Infant Mortality: Laramie County, Wyoming," Rocky Mountain Medical Journal, 74 (July-August, 1977), 196-198.

4694. Heifetz, M.D. "Ethics in Human Biology," in Garfield, C.A. (ed) Psychosocial Care of the Dying Patient. New York: McGraw-Hill, 1978, 304-316.

4695. Heim, E. et al. "Defense Mechanisms and Coping Behavior in Terminal Illness. An Overview," Psychotherapy and Psychosomatics, 30 (1978), 1-17.

4696. Heller, D.B., C.D. Schneider. "Interpersonal Methods for Coping With Stress: Helping Families of Dying Children," Omega, 8 (1977-1978), 319-331.

4697. Hellegers, A.E., E. Wakin. "Is the Right-To-Die Wrong?," U.S. Catholic, 43 (March, 1978), 13-17.

4698. Helmrath, T.A., M.D., E.M. Steinitz. "Death of an Infant: Parental Grieving and the Failure of Social Support," The Journal of Family Practice, 6 (April, 1978), 785-790.

4699. Helms, J. "Human Life Amendment," Congressional Record (Daily Edition), 123 (11 January, 1977), S436-S445.

4700. ________. "A Human Life Amendment," Human Life Review, 3 (Spring, 1978), 7-42.

4701. ________. et al. "Proposed Right of Life Amendment to the Constitution," Congressional Record (Daily Edition), 122 (28 April, 1976), S6116-S6142.

4702. Hendin, H. "Student Suicide: Death as a Life Style," Journal of Nervous and Mental Disease, 160 (March, 1975), 204-219.

4703. Hendricks, W.L. The Conception of Death in the Theology of Karl Barth. Thesis, University of Chicago, 1972.

4704. Hendrix, L. "Death Themes in Anglo-American Folk Balladry," Southern Illinois University, Carbondale, 1977.

4705. Henry, A.F., J.F. Short. Suicide and Homocide: Some Economic, Sociological and Psychological Aspects of Aggression. New York: Arno Press, 1976. (Orig. Pub. 1954)

4706. Herhold, R. Learning to Die, Learning to Live. Philadelphia: Fortress, 1976.

4707. Hershey, D.W. "Time Experience and a Certain Type of Mourning," Journal of the American Psychoanalytic Association, 26 (1978), 109-130.

4708. Hershiser, M.R., E.L. Quarantelli. "The Handling of The Dead in a Disaster," Omega, 76 (1976), 195-208.

4709. Hertel, B. et al. "Religion and Attitudes Toward Abortion: A Study of Nurses and Social Workers," Journal for the Scientific Study of Religion, 13 (March, 1974), 23-34.

4710. Herve, L. "New Approach to Sudden Death," Revista Medica De Chile, 104 (July, 1976), 491-495.

4711. Herzovi, F., R. Dumitrescu. "Epidemiology of Infant Deaths at Home and The Problem of Sudden Death," Review of Pediatrics, Obstetrics, Gynecology and Pediatrics, 25 (January-March, 1976), 69-78.

4712. Hessler, F.M., J.P. Carse (eds). Philosophical Aspects of Thanatology. Volume 1. Volume II. New York: MSS Information Corportion, 1976.

4713. Hessler, F.M., A. Kutscher (eds). Philosophical Aspects of Thanatology. Volume II. New York: MSS Information Corportion, 1978.

4714. Hetzler, F. Death and Creativity: An Interdisciplinary Encounter. New York: Health Sciences Publishing Company, 1976.

4715. Heuse, G. Guide De La Mort. Paris: Masson, 1975.

4716. Hick, J.H. Death and Eternal Life. New York: Harper and Row, 1976.

4717. Higgins, G.L. "Grief Reactions," Practitioner, 218 (May, 1977), 689-695.

4718. High, D.M. "Is 'Natural Death' An Illusion?" Hastings Center Report, 8 (August, 1978), 37-42.

4719. Hill, E. "Psychologic Giving Up: An Often Fatal Choice (letter)," Minnesota Medicine, 60 (November, 1977), 811-912.

4720. Hilton, J. "Cot Death Syndrome," Australia Nurses Journal, 3 (April, 1975), 3.

4721. Hiltz, S.R. "Evaluating a Pilot Social Service Project for Widows: A Chronicle of Research Problems," Journal of Sociology and Social Welfare, 1 (Summer, 1974), 217-224.

4722. ________. "Helping Widows: Group Disscussions as a Therapeutic Technique," Family Coordinator, 24 (July, 1975), 331-336.

4723. Hine, V.H. "Altered States of Consciousness: A Form of Death Education," Death Education, 1 (Winter, 1978), 377-396.

4724. Hinton, J. "Comparison of Places and Policies for Terminal Care," Lancet, 1 (January, 1979), 29-32.

4725. ________. "Speaking of Death With the Dying," in: Schneidman, E.S. (ed) Death: Current Perspectives. Palo Alto, California: Mayfield Publishing Company, 1976.

4726. ________. "Patient's Attitudes to Dying," Documentation in Medical Ethics, 5 (1975), 4.

4727. Hirth, H.L. "Not Until Death Do You Part," Journal of Legal Medicine, 5 (February, 1977), 25-28.

4728. Hirschfeld, B. "Grief and Grief Reactions," Royal Australian Nursing Federation (Brisbane), 7 (October, 1976), 4 & 6.

4729. Hixon, K. "Care for the Dying--Ideal Versus Actual Care," New Zealand Nursing Journal, 71 (December, 1978), 19-20.

4730. Hobson, D.P. "'Perithan Experience': Naming the Beyond," Perspectives in Biology and Medicine, 21 (Summer, 1978), 626-628.

4731. Hockey, L. "Dying at Home," Nursing Times, 72 (March, 1976), 324-325.

4732. Hocking, W.E. The Meaning of Immortality In Human Experience, Including Thoughts on Death and Life. (Rev. Ed.) Westport, Conneticut: Greenwood, 1973.

4733. Hodge, T.E. "Pastoral Care of the Family of the Critically Ill Patient," Dissertation Abstracts International, 36 (February, 1976), 4159.

4734. Hoeger, J.A. "Helping the Family Struggle With Death," Journal of American Health Care Association, 3 (March, 1977), 18-20.

4735. Hoekelman, R.A. "A New Perspective on Sudden Infant Death Syndrome Editorial," American Journal of Diseases of Children, 130 (November, 1976), 1191-1192.

4736. Hoelter, J.A., J.W. Hoelter. "An Examination of Fear of Death, Anxiety and Exposure to Death and Dying," Bowling Green State University, Ohio, 1978.

4737. ________. "The Relationship Between Fear of Death and Anxiety," The Journal of Psychology, 99 (July, 1978), 225-226.

4738. Hoelter, J.W. "A Multidimentional Fear of Death Scale," Bowling Green State University, Ohio, 1978.

4739. ________,L. Street. "Sex Differences on Fears of Death," Bowling Green State University, Ohio, 1978.

4740. ________, R.J. Epley. "Death Education and Death-Related Attitudes," Death Education, 3 (1979), 67-75.

4741. Hoffman, A.D. et al. "The Dying Adolescent," in: their The Hospitalized Adolescent: A Guide to Managing the Ill and Injured Youth. New York: Free Press, 1976.

4742. Hogan, J.E. "The Conscience of the Law," Catholic Lawyer, 21 (Summer, 1975), 190-196.

4743. Hogberg, U. "The Decline of Infant Mortality in Sweden--A Comparison With Developing Countries," Lakartidningen, 74 (September, 1977), 3187-3190.

4744. Hogatt, L., B. Spilka. "The Nurse and the Terminally Ill Patient: Some Perspectives and Projected Actions," Omega, 9 (1978-1979), 255-266.

4745. Holck, F.H. "Life Revisited - Parällels in Death Experiences," Omega, 9 (1979), 1-11.

4746. Holden, C. "Hospices: For the Dying, Relief From Pain and Fear," Science, 193 (30 July, 1976), 389-391.

4747. ________. "Pain, Dying, and the Health Care System," Science, 203 (9 March, 1979), 984-985.

4748. Holford, J.M. "Terminal Care," Nursing Times, 69 (1973), 113-115.

4749. Holinger, S.W. "The Hospice Movement Letter," Journal of the American Medical Association, 241 (June, 15, 1979), 2600.

4750. Hollander, N., D. Ehrenfried. "Reimbursing Hospice Care: A Blue Cross and Blue Shield Perspective," Hospital Progress, 60 (March, 1979), 54-56 & 76.

4751. Hollingsworth, C.E., R.O. Pasnau (eds). The Family in Mourning: A Guide for Health Professionals. New York: Grune & Stratton, 1977.

4752. Hollowell, E.E. "The Right to Die. How Legislation is Defining the Right," Journal of Practical Nursing, 27 (October, 1977), 20-21 & 36.

4753. Holmes, J. "Teaching About Death: A Review of Selected Materials," Social Studies Journal, 4 (Winter, 1975), 48-50.

4754. Holt, J. "The Right of Children to Informed Consent," in: Van Eys, J. (ed). Research on Children: Medical Imperatives, Ethical Quandries and Legal Constraints. Baltimore: University Park Press, 1978, 5-16.

4755. Homan, R.W. "Ethical, Legal, and Medical Aspects of Brain Death--Review and Proposal," Texas Medicine, 75 (1979), 36-43.

4756. Hommen, D.L. An Assessment of the Effects of a Community Mental Health Center Laboratory Training-Education-Consultation Program in Bereavement Ministry for Parish Clergymen. Thesis - Boston University, Boston, 1978.

4757. Hong, S.B., C. Tietze. "Survey of Abortion Providers in Seoul, Korea," Studies in Family Planning, 10 (1979), 161-613.

4758. Hopkins, C. "The Right to Die With Dignity," in: Caughill, R.E. (ed). The Dying Patient: A Supportive Approach. Boston: Little-Brown, 1976, 73-94.

4759. Hopping, B.K. "Nursing Students' Attitudes Toward Death," Nursing Research, 26 (November-December, 1977), 443-447.

4760. Horan, D.J. "Euthanasia and Brain Death: Ethical and Legal Considerations," Annals of the New York Academy of Sciences, 315 (November 17, 1978), 363-375.

4761. ________, D. Mall (eds). Death, Dying and Euthanasia. Washington: University Publications of America, 1977.

4762. Horkan, T.A., Jr. "Death With Dignity: California Style," Hospital Progress, 58 (February, 1977), 12-13.

4763. Horn, P.A. "Moral Rights to Live and Decisions About Death," Ann Arbor, Michigan: University Microfilms International, 1977. 279 pages.

4764. Hornby, A. "Death, Dying and Bereavement," Nursing Mirror, 146 (February, 1978), 18.

4765. Horrobin, D.F. Medical Hubris: A Reply to Ivan Illich. Montreal: Eden Press, 1977.

4766. Houghton, I. "Death With Dignity," New Zealand Medical Journal, 87 (April, 1978), 248-251.

4767. Howard, J.H. "The Nanticoke-Delaware Skeleton Dance," American Indian Quarterly, 2 (Spring, 1975), 1-13.

4768. Howell, K.A. "Death and The Consumer," Health Education, 6 (November-December, 1975), 15-17.

4769. Howell, M.M. "The Lone Eagle's Last Flight," Journal of the American Medical Association, 232 (May 19, 1975), 715.

4770. Howell, W. "Attitudes Toward Death and Toward the Future in Aged and Young Adults," Dissertation Abstracts International, 37 (March, 1977), 4685.

4771. Howells, J.G. "Whose Responsibility--Parent, Foster Parent or Local Authority? (A Separation or Death?)," Royal Society of Health Journal, 95 (October, 1975), 257-261.

4772. Howells, W.D. et al. In After Days: Thoughts on the Future Life. New York: Arno Press, 1976. (Orig. Pub. 1910)

4773. Hoyman, H.S. "Rethinking an Ecologic-System Model of Man's Health, Disease, Aging, Death," Journal of School Health, 45 (November, 1975), 509-518.

4774. Huber, L.V. et al. The Cemeteries. Gretna, Louisiana: Pelican Publishing Company, 1974.

4775. Hudson, R.P. "Death, Dying and the Zealous Phase," Annals of Internal Medicine, 88 (May, 1978), 696-702.

4776. Hughes, C.W., J.J. Lynch. "A Reconsideration of Psychological Precursors of Sudden Death in Infrahuman Animals," American Psychologist, 33 (May, 1978), 419-429.

4777. Humber, J.M. "Abortion, Fetal Research and the Law," Social Theory and Practice, 4 (Spring, 1977), 127-147.

4778. Hummell, R.F. "Death With Dignity Legislation: A Foot in the Door," Hospital Progress, 57 (June, 1976), 50-57.

4779. Humphrey, D. Jean's Way. London: Quartet, 1978.

4780. Humphrey, J.A. "Social Loss: A Comparison of Suicide Victims, Homicide Offenders and Non-Violent Individuals," Diseases of the Nervous System, 38 (March, 1977), 157-166.

4781. Humphries, S.V. "Editorial: The Alternative to Euthanasia," Central African Journal of Medicine, 22 (May, 1976), 99-102.

4782. ________. "The Problems of Therapeutic Abortion and Infanticide," Central African Journal of Medicine, 24 (April, 1978), 77-79.

4783. Hunt, R., J. Arras (eds). Ethical Issues in Modern Medicine. Palo Alto: Mayfield Publishing Company, 1977.

4784. Hunter, K.I., R.H. Shane. "Time of Death and Bio-Rhythmic Cycles," Perceptual and Motor Skills, 48 (1979), 220.

4785. Hunter, T.H. "On Letting Die," Pharos, 40 (January, 1977), 31.

4786. Huntington, R., P. Metcalf. Celebrations of Death. New Rochelle, New York: Cambridge University Press, 1979.

4787. Huttunen, M.O., P. Niskanen. "Prenatal Loss of Father and Psychiatric Disorders," Archives of General Psychiatry, 35 (April, 1978), 429-431.

4788. Hymovitz, L. "Death as a Discipline: The Ultimate Curriculum," Oceanside, Oregon: Curriculum Bulletin #342.

4789. Hynson, L.M. "Belief in Life After Death and Societal Intergration," Omega, 9 (1979), 13-18.

4790. Iammarino, N.K. "Relationship Between Death Anxiety and Demographic Variables," Psychological Report, 37 (August, 1975), 262.

4791. Idinopulos, T.A. "Death-Of-God Theology," Intellect, 104 (May-June, 1976), 598-599.

4792. Ikerman, R.C. A Little Book of Comfort. Nashville: Abingdon, 1976.

4793. Imboden, J.B., J.C. Urbaitis. Practical Psychiatry in Medicine. New York: Appleton-Centrue-Crofts, 1978.

4794. Inoue, S., D.W. Plath. "The Loss of Meaning in Death," The Japan Interpreter, 9 (Winter, 1975), 331-343.

4795. Insel, S.A. "On Counseling the Bereaved," Personnel and Guidance Journal, 55 (November, 1976), 127-129.

4796. Irion, P.E. The Funeral: Vestige or Value? New York: Arno Press, 1976. (Orig. Pub. 1966)

4797. ________. Cremation. Philadelphia: Fortress Press, 1968.

4798. Isaacs, L. "Death, Where is Thy Distinguishing?" Hastings Center Report, 8 (February, 1978), 5-8.

4799. Isler, C. "Breaking Down the Barriers to Total Cancer Care. Approaching the Final Days," Registered Nurse, 41 (April, 1978), 63-65.

4800. Istvan, S. et al. "Determination of Death in the Case of Organ Removal For Transplantation," Orvosi Hetilap, 118 (May 29, 1977), 1271-1274.

4801. Jackson, E. "Counseling the Dying," Death Education, 1 (Spring, 1977), 27-39.

4802. ________. The Many Faces of Grief. New York: Abingdon Press, 1977.

4803. ________. "Wisely Managing Our Grief: A Pastoral Viewpoint," Death Education, 3 (Summer, 1979), 143-155.

4804. Jacobs, S., A. Ostfeld. "An Epidemiological Review of Mortality of Bereavement," Psychosomatic Medicine, 39 (September-October, 1977), 344-357.

4805. ________, L. Douglas. "Grief - Mediating Process Between a Loss and Illness," Comprehensive Psychiatry, 20 (1979), 165-176.

4806. Jacobsen, M., N. Hennignsen. "With a Living Will - Right to Dignified Death. We Should Take a Position About Death," Sygeplejersken, 76 (May 19, 1976), 10-13.

4807. Jacobson, L. et al. "Repeat Aborters: First Aborters: A Social-Psychiatric Comparison," Social Psychiatry, 11 (April, 1976), 75-86.

4808. Jaksetic, E. "Bioethics and the Law: A Bibliography, 1974-1976," American Journal of Law and Medicine, 2 (Winter, 1976-1977), 263-281.

4809. Jamski, W. "Using Mortality Data to Introduce Social Issues," Social Studies, 70 (January-February, 1978), 20-21.

4810. Janes, R.G. "A Clinical Perspective on Dying," Canadian Medical Association Journal, 107 (September, 1972), 425-430.

4811. Jaretzki, A. "Death With Dignity--Passive Euthanasia. Guide to Physician Dealing With Dying Patients," New York State Journal of Medicine, 76 (April, 1976), 539-544.

4812. Jarvis, S.S., B.W. Jarvis. "Failure to Define Death: The Unsettled Question," Southern Medical Journal, 70 (May, 1977), 607-610.

4813. Jayewardene, C.H.S. The Penalty of Death: The Canadian Experiment. Lexington, Massachusetts: Lexington Books, 1977.

4814. Jeddeloh, N.P. "The Uniform Anatomical Gift Act and a Statutory Definition of Death," Transplantation Proceedings, 8 (June, 1976), 245-249.

4815. Jennett, B. "The Donor Doctor's Dilemma: Observations on the Recognition and Management of Brain Death," Journal of Medical Ethics, 1 (July, 1975), 63-66.

4816. ________. "Irrecoverable Brain Damage After Resuscitation: Brain Death and Other Syndromes," Resuscitation, 5 (1976), 49-52.

4817. ________. "Diagnosis of Brain Death," Journal of Medical Ethics," 3 (March, 1977), 4-5.

4818. Jennings, L.E., R.D. France. "Management of Grief in the Hypochondriac," Journal of Family Practice, 8 (May, 1979), 957-960.

4819. Jernigan, H.L. "Bringing Together Psychology and Theology: Reflections on Ministry to the Bereaved," Journal of Pastoral Care, 30 (June, 1976), 88-102.

4820. Johannson, F.F. (ed). The Last Rights: A Look at Funerals. Maryland Center for Public Broadcasting. Mills, Maryland: Owings, 1975.

4821. Johnson, A. "Recent Trends in Sex Mortality Differentials in the United States," Journal of Human Stress, 3 (March, 1977), 22-32.

4822. Johnson, M.W. We Lived With Dying. Waco, Texas: Word Books, 1975.

4823. Johnston, L.C. "Terminal Illness: A Psychosocial Approach to the Experience," Dissertation Abstracts International, 36 (February, 1976), 4163-4164.

4824. Jolly, H. "Family Reactions to Stillbirth," Proceedings of the Royal Society of Medicine, 69 (November, 1976), 835-837.

4825. ________. "Loss of a Baby," Australia Nurses Journal, 7 (October, 1977), 40-41.

4826. Jonas, H. "The Right to Die," Hastings Center Report, 8 (August, 1978), 31-36.

4827. Jonch'eres, J. "The Right to Live," World Health, (January, 1976), 8-12.

4828. Jones, A.M., J.T. Weston. "The Examination of the Sudden Infant Death Syndrome Infant: Investigative and Autopsy Protocols," Journal of Forensic Science, 21 (October, 1976), 833-841.

4829. Jones, W. "Learning From a Dying Patient," Nephrology Nursing, 1 (March-April, 1979), 37-39.

4830. Jones, W.H. "Death Related Grief Counseling: The School Counselor's Responsibility," School Counselor, 24 (May, 1977), 315-320.

4831. ________. "Grief and Involuntary Career Change - Its Implications for Counseling," Vocational Guidance Quarterly, 27 (1979), 196-201.

4832. ________. "Emergency Room Sudden Death: What Can Be Done for the Survivors," Death Education, 2 (Fall, 1978), 231-245.

4833. Jonsen, A.R., M.J. Garland. "A Moral Policy for Life/Death Decisions in the Intensive Care Nursery," Ethics of Newborn Intensive Care. San Francisco University of California Health Policy Program, 1976.

4834. Jozefowski, J. "Paula's Legacy," Registered Nurse, 40 (November, 1977), 81-83.

4835. Jury, M., D. Jury. Gramp. New York: Grossman Publishers, 1976.

4836. Kadlub, K.J., K.G. Kadlub. "SIDS: Working a Model Letter," Illinois Journal of Medicine, 150 (December, 1976), 591-592.

4837. Kahana, R.J. "On Widowhood," Journal of Geriatric Psychiatry, 8 (1975), 5-8.

4838. Kahn, J.H. Job's Illness--Loss, Grief and Integration. Oxford, New York: Pergamon Press, 1975.

4839. Kahnedrington, M. "Abortion Counseling," Counseling Psychologist, 8 (1979), 37-38.

4840. Kahoe, R.D., R.F. Dunn. "Fear of Death and Religious Attitudes and Behavior, Journal for the Scientific Study of Religion, 14 (December, 1976), 379-382.

4841. Kalant, H., O.J. Kalant. "Death in Amphetamine Users: Causes and Rates," Canada Medical Association, 112 (February, 1975), 299-304.

4842. Kalish, R.A., L. Dunn. "Death and Dying: A Survey of Credit Offerings in Theological Schools and Some Possible Implications," Review of Religious Research, 17 (Winter, 1976), 134-140.

4843. ________, H. Goldberg. "Clergy Attitudes Toward Funeral Directors," Death Education, 2 (Fall, 1978), 247-260.

4844. ________, D. Reynolds. Death and Ethnicity: A Psychocultural Study. Los Angeles: University of Southern California Press, 1976.

4845. ________. "The Role of Age in Death Attitudes," Death Education, 1 (Summer, 1977), 205-230.

4846. Kamiya, K. "Karen Quinlan Case--Dignified Death and Nursing. Nursing for the Purpose of Restoration of a More Humane Life. A Case Study of a Vegetative Patient," Japan Journal of Nursing, 40 (August, 1976), 812-815.

4847. Kane, B. "Children's Concepts of Death," Journal of Genetic Psychology, 134 (1979), 141-153.

4848. Kaplan, D.G. "The Relationship of Death Concern and Ego Strength, Security-Insecurity, and Repression-Sensitization," Dissertation Abstracts International, 37 (March, 1977), 4686.

4849. Kaplan, L.S. "A Matter of Loss: Living On, Surviving Sadness," School Counselor, 26 (March, 1979), 229-235.

4850. Karo, N., A. Michelson. Adventure in Dying. Northbrook, Illinois: Moody, 1976.

4851. Kashiwagi, T. "Nursing of a Dying Patient. A Need for Team Approach," Japan Journal of Nursing, 41 (January, 1977), 65-69.

4852. ________. "Terminal Care. Need to Inform the Patient and His Family of the Result of the Diagnosis: In A Case of Gastric Cancer," Japan Journal of Nursing, 41 (February, 1977), 172-177.

4853. ________. "Nursing in Terminal Care. Team Approach in Fulfilling the Patients' Needs: An Experience in a Case of Ovarian Cancer," Japan Journal of Nursing, 41 (March, 1977), 282-286.

4854. ________. "Nursing in Terminal Care. Conditions for Sympathetic Listening--Examples in three Terminal Cases," Japan Journal of Nursing, 41 (April, 1977), 393-397.

4855. ________. "Nursing a Dying Patient. Importance of a Sympathetic Personal Relationship--A Study of a Patient with Gastric Cancer Who Attempted Suicide," Japan Journal of Nursing, 41 (May, 1977), 497-501.

4856. ________. "Nursing A Dying Patient. Religious Need of a Patient," Japan Journal of Nursing, 41 (June, 1977), 606-610.

4857. ________. "Nursing a Dying Patient. The Role of His Family," Japan Journal of Nursing, 41 (August, 1977), 825-830.

4858. Kasl, S.V., F. Reichman. Advances in Psychosomatic Medicine. Basel, Switzerland: S. Karger, 1977.

4859. Kaspar, F.E., J.J. Vesper. "Death Anxiety in a Risk-Taking Group," Essence, 1 (1976), 95-97.

4860. Kastenbaum, R. Death, Society and Human Experience. St. Louis: C.V. Mosby, 1977.

4861. ________. "Toward Standards of Care for the Terminally Ill. A Few Guiding Principles," Omega, 76 (1976), 191-193.

4862. ________. Care of Aging, Dying and the Dead. New York: Arno Press, 1977.

4863. ________. "We Covered Death Today," Death Education, 1 (Spring, 1977), 85-92.

4864. ________. "Healthy Dying--Paradoxical Quest Continues," Journal of Social Issues, 35 (1979), 185-206.

4865. ________. "Fertility and the Fear of Death," Journal of Social Issues, 30 (1974), 63-78.

4866. ________ (ed). Death and Dying, 40 vols. New York: Arno Press, 1977.

4867. ________, R. Aisenberg. The Psychology of Death. New York: Springer Publishing Company, 1976.

4868. ________, P.T. Costa, Jr. "Psychological Perspectives on Death," Annual Review of Psychology, 28 (1977), 225-249.

4869. ________ et al. Death as a Speculative Theme in Religious, Scientific and Social Thought. New York: Arno Press, 1976.

4870. ________ et al. Death and the Visual Arts. New York: Arno Press, 1976.

4871. ________ et al. Return to Life: Two Imaginings of the Lazarus Theme. New York: Arno Press, 1976.

4872. Kates, R.W. et al. "Human Impact of the Managua Earthquake," Science, 182 (December, 1973), 981-990.

4873. Katterhagen, G. "The Hospice Movement Letter," Journal of the American Medical Association, 241 (June 15, 1979), 2600.

4874. Kaufman, L.W., C.K. Rovee-Collier. "Arousal-Induced Changes in the Attitude of Death Feigning and Periodicity," Psychology and Behavior, 20 (April, 1978), 453-458.

4875. Kavanaugh, R.E. "Dealing Naturally With the Dying," Nursing (Jenkintown), 6 (October, 1976), 23-29.

4876. Kawamjra, S. "Karen Quinlan Case--Dignified Death and Nursing. Need for Development of Nursing Technology for Functional Recovery of Affected Patients," Japan Journal of Nursing, 40 (August, 1976), 807-809.

4877. Keane, M. "Implications of Euthanasia--A Nursing Perspective," Journal of the New York State Nurses Association, 8 (March, 1977), 15-18.

4878. Keddie, K.M. "Pathological Mourning After the Death of a Domestic Pet," British Journal of Psychiatry, 131 (July, 1977), 21-25.

4879. Keeling, B. "Giving and Getting the Courage to Face Death," Nursing (Horsham), 8 (November, 1978), 38-41.

4880. Keith, C.R., D. Ellis. "Reactions of Pupils and Teachers to Death in the Classroom," School Counselor, 25 (March, 1978), 228-234.

4881. Keith, P.M., M.R. Castles. "Expected and Observed Behavior of Nurses and Terminal Patients," International Journal Nursing Studies, 16 (1979), 21-28.

4882. Keleman, S. Living Your Dying. New York: Random, 1976.

4883. Kelleher, K.L. "Go Gentle," Nursing (Horsham), 9 (July, 1979), 96.

4884. Kennedy, B.J. "Letter: Pleasures and Tragedies of Death," Journal of the American Medical Association, 234 (October 6, 1975), 24.

4885. Kennedy, B. Gerhard. Canada: Macmillan, 1976.

4886. Kennedy, I. "The Doctor and the Dying Patient," Times (London), (December 21, 1976), 13.

4887. ________. "The Definition of Death," Journal of Medical Ethics, 3 (March, 1977), 5-6.

4888. ________. "Case Conference: Strive Officiously to Keep Alive Letter," Journal of Medical Ethics, 4 (March, 1978), 49-50.

4889. Kerner, J. et al. "Impact of Grief-Retrospective Study of Family Function Following the Loss of a Child with Cystic Fibrosis," Journal of Chronic Diseases, 32 (1979), 221-225.

4890. Kerr, J.C. "Dying in the Hospital," Canadian Nurse, 74 (November, 1978), 17-19.

4891. Kestenbaum, C.J. "The Effects of Fatherless Homes Upon Daughters: Clinical Impression Regarding Paternal Deprivation," Journal of American Academy of Psychoanalysis, 4 (April, 1976), 171-190.

4892. Keyser, M. "At Home With Death: A Natural Child-Death," Journal of Pediatrics, 90 (March, 1977), 486-487.

4893. Khosla, T. "Letter: Sudden Death and Sport," Lancet, 1 (February, 1975), 395.

4894. Kierniesky, N., L. Groelinger. "General Anxiety and Death Imagery in Catholic Seminarians and College Students," Journal of Psychology, 97 (November, 1977), 199-203.

4895. Kihara, Y. "Karen Quinlan Case--Dignified Death and Nursing. Detection of the Proof of Life in Vegetative Patients," Japan Journal of Nursing, 40 (August, 1976), 908-810.

4896. Killian, R.A. "Attitudes to Death and Bereavement Among the Elderly," World Journal of Nursing, 7 (May, 1978), 2-3.

4897. Killip, T. "Time, Place, Event of Sudden Death," Circulation, 52 (Suppl. 3), (December, 1975), 160-163.

4898. Kimble, D.W. "The Fine Example," Nursing (Jenkintown), 6 (July, 1976), 44.

4899. Kimzey, L.M. "A Time to Die," Imprint, 25 (February, 1978), 47-60.

4900. Kincaid, J.E. "The Right to a Natural Death," Michigan Medicine, 75 (April, 1976), 208-211.

4901. Kinoshita, Y. "Karen Quinlan Case--Dignified Death and Nursing. Questions on 'Dignified Death'," Japan Journal of Nursing, 40 (August, 1976), 802-804.

4902. Kinston, W., R. Rosser. "Disaster: Effects on Mental and Physical State," Journal of Psychosomatic Research, 18 (December, 1974), 437-456.

4903. Kirven, G. "The Right to Die," Kentucky Bench and Bar, 39 (July, 1975), 16.

4904. Kittleson, J.A. "Nursing Experience: In Spite of Everything Tommy Died in Peace," Registered Nurse, 41 (February, 1978), 97-102.

4905. Kivett, V.R. "Loneliness and the Rural Widow," Family Coordinator, 27 (October, 1978), 389-394.

4906. Klagsbrun, S. "Cancer, Emotions and Nurses," American Journal of Psychiatry, 126 (March, 1970), 1237-1244.

4907. ________. "Communication in the Treatment of Cancer," American Journal of Nursing, 71 (May, 1971), 944-948.

4908. Klass, D., A. Gordon. "Varieties of Transcending Experience at Death - Videotaped Based Study," Omega, 9 (1979), 19-36.

4909. Klein, K.M. "Death Education: An Appraisal," Dissertation Abstracts International, 38 (April, 1978), 5026-5027.

4910. Klein, R. "The New Life-Or-Death Choices," Connecticut Medicine, 43 (March, 1979), 153.

4911. Kleinman, J.C. et al. "Geographic Variations in Infant Mortality," Public Health Report, 91 (September-October, 1976), 423-432.

4912. Kleinman, M.A. et al. "RX for Social Death: The Cancer Patient as Counselor," Community Mental Health Journal, 13 (Summer, 1977), 115-124.

4913. Klepser, M.J. "Grief: How Long Does Grief Go On?" American Journal of Nursing, (March, 1978), 420-422.

4914. Klopfer, F.J., W.F. Price. "Euthanasia Acceptance as Related to After Life Belief and Other Attitudes," Omega, 9 (1979), 245-253.

4915. Klug, L. M. Boss. "Factorial Structure of the Death Concern Scale," Psychological Reports, 38 (February, 1976), 107-112.

4916. ________. "Further Study on the Validity of the Death Concern Scale," Psychological Reports, 40 (June, 1977), 907-910.

4917. Kluge, E.W. The Practice of Death. New Haven, Conneticut: Yale University Press, 1976.

4918. Klutch, M. "Survey Results After One Year's Experience With the Natural Death Act, September 1, 1976- August 31, 1977," Western Journal of Medicine, 128 (April, 1978), 329-330.

4919. ________. "Hospices for the Terminally Ill Patients: The California Experience," Western Journal of Medicine, 129 (July, 1978), 82-84.

4920. Knecht, T.S. "Crib Death and Primal Pain," Journal of Primal Therapy, 3 (Summer, 1976), 214-219.

4921. Kneisl, C.R. "Thoughtful Care for the Dying," American Journal of Nursing, 68 (March, 1968), 550-552.

4922. ________. "Dying Patients and Their Families: How Staff Can Give Support," Hospital Topics, (November, 1967), 37-39.

4923. Knight, B. "Forensic Problems in Practice--The Doctor at the Scene of Death," Practitioner, 216 (June, 1976), 721-724.

4924. Knobel, G.J. "Aircraft Fatality Investigation: The Non-Natural Death," South African Medical Journal, 52 (July, 1977), 150-152.

4925. Knott, J.E., R.W. Prull. "Death Education: Accountable to Whom? For What?," Omega, 76 (1976), 177-181.

4926. Kodama, M. "Bedside Nursing. A Study on Acceptance of Death by a Patient With a Poor Prognosis," Japan Journal of Nursing, 40 (June, 1976), 596-598.

4927. Koestenbaum, P. Vitality of Death: Essays in Existential Psychology and Philosophy. Westport, Conneticut: Greenwood, 1971.

4928. ________. Is There an Answer to Death? Englewood Cliffs, New Jersey: Spectrum/Prentice Hall, 1976.

4929. Kohl, M. "Karen Ann Quinlan, Human Rights and Wrongful Killing," Connecticut Medicine, 42 (September, 1978), 579-583.

4930. ________. "Euthanasia and the Right to Life," in: Spicker, S.F., H.T. Engelhardt (eds). Philosophical Medical Ethics: Its Nature and Significance. Boston: Teidel, 1977.

4931. Kohn, J. "Hospice Movement Provides Human Alternative For Terminally Ill," Modern Health Care, 6 (1976), 26-28.

4932. ________. "Hospice Group Seeks Reimbursement," Modern Health Care, 8 (October, 1978), 29.

4933. Kojima, U. "Nursing of a Dying Friend," Japan Journal of Nursing, 41 (April, 1977), 371-374.

4934. Kolke, R. "Inside the English Hospice," Hospitals, (July, 1975), 65.

4935. Kolls, M. "Reflections on My Children's Experiencing Death," Death Education, 1 (Summer, 1977), 231-234.

4936. Kolman, R.R. "Bioethics," in her: Health Care. Rochelle Park, New Jersey: Hayden Book Company, 1976, 98-117.

4937. Konior, G.S., A.S. Levine. "The Fear of Dying: How Patients and Their Doctors Behave," Seminars in Oncology, 3 (December, 1975), 311-316.

4938. Koob, P.B., S.F. Davis. "Fear of Death in Military Officers and Their Wives," Psychological Reports, 40 (February, 1977), 261-262.

4939. Koocher, G.P. et al. "Death Anxiety in Normal Children and Adolescents," Psychiatria Clinica (Basel), 9 (1976), 220-229.

4940. Koolman, G. When Death Takes a Father. Grand Rapids, Michigan: Baker Book House, 1968.

4941. Kooiman, G. After the Flowers Have Gone. Grand Rapis, Michigan: Zondervan Publishing Company, 1973.

4942. Koop, C.E. "The Slide to Auschwitz," Human Life Review, 3 (Spring, 1977), 101-114.

4943. ________. The Right to Life; The Right to Die. Wheaton, Illinois: Tyndale House, 1976.

4944. Kopel, K., L.A. Mock. "The Use of Group Sessions for the Emotional Support of Families of Terminal Patients," Death Education, 1 (Winter, 1978), 409-421.

4945. Kopel, R.F. "Death on Every Weekend," Suicide and Life Threatening Behavior, 7 (Summer, 1977), 110-119.

4946. Korein, J. "Neurology and Cerebral Death--Definitions and Differential Diagnosis," Tranamerican Neurological Association, 100 (1976), 210-212.

4947. Koslowsky, M. et al. "The Application of Guttman Scale Analysis to Physician Attitudes Regarding Abortion," Journal of Applied Psychology, 61 (January, 1976), 301-304.

4948. Kovacs, M., A.T. Beck. "The Wish to Die and The Wish to Live in Attempted Suicide," Journal of Clinical Psychology, 33 (April, 1977), 361-365.

4949. Kovalesky, A. "That Night in the Neonate Nursery," American Journal of Nursing, (March, 1978), 414-416.

4950. Kowalsky, E.L. "Grief: A Lost Life-Style," American Journal of Nursing, (March, 1978), 418-420.

4951. Kowalsky, K., M.R. Osborn. "Helping Mothers of Stillborn Infants to Grieve," Maternal Child Nursing Journal, 2 (January-February, 1977), 29-32.

4952. Koza, P. "Euthanasia: Some Legal Considerations," Essence, 76 (1976), 79-88.

4953. Krakoff, I.M. "The Case for Active Treatment in Patients With Advanced Cancer: Not Everyone Needs a Hospice," Cancer, 29 (March-April, 1979), 108-111.

4954. Krant, M.J. "Sounding Board. The Hospice Movement," New England Journal of Medicine, 299 (September, 1978), 546-549.

4955. ________, et al. "The Role of a Hospital-Based Psychosocial Unit in Terminal Cancer, Illness and Bereavement," Journal of Chronic Diseases, 29 (February, 1976), 115-127.

4956. Kraisman, A.U. "The Nature of Change in a Fatally Ill Individual," Dissertation Abstracts International, 37 (June, 1977), 6406.

4957. Kraus, A.S. et al. "Potential Interest of the Elderly in Active Euthanasia," Canadian Family Physician, 23 (March, 1977), 123.

4958. Kravitz, H., R.G. Scherz. "Sudden Infant Death Syndrome: A New Hypothesis," Illinois Medical Journal, 149 (May, 1976), 444-447.

4959. Kreeft, P.J. Love Is Stronger Than Death. New York: Harrow, 1979.

4960. Krieger, G.W. "Loss and Grief in Rehabilitation Counseling of the Severely Traumatically Disabled," Journal of Applied Rehabilitation Counseling, 7 (Winter, 1977), 223-227.

4961. ________, L.D. Bascue. "Terminal Illness: Counseling With a Family Perspective," Family Coordinator, 24 (July, 1975), 351-354.

4962. Krieger, S.R. "Death Orientation and the Specialty Choice and Training of Physicians," Dissertation Abstracts International, 37 (January, 1977), 3616.

4963. Kron, J. "Designing a Better Place to Die," Lamp, 35 (March, 1978), 6-13.

4964. Kubler-Ross, E. To Live Until We Say Good-Bye. New York: Prentice-Hall, 1978.

4965. ________. "Coping With the Reality of Terminal Illness in the Family," in: Shneidman, E.S. (ed) Death: Current Perspectives. Palo Alto, California: Mayfield Publishing Company, 1976.

4966. ________. Images of Growth and Death. New York: Prentice-Hall, 1976.

4967. ________. "Therapy With the Terminally Ill," in: Schneidman, E.S. (ed) Death: Current Perspectives. Palo Alto, California: Mayfield Publishing Company, 1976.

4968. ________, W.J. Worden. "Attitudes and Experiences of Death Workshop Attendees," Omega, 8 (1977-1978), 91-106.

4969. Kukolich, M.K. et al. "Sudden Infant Death Syndrome: Normal Interval on ECGs of Relatives," Pediatrics, 60 (July, 1977), 51-54.

4970. Kuperman, S.K., C.J. Golden. "Personality Correlates of Attitude Toward Death," Journal of Clinical Psychology, 34 (July, 1978), 661-663.

4971. Kurlychek, R.T. "Assessment of Attitudes Toward Death and Dying - Critical Review of Some Available Methods," Omega, 9 (1979), 37-47.

4972. ________. "Death Education: Some Considerations of Purpose and Rationale," Educational Gerontology, 2 (January, 1977), 43-50.

4973. ________. "Level of Belief in Afterlife and Four Categories of Fear of Death in a Sample of 60+ Year Olds," Psychological Reports, 38 (February, 1976), 228.

4974. ________. "Assessment of Death Acceptance: A Proposed Scale," Psychology, 13 (February, 1976), 19-20.

4975. ________. "The Evaluation and Comparison of the Effects of Two Methods of Death Education on Participants' Attitudes Toward Life and Death," Dissertation Abstracts International, 38 (January, 1978), 3368.

4976. Kurtz, D.C., J. Boardman. Greek Burial Customs. Ithica, New York: Cornell University Press, 1971.

4977. Kurtzman, J., P. Gordon. No More Dying. Los Angeles: Tarcher, 1976.

4978. Kurz, A. et al. "Dying--Aid to the Dying--Hospice for the Dying," Krandenrflege, 31 (June, 1977), 198-201.

4979. Kushner, L. "Infant Death and the Childbirth Educator," Maternal Child Nursing Journal, 4 (July-August, 1979), 231-233.

4980. Kutner, L. "Euthanasia - Due Process for Death With Dignity - Living Will," Indiana Law Journal, 54 (1979), 201-228.

4981. Kutscher, A.H., Jr., M.A. Kutscher. Bibliography of Books on Death, Bereavement, Loss and Grief 1935-1968. New York: Health Sciences Publishing Corporation, 1969.

4982. ________. Bibliography of Books on Death, Bereavement, Loss and Grief 1968-1972. New York: Health Sciences Publishing Corporation, 1974.

4983. ________ et al (eds). Death, The Press and the Public. New York: MSS Information Company, 1978.

4984. ________ et al (eds). A Comprehensive Bibliography of the Thanatology Literature. New York: MSS Information Company, 1976.

4985. ________ et al (eds). A Cross Index of Indices of Books on Thanatology. New York: MSS Information Company, 1976.

4986. Lack, S.A. "I Want To Die While I'm Still Alive," Death Education, 1 (Summer, 1976), 165-176.

4987. ________, R.W. Buckingham III. The First American Hospice: Three Years of Home Care. New Haven, Connecticut: Hospice, Inc., 1978.

4988. ________, W. Fischer. "The Hospice Movement Letter," Journal of the American Medical Association, 241 (June 15, 1979), 2599-2600.

4989. Laing, R.D. Conversations With Adam and Natasha. New York: Pantheon, 1977.

4990. Lally, J.J. "Social Determinants of Differential Allocation of Resources to Disease Research: A Comparative Analysis of Crib Death and Cancer Research," Journal of Health & Social Behavior, 18 (June, 1977), 125-138.

4991. Lally, M.M. "Last Rites and Funeral Customs of Minority Groups," Midwife Health Visit Community Nurse, 14 (July, 1978), 224-225.

4992. Lambert, C.E., V.A. Lambert. "Divorce: A Psychodynamic Development Involving Grief," Journal of Psychiatric Nursing, 15 (January, 1977), 37-42.

4993. Lambert, R. "Books on Death and Dying," Media and Methods, 13 (February, 1977), 66-67.

4993a. Lamberton, R. "Going Deeper Into Care of the Dying," Nursing Mirror, 144 (March, 1977), 64-65.

4994. ________. "Nurse Could You Care More," Nursing Times, 75 (May 31, 1979), 905-906.

4995. ________. "The Care of the Dying: A Specialty," Nursing Times, 74 (March 16, 1978), 436.

4996. Lamont, A.M. "Bereavement," Central African Journal of Medicine, 23 (August, 1977), 167-170.

4997. Lampl-De Groot, J. "Mourning in a 6 Year Old Girl," Psychoanalytic Study of the Child, 76 (1976), 273-281.

4998. Lampton, L.M., C.H. Winship. "The 'No Code Blue' Issue: Missouri is not Massachusetts," Missouri Medicine, 76 (May, 1979), 259-261.

4999. Landau, E. Death: Everyone's Heritage. New York: Julian Messner, 1976.

5000. Landsberg, P. The Experience of Death: The Moral Problem of Suicide. New York: Arno Press, 1976. (Orig. Pub. 1953)

5001. Lane, J.C., T.C. Brown. "Probability of Casualties in an Airport Disaster," Aviation Space and Environmental Medicine, 46 (July, 1975), 958-961.

5002. Lang, J.A., M.M. Seltzer. "Review of Two Books on Death and Dying," DePaul Law Review, 26 (Summer, 1977), 891-901.

5003. Langer, L. "The Fear of Death: An Exploratory Study," Dissertation Abstracts International, 36 (March, 1976), 4694-4695.

5004. ______. The Age of Atrocity: Death in Modern Literature. Boston: Beacon Press, 1978.

5005. Langner, M.B. The Private Worlds of Dying Children. Princeton University Press, 1978.

5006. Langston, C. "Sudden Infant Death Syndrome," Human Pathology, 7 (September, 1976), 492-494.

5007. Lannerstad, O. et al. "Risk Factors For Premature Death in Men 56-60 Years Old," Scandanavian Journal of Social Medicine, 7 (1979), 41-47.

5008. Lappe, M. "Dying While Living: A Critique of Allowing To-Die Legislation," Journal of Medical Ethics, 4 (December, 1978), 195-199.

5009. Larrabee, M.J. "Measuring Fear of Death: A Rehabilitation Study," Journal of Psychology, 100 (September, 1978), 33-37.

5010. Larsch, C. "Birth, Death and Technology: The Limits of Cultural Laissez-Faire," Hastings Center Report, 2 (June, 1972), 1-4.

5011. Lascardi, A.D. "The Dying Child and the Family," Journal of Family Practice, 6 (January, 1978), 1279-1286.

5012. Lattimore, R. Themes in Greek and Latin Epitaphs. Urbana: University of Illinois Press, 1962.

5013. Laube, J. "Death and Dying Workshop for Nurses: Its Effect on Their Death Anxiety Level," International Journal of Nursing Students, 14 (1977), 111-120.

5014. Lawton, R.L., J. Davis. "Importance of Recent Legislation Regarding the Recognition of Brain Death, and the Identification of Organ Donors," Journal of the Iowa Medical Society, 67 (January, 1977), 11-13.

5015. Leach, W.H. The Cokesburn Funeral Manual. Nashville: Cokesbury, 1932.

5016. ________. The Improved Funeral Manual. Grand Rapids: Baker Book House, 1956.

5017. Leblang, T.R. "Death With Dignity: A Tripartite Legal Response," Death Education, 2 (Spring-Summer, 1978), 173-186.

5018. Lebovici, S. et al. "Remarks Concerning Several Cases of Children Being Present at the Violent Death of a Parent," Psychiatrie De L' Enfant, 18 (1975), 401-402.

5019. Le Bourdais, E. "The Hospital Inquest: Lessons in Death," Dimensions of Health Service, 51 (February, 1974), 12-17.

5020. Lechat, M.F. "Disasters and Public Health," Bulletin of the World Health Organization, 57 (1979), 11-17.

5021. Lee, A. "The Lazarus Syndrome, Caring for Patients Who've 'Returned From the Dead'," Registered Nurse, (June, 1978), 52-63.

5022. Lee, J.Y. Death and Beyond in the Eastern Perspective; A Study Based on the Bardo Thodol and the I Ching. New York: Gordon and Breach, 1974.

5023. Leetz, I. "Medical-Statistical Data on Sudden Infant Death in the GDR," Kinderaerztl Frax, 45 (April, 1977), 145-150.

5024. Legg, C., I. Sherick. "The Replacement Child--A Developmental Tragedy: Some Preliminary Comments," Child Psychiatry and Human Development, 7 (Winter, 1976), 113-126.

5025. Lehtinen, M.W., G.W. Smith. "The Value of Life: An Argument for the Death Penalty," Crime and Delinquency, 23 (July, 1977), 237-252.

5026. Lehtinen, M.W. "Death Penalty - Life and Death Issue," USA Today, 107 (1979), 32-36.

5027. Leibel, R.L. "Sounding Board. Thanatology and Medical Economics," New England Journal of Medicine, 296 (March 3, 1977), 511-513.

5028. Leighton, P. et al. "Malignant Disease in the Parents of Children Dying of Hodgkins Disease," British Journal of Cancer, 30 (October, 1974), 373-375.

5029. Lemasters, G. "The Effects of Bereavement on the Elderly and the Nursing Implications," Journal of Gerontology Nursing, 4 (November-December, 1978), 21-25.

5030. Leming, M.R. "The Relationship Between Religiosity and the Fear of Death," Dissertation Abstracts International, 36 (May, 1976), 7674.

5031. ________, et al. "The Dying Patient: A Symbolic Analysis," International Journal of Symbology, 8 (July, 1977), 77-86.

5032. Leon, J.J., P.G. Steinhoff. "Catholics' Use of Abortion," Sociological Analysis, 36 (Summer, 1975), 125-136.

5033. Leonard, G., A.J. Martin. "The Doctor and the Dying Patient," Times (London), (December 31, 1976), 15.

5034. Leonard, V.R. "Death Education in the Helping Professions," Australian Journal of Social Issues, 11 (May, 1976), 108-119.

5035. Lepontois, J. "Adolescents With Sickle-Cell Anemia Deal With Life and Death," Social Work Health Care, 1 (Fall, 1975), 71-80.

5036. Lerner, G. Death of One's Own. New York: Harrow, 1980.

5037. Lerner, R.C. et al. "Abortion Programs in New York City: Services, Policies & Potential Health Hazards," The Milbank Memorial Fund Quarterly, 52 (Winter, 1974), 15-38.

5038. Le Roux, R.S. "Communicating With the Dying Person," Nursing Forum, 16 (1977), 144-155.

5039. Lescoe, R.J. "Legislative Proposals for Death With Dignity," Journal of Legal Medicine, 3 (September, 1975), 34-35.

5040. LeShan, E. Learning to Say Goodbye When a Parent Dies. New York: Macmillan, 1976.

5041. LeShan, L. You Can Fight For Your Life: Emotional Factors in the Causation of Cancer. New York: M. Evans & Co., 1977.

5042. Lester, D., L.M. Colvin. "Fear of Death. Alienation and Self-Actualization," Psychological Reports, 41 (October, 1977), 526.

5043. ________ et al. "Prediction of Homicide and Suicide: A Test in Health Risk-Taking Group," Perceptual and Motor Skills, 44 (February, 1977), 222.

5044. Levenstein, R.M. "Jewish Teaching Concerning Death," Nursing Times, 74 (March, 1978), 35-36 (suppl.).

5045. Levin, S. "On Widowhood, Discussion," Journal of Geriatric Psychiatry, 8 (1975), 57-59.

5046. Levine, A. "Viewpoints on Life and Death," Journal of the New York State Nurses Association, 8 (March, 1977), 20-24.

5047. Levit, R. Ellen: A Short Life Long Remembered. New York: Bantam, 1975.

5048. Leviton, D. "The Stimulus of Death," Health Education, 7 (March-April, 1976), 17-20.

5049. ________. "The Scope of Death Education," Death Education, 1 (Spring, 1977), 41-55.

5050. ________. "Life and Death Attitudes of Parents of Children With Problems: Interview Data," Omega, 8 (1977-1978), 333-357.

5051. ________. "The Intimacy/Sexual Needs of the Terminally Ill and The Widowed," Death Education, 2 (Fall, 1978), 261-280.

5052. ________, B. Fretz. "Effects of Death Education on Fear of Death and Attitudes Towards Death and Life," Omega, 9 (1979), 267-277.

5053. Levy, B. "A Study of Bereavement in General Practice," Journal of the Royal College of General Practitioners, 26 (May, 1976), 329-336.

5054. Lewak, N. "Sudden Infant Death Syndrome in a Hospitalized Infant on an Apnea Monitor," Pediatrics, 56 (August, 1975), 296-298.

5055. Lewis, E. "Mourning By the Family After a Stillbirth or Neonatal Death," Archives of Diseases in Childhood, 54 (April, 1979), 303-306.

5056. ________, A. Page. "Failure to Mourn a Stillbirth: An Overlooked Catastrophe," British Journal of Medical Psychology, 51 (September, 1978), 237-241.

5057. Lewis, G.W. "Differences in Concerns About Death and Dying in Medical and Law Students at Different Levels of Training," Dissertation Abstracts International, 38 (November, 1977), 2372-2373.

5058. Lewis, J. "How the Nurse Copes With Grief: Care of the Child With Cancer," Australas Nurses Journal, 8 (January-February, 1979), 16-17.

5059. Lewis, K. "The Elderly and the Imminence of Death," Journal of the American Health Care Association, 3 (March, 1977), 10-12, 14, 16-18.

5060. Lewis, R.L. "The Effects of Type of Death and Preparation Time on Bereavement," Dissertation Abstracts International, 38 (March, 1978), 4466-4467.

5061. Lewis, S., S.H. Armstrong. "Children With Terminal Illness: A Selected Review," International Journal of Psychiatry in Medicine, 8 (1977-1978), 73-82.

5062. Leyn, R.M. "Letters of a Mother in Mourning," Maternal Child Nursing Journal, 4 (Summer, 1975), 83-94.

5063. ________. "Terminally Ill Children and Their Families: A Study of the Variety of Responses to Fatal Disease," Maternal Child Nursing Journal, 5 (Fall, 1976), 179-188.

5064. Libman, J. "The Hospice Movement," Medical Times, 107 (May, 1979), 108 (1D-3-D).

5065. Lichtenstein, S. et al. "Judged Frequency of Lethal Events," Journal of Experimental Psychology, 4 (November, 1978), 551-578.

5066. Lidz, T. The Person: His & Her Development Throughout the Life Cycle. New York: Basic Books, 1976.

5067. Lieberman, S. "Nineteen Cases of Morbid Grief," *British Journal of Psychiatry*, 132 (February, 1978), 159-163.

5068. Lief, H.I. "Commentary on Dr. Ian Stevenson's 'The Evidence of Man's Survival After Death'," *Journal of Nervous and Mental Disease*, 165 (September, 1977), 171-173.

5069. Liemak, F. et al. "Husbands of Abortion Applicants - Comparison With Husbands of Women Who Complete Their Pregnancies," *Social Psychiatry*, 14 (1979), 59-64.

5070. Liftshitz, M. "Long-Renge Effects of Father's Loss: The Cognitive Complexity of Bereaved Children and Their School Adjustment," *British Journal of Medicine and Psychology*, 49 (June, 1976), 189-197.

5071. ________ et al. "Bereaved Children. The Effects of Mother's Perception and Social-System Organization on Their Short-Range Adjustment," *Journal of the American Academy of Child Psychiatry*, 16 (Spring, 1977), 272-284.

5072. Lifton, R.J. *The Life of the Self: Toward a New Psychology*. New York: Simon & Schuster, 1977.

5073. ________. *Death in Life: Survivors in Hiroshima*. New York: Simon & Schuster, 1976.

5074. ________, E. Olson. "The Human Meaning of Total Disaster. The Buffalo Creek Experience," *Psychiatry*, 39 (February, 1976), 1-18.

5075. ________. *Boundaries: Psychological Man in Revolution*. New York: Simon & Schuster, 1977.

5076. ________. *Home From the War: Transformations of Vietnam Veterans*. New York: Simon & Schuster, 1977.

5077. ________. "The Sense of Immortality: On Death and the Continuity of Life," *American Journal of Psychoanalysis*, 33 (1973), 1.

5078. Ligouri, St. A. *How to Face Death Without Fear*. Ligouri, Missouri: Ligouri Press, 1976.

5079. Limerick, L. "Support and Counseling Needs of Families Following a Cot Death Bereavement," *Proceedings of the Royal Society of Medicine*, 69 (November, 1976), 839-842.

5080. Lindeman, E. "Grief and Grief Management: Some Reflections," Journal of Pastoral Care, 30 (September, 1976), 198-207.

5081. Lindenberg, S.P. "The Effects of an Existential Type of Group Therapy on a Time-Limited Group of Members For Whom the Imminence of Death is a Pressing Reality," Dissertation Abstracts International, 38 (January, 1978), 3404.

5082. Lindholm, D. Death is a Miracle. Hicksville, New York: Exposition, 1977.

5083. Lindsay, R. Alone and Surviving: A Guide for Today's Widow. New York: Walker Publishing, 1977.

5084. Lindsey, H.L. "Statistical and Modeling Techniques for Studying the Sudden Infant Death Syndrome," Education, 96 (Spring, 1976), 226-234.

5085. Lingg, B.A. "Widowed-Father Beneficiaries," Social Security Bulletin, 40 (February, 1977), 26-29.

5086. Linzer, N. (ed). Understanding Grief and Bereavement. Yeshiva University Press: KTAV Publishing House, 1977.

5087. Lister, L. H. Gochros. "Preparing Students for Effective Social Work Practice Related to Death," Journal of Education for Social Work, 12 (Winter, 1976), 35-90.

5088. Lofland, L.H. The Craft of Dying: The Modern Face of Death. Beverly Hills: Sage, 1978.

5089. ________. Sage Contemporary Social Science Issues: XXVIII, Toward a Sociology of Death and Dying. Beverly Hills: Sage, 1976.

5090. Logan, J.P. "The 'Right to Die' and the Language of Christian Personalist Ethics," Ann Arbor: University Microfilms International, 1977.

5091. Lombana, J.H. "Toward Death Integration: Implications for Counselors," Counseling and Values, 23 (February, 1979), 97-105.

5092. Lombardo, L. "Brain Death," Gaceta Medica de Mexico, 113 (January, 1977), 10-13.

5093. Lonetto, R. et al. "The Perceived Sex of Death and Concerns About Death," Essence, 76 (1976), 66-84.

5094. Longley, C. "Wrong to Prolong Life at any Cost, Dr. Coggan Says," Times (London), (December 14, 1976), 1.

5095. Longmore, D.B., M. Rehahn. "The Cumulative Cost of Death," Lancet, 1 (May, 1975), 1023-1025.

5096. Longo, D.R., K. Darr. "Hospital Care for the Terminally Ill: A Model Program," Hospital Progress, (March, 1978), 62-70.

5097. Loomba, M.A. "Attitudes of the Aged Toward Death and Dying," Journal of Long Term Care Administration, 3 (Spring, 1975), 35-43.

5098. Lorber, J., R.B. Zachary. "Spina Bifada: To Treat or Not to Treat? Selection - The Best Policy Available," Nursing Mirror, 147 (September, 1978), 13-19.

5099. Lord, R. et al. "Patients' Reactions to the Death of the Psychoanalyst," International Journal of Psychoanalysis, 59 (1978), 189-197.

5100. Lowe, W.C., S.D. Thomas. "Death Expectancies in Alcoholic and Non-Alcoholic Persons," Journal of Clinical Psychology, 33 (October, 1977), 1154-1156.

5101. Luckman, D. "The Dark Side of Nursing: The Nurse Who Asked Why," Nursing Mirror, 148 (April, 1979), 18-19.

5102. Lugt, H.V. Light In the Valley. Wheaton, Illinois: Victor Books, 1977.

5103. Lunceford, R., J. Lunceford. Attitudes on Death and Dying: A Cultural View. Los Alamitos: Hwong Press, 1976.

5104. Luntz, L.L., P. Luntz. "Dental Identification of Disaster Victims by a Dental Disaster Squad," Journal of Forensic Science, 17 (January, 1972), 63- 69.

5105. Lutticken, C.A. et al. "Attitudes of Physical Therapists Toward Death and Terminal Illness," Physical Therapy, 54 (March, 1974), 226-232.

5106. Lynch, J.L. The Broken Heart: The Medical Consequences of Loneliness. New York: Basic Books, 1977.

5107. MacDonald, A.J. "Mourning After Pets (Letter)," British Journal of Psychiatry, 131 (November, 1977), 551.

5108. MacDonald, M.B., K.C. Meyer. "Defining Death," Mt. Sinai Journal of Medicine New York, 43 (May-June, 1976), 300-302.

5109. Madigan, F.C. et al. "Purposive Concealment of Death in Household Surveys in Misamis Oriental Province," Population Studies, 30 (July, 1976), 295-303.

5110. Maddison, D. "Coping With Crisis," The Australas Nurses Journal, 7 (March, 1978), 31-35.

5111. Maeterlinck, M. Before the Great Silence. New York: Arno Press, 1976. (Orig. Pub. 1937).

5112. ________. Death. New York: Arno Press, 1976. (Orig. Pub. 1912).

5113. Magee, B. Facing Death. London: William Kimber, 1977.

5114. Maguire, D.C. "Death and the Moral Domain," St. Luke's Journal of Theology, 20 (June, 1977), 197-216.

5115. Magura, S. "Letter: Sudden Death in Infancy," Nature, 256 (August, 1975), 519.

5116. Mahew, H.E., R.D. Gillette. "The Forensic Pathologist: 'Family Physician' to the Bereaved," Journal of the American Medical Association, 238 (October, 1977), 1496.

5117. Mahon, E., D. Simpson. "The Painted Guinea Pig," Psychoanalytic Study of the Child, 32 (1977), 283-303.

5118. Mahoney, E.J. "The Mortality of Terminating Life versus Allowing to Die," Louvain Studies, 6 (Spring, 1977), 256-272.

5119. Maine, D. "Does Abortion Affect Later Pregnancies," Family Planning Perspectives, 11 (1979), 98-101.

5120. Male, N.S. "The Effects of Thanatology Instruction on Attitudes and Fears About Death and Dying," Dissertation Abstracts International, 39 (August, 1978), 688.

5121. Malkin, S. "Care of the Terminally Ill at Home," Canadian Medical Association Journal, 115 (1976), 129-130.

5122. Mancini, M. "Death With Dignity: Are Living Wills an Answer," American Journal of Nursing, 78 (December, 1978), 2133-2134.

5123. Mandell, F., B. Belk. "Sudden Infant Death Syndrome. The Disease and its Survivors," Postgraduate Medicine, 62 (October, 1977), 193-197.

5124. ________, L.C. Wolfe. "Sudden Infant Death Syndrome and Subsequent Pregnancy," Pediatrics, 56 (November, 1975), 774-776.

5125. Manganello, J.A. "An Investigation of Counselor Empathy with Terminally Ill Patients on Attitude Toward Afterlife," Dissertation Abstracts International, 38 (October, 1977), 1891-1892.

5126. Mann, B.A. "Cracking the Ice: An Examination of 'Instantaneous Thanatology'," Suicide and Life Threatening Behavior, 7 (Winter, 1977), 246-256.

5127. Mann, J. et al. "Feigned Bereavement Letter," British Journal of Psychiatry, 134 (January, 1979), 127.

5128. Manning, J.A. "Sudden, Unexpected Death in Children," American Journal of Diseases of Children, 131 (November, 1977), 1201-1202.

5129. Manning, W.H., H.J. Vogel. "Case For Brain Death Legislation - Response," Minnesota Medicine, 62 (1979), 121-127.

5130. Mappes, T.A., J.S. Zembaty (eds). Social Ethics: Mortality and Social Policy. New York: McGraw-Hill, 1977.

5131. Margolis, O.S. et al (eds). Thanatology Course Outlines. (vol. 2). New York: MSS Information Company, 1978.

5132. Marie, H. "Reorienting the Staff Attitudes Toward the Dying," Hospital Progress, 59 (August, 1978), 74-76 & 92.

5133. Marino, C.D., R.J. McCowan. "The Effects of Parent Absence on Children," Child Study Journal, 6 (1976), 165-182.

5134. Markel, W.M., V.B. Sinon. "The Hospice Concept," Journal of Practical Nursing, 29 (March, 1979), 24-29.

5135. Markides, K.S., D. Barnes. "A Methodological Note on the Relationship Between Infant Mortality and Socioeconomic Status with Evidence From San Antonio, Texas," Social Biology, 24 (Spring, 1977), 38-44.

5136. Marks, M.L. "Dealing With Death. The Grieving Patient and Family," American Journal of Nursing, 76 (September, 1976), 1488-1491.

5137. Marks, S.C., S.L. Bertam. "Experiences With and Resources for Learning About Death and Dying Within the Undergraduate Anatomy Curriculum," Anatomical Record, 193 (1979), 735.

5138. Markusen, E. et al. "SIDS: The Survivor as Victim," Omega, 8 (1977-1978), 277-284.

5139. Marnocha, M. "Clinical Perspectives on Death and Self-Awareness," Human Development, 20 (1977), 199-203.

5140. Maron, B.J. et al. "Sudden Infant Death Syndrome (SIDS). Echocardiographic Studies in Relatives of Infants with SIDS," Journal of Clinical Ultrasound, 5 (October 1977), 313-315.

5141. Marshall, J.R. "The Geriatric Patient's Fears About Death," Postgraduate Medicine, 57 (April, 1975), 144 & 147-149.

5142. Marshall, V.W. "Socialization For Impending Death in a Retirement Village," American Journal of Sociology, 80 (March, 1975), 1124-1144.

5143. Martin, A. "Nurses and the Law--Euthanasia," Nursing Times, 74 (May, 1978), 800.

5144. Martin, M.C. "Cooperation Marks Development of Hospice," Hospitals, 53 (July, 1979), 32, 41 &44.

5145. Martinson, I.M. "Why Don't We Let Them Die at Home?" Registered Nurse, 39 (January, 1976), 58-65.

5146. ________. The Dying Child, the Family & the Health Professionals. Englewood Cliffs, New Jersey: Prentice-Hall, 1976.

5147. ________. Home Care for the Dying Child: Professional and Family Perspectives. New York: Appleton-Century-Crofts, 1976.

5148. ________ et al. "The Dying Patient: Death and Dying: Selected Attitudes and Experiences of Minnesota's Registered Nurses," Communicating Nursing Research, 9 (April, 1977), 1815-1817.

5149. ________ et al. "When the Patient is Dying: Home Care for the Child," American Journal of Nursing, 77 (November, 1977), 1815-1817.

5150. Marx, P. "Abortion/Euthanasia," Persona y Derecho: Revista de Fundamentacion de la Instituciones Juridicas, 2 (1975), 283-410.

5151. Mathers, J. "'Brain Death' or 'Heart Death'? Reflections on an Ethical Dilemma," Expository Times, 87 (August, 1976), 328-332.

5152. Mathis, J.L. "The Terminally Ill Patient," Primary Care, 1 (June, 1974), 211-219.

5153. Matson, A. The Waiting World: What Happens After Death. New York: Harper & Row, 1975.

5154. ________. Afterlife: Reports From the Threshold of Death. New York: Harper & Row, 1977.

5155. Matthews, G.B. "Life and Death as the Arrival and Departure of the Psyche," American Philosophical Quarterly, (1979), 151-157.

5156. Mattis, J.I. "Marilyn Died, But on Her Own Terms," Registered Nurse, 40 (October, 1977), 59.

5157. Maxwell, M. "Elisabeth Kubler-Ross Revisited: A Personal Account of a 'Life and Transitions' Workshop," Oncology Nursing Forum, 6 (January 1979), 26-27.

5158. Maxwell, R. et al. "Incidence of Sudden Infant Death Syndrome in Texas, 1969-1972: Estimation By the Surrogate Method," Texas Medicine, 72 (October, 1976), 58-66.

5159. May, R. "The Confrontation With Death," Preventive Medicine, 5 (December, 1976), 508-517.

5160. May, W.E. "Death, Dying and Organ Donation," in: his Human Existence, Medicine and Ethics: Reflections on Human Life. Chicago: Franciscan Herald Press, 1977, 159-167.

5161. ________. Human Existence, Medicine and Ethics: Reflections on Human Life. Chicago: Franciscan Herald Press, 1977.

5162. ________. "Care of the Dying," in: his Human Existence, Medicine and Ethics: Reflections on Human Life. Chicago: Franciscan Herald Press, 1977, 131-158.

5163. May, W.F. "The Right to Die and the Obligation to Care: Allowing to Die, Killing for Mercy and Suicide," in: McMullin, E. (ed) Death and Decision. Boulder: Westview Press, 1978.

5164. Mayer, G. Behind the Veils of Death and Sleep. New York: Krishna Press, 1973.

5165. McCarthy, D.G. "Euthanasia: Meaning and Challenge," in: Ethical Issues in Nursing: A Proceedings. St. Louis: Catholic Hospital Association, 1976, 55-64.

5166. ________. "Should Catholic Hospitals Sponsor Hospices?," Hospital Progress, 57 (December, 1976), 61-65.

5167. ________ (ed). Responsible Stewardship of Human Life: Inquiry Into Medical Ethics. St. Louis: Catholic Hospital Association, 1976.

5168. McCarthy, J. Fearful Living: The Fear of Death. New York: Halsted Press, 1979.

5169. McCarthy, M. "Life Issues and Group Psychotherapy With Terminal Cancer Patients," Dissertation Abstracts International, 36 (January, 1976), 3615-3616.

5170. McCawley, A. "Grief and the Primary Physician," Connecticut Medicine, 40 (February, 1976), 115-122.

5171. McCorkle, M.T. "Human Attachments and Intended Goals During Terminal Illness," Dissertation Abstracts International, 36 (February, 1976), 3866-3867.

5172. McCorkle, R. "The Advanced Cancer Patient: How He Will Life--And Die," Nursing (Jenkintown), 6 (October, 1976), 46-49.

5173. ________. "Effects of Touch on Seriously Ill Patients," Nursing Research, 23 (March-April, 1974), 125-132.

5174. McCormick, R.A. "The Quality of Life: The Sanctity of Life," Hastings Center Report, 8 (February, 1978), 30-36.

5175. McCourt, W.F. et al. "We Help Each Other: Primary Prevention for the Widowed," American Journal of Psychiatry, 133 (January, 1976), 98-100.

5176. McDowell, M.M. "American Attitudes Toward Death: 1825-1865," Dissertation Abstracts International, 38 (June, 1978), 7335.

5177. McEllhenney, J.G. Cutting the Monkey Rope. Valley Forge, Pennsylvania: Judson Press, 1973.

5178. McGeachy, D.P. A Matter of Life and Death. Richmond: John Knox, 1966.

5179. McGuire, M.A. "Have You Ever Let a Patient Die by Default," Registered Nurse, 40 (November, 1977), 56-59.

5180. McGurn, W.M. "The Will to Life, The Will to Die: Correlates of Disengagement in Hospitalized Cancer Patients," Dissertation Abstracts International, 37 (January, 1977), 4648.

5181. McHugh, J.T. (ed). Death, Dying and the Law. Huntington, Indiana: Our Sunday Visitor Press, 1976.

5182. McIntier, T.M. "Hillhaven Hospice: A Free-Standing, Family Centered Program," Hospital Progress, 60 (March, 1979), 68-72.

5183. McIntosh, J. Communication & Awareness in a Cancer Ward. London: Croom Helm, 1977.

5184. McIntosh, W.A., J.P. Alston. "Acceptance of Abortion Among White Catholics and Protestants: 1962-1975," Journal for the Scientific Study of Religion, 16 (September, 1977), 295-303.

5185. McIntyre, R.L. "Euthanasia: A Soft Paradign for Medical Ethics," Linacre Quarterly, 45 (February, 1978), 41-54.

5186. McKenney, E.J. "Death and Dying in Tennessee," Memphis State University Law Review, 7 (Summer, 1977), 503-554.

5187. McKissock, M. "Bereavement Education for Nurses," The Nurse's Lamp, 35 (March, 1978), 14-15.

5188. McLaren, A. "Abortion in France - Women and Regulation of Family Size 1800-1914," French Historical Studies, 10 (1978), 461-485.

5189. McLaughlin, M.F. "Grief: Who Helps the Living?," American Journal of Nursing, (March, 1978), 422-433.

5190. McLendon, G.H. "One Teacher's Experience With Death Education for Adolescents," Death Education, 3 (1979), 57-65.

5191. McLuckie, B.F. "Centralization and Natural Disaster Response: A Preliminary Hypothesis and Interpretation," Mass Emergencies, 1 (October, 1975), 1-9.

5192. McMillen, M.M. "Differential Mortality by Sex in Fetal and Neofetal Deaths," Science, 204 (1979), 89-91.

5193. McMullin, E. (ed). Death and Decision. Boulder, Colorado: Westview Press, 1978.

5194. McNamara, E.M. "Continuing Health Care: Attention Turns to Day Care and Hospice Services," Hospitals, 52 (April, 1978), 82-83.

5195. McNulty, B. "Discharge of the Terminally Ill Patient," Nursing Times, 66 (September, 1970), 1160-1162.

5196. ________. "St. Christopher's Outpatients," American Journal of Nursing, 71 (December, 1971), 2328-2330.

5197. ________. "The Problem of Pain in the Dying Patient," Queen's Nursing Journal, 16 (1973), 152-161.

5198. ________. "The Nurses Contribution in Terminal Care," Nursing Mirror, 139 (1974), 59-61.

5199. McPhee, M.S. et al. "Taking the Stigma Out of Hospital Care: Flexible Approaches for the Terminally Ill," Canadian Medical Association Journal, 120 (May, 1979), 1284-1288.

5200. Mehr, R.I. "Changing Responsibility for Personal Risks and Societal Consequences - Premature Death and Old Age," Annals of the Academy of Political Science and Social Science, 443 (May, 1979), 1-11.

5201. Mehta, R. The Journey With Death. Mystic, Conneticut: Verry, 1977.

5202. Meilaender, G. "The Distinction Between Killing and Allowing to Die," Theological Studies, 37 (September, 1976), 467-470.

5203. Melzak, R. et al. "The Brompton Mixture: Effects on Pain in Cancer Patients," Canadian Medical Association Journal, 115 (1976), 125-129.

5204. Menig-Peterson, C.L., A. McCabe. "Children Talk About Death," Omega, 8 (1977-1978), 305-317.

5205. Merkin, L. "Problem of 'Dying With Dignity'," New York State Journal of Medicine, 79 (January, 1979), 101-106.

5206. Merritt, T.A. et al. "Sudden Infant Death Syndrome: The Role of the Emergency Room Physician," Clinical Pediatrics (Philadelphia), 14 (December, 1975), 1095-1097.

5207. Meserve, H.C. "Getting Out of It," Journal of Religion and Health, 14 (January, 1975), 3-6.

5208. Mester, R.C. "Requests for Abortions: A Psychiatrist's View," Israel Annals of Psychiatry and Related Disciplines, 14 (September, 1976), 294-299.

5209. Metchnikoff, E. The Nature of Man. New York: Arno Press, 1976. (Orig. Pub. 1910).

5210. ________. The Prolongation of Life: Optimistic Studies. New York: Arno Press, 1976. (Orig. Pub. 1908).

5211. Meuller, M.L. "Death Education and Fear of Death Education," Education, 97 (Winter, 1976), 145-148

5212. Meyer, J.E. "The Theme of Death and the Origin and Course of Obsessional Neuroses," (author's translation), Psychotherapie Medizinische Psychologie, 25 (July, 1975), 124-128.

5213. Meyers, J., N.W. Pitt. "A Consultation Approach to Help a School Cope With the Bereavement Process," Professional Psychology, 7 (November, 1976), 559-564.

5214. Michalowski, R.J., Jr. "Violence in the Road: The Crime of Vehicular Homicide," Journal of Research in Crime and Delinquency, 12 (January, 1975), 30-43.

5215. Midgley, J. "Public Opinion and the Death Penalty in South Africa," The British Journal of Criminology, 14 (October, 1974), 345-358.

5216. Migre, D. "Death and Suicide in Modern Lyrics," Suicide, 5 (Winter, 1975), 232-245.

5217. Mikolaitis, S.M. "Choosing the Circumstances of Death," Forum, 2 (1978), 19-23.

5218. Miles, H.S., D.R. Hays. "Widowhood," American Journal of Nursing, 75 (February, 1975), 280-282.

5219. Miles, M.S. "SIDS: Parents are the Patients," Journal of Emergency Nursing, 3 (March-April, 1977), 29-32.

5220. ________. "The Effects of a Small Group Education/Counseling Experience on the Attitudes of Nurses Toward Death and Toward Dying Patients," Dissertation Abstracts International, 38 (August, 1977), 636.

5221. Miller, A. "The Wages of Neglect: Death and Disease in the American Workplace," American Journal of Public Health, 65 (November, 1975), 1217-1220.

5222. ________, A. Acri. Death: A Bibliographical Guide. Metuchen, New Jersey: Scarecrow Press, 1977.

5223. Miller, D. "Management of the Dying Patient With Head and Neck Cancer," Annals of Otology, Rhinology, and Laryngology, 86 (November-December, 1977), 801-805.

5224. Miller, G.W. "Moral and Ethical Implications of Positive and Negative Euthanasia," Bulletin of American Protestant Hospital Association, 40 (March, 1976), 89-92.

5225. Miller, J. The Healing Power of Grief. New York: Seabury, 1978.

5226. Miller, J. "Community Development in a Disaster Community," Community Development Journal, 8 (October, 1973), 161-165.

5227. Miller, R.C. Live Until You Die. Philadelphia: United Church Press, 1973.

5228. Millerd, E.J. "Health Professionals as Survivors," Journal of Psychiatric Nursing, 15 (April, 1977), 33-37.

5229. Millett, N. "Hospice: Challenging Society's Approach to Death," Health and Social Work, 4 (February, 1979), 131-150.

5230. Milligan, H.C. "Discussion of Papers on the Inner London Survey on Sudden Death in Infancy," Public Health, 89 (May, 1975), 159-160.

5231. Mills, D.H. "California's Natural Death Act," Journal of Legal Medicine, 5 (January, 1977), 22-23.

5232. ________. "The Death Certificate," Journal of the American Dental Association, 76 (June, 1977), 19-20.

5233. Mills, G.C. "Nurses Discuss Dying--A Simulation Experience," Journal of Continuing Education for Nurses, 8 (September-October, 1977), 35-40.

5234. ________. "Books to Help Children Understand Death," American Journal of Nursing, 79 (1979), 291-295.

5235. ________ et al. Discussing Death: A Guide to Death Education. Homewood, Illinois: ETC Publications, 1976.

5236. Minear, P.S. To Die and to Live. New York: Seabury Press, 1977.

5237. Mirande, A.M., E.L. Hammer. "Love, Sex, Permissiveness and Abortion: A Test of Alternative Models," Archives of Sexual Behavior, 5 (November, 1976), 553-566.

5238. Mircea, N. et al. "Criteria of Brain Death (Personal Opinions)," Revista De: Chirurgie Oncologie Radiologie Orl Oftalmologie Stomatologie, 26 (July-August, 1977), 275-280.

5239. Mitchell, P. Act of Love. New York: Alfred A. Knopf, 1976.

5240. Mitscherlich, A., M. Mitscherlich. The Inability to Mourn: Prinicipies of Collective Behavior. New York: Grove Press, 1975.

5241. Miyano, H. "Karen Quinlan Case--Dignified Death and Nursing. Solution to the Medico-Legal Dilemma. The Choice Between Life and Death - Current Development in Europe and the United States," *Japan Journal of Nursing*, 40 (August, 1976), 816-824.

5242. ________. "Choice Between Life and Death: Current Trends in Western Societies. Legislation and Establishment of Criteria: Popular Opinions and the Danger of Diversion from the Fundamental Problems," *Japan Journal of Nursing*, 41 (February, 1977), 153-160.

5243. Miyuki, M.K. "Dying Isagi-Yoku," *Journal of Humanistic Psychology*, 18 (Fall, 1978), 37-44.

5244. Mize, E. "As A Nurse, How Can You Help?" *Journal of Practical Nursing*, 25 (October, 1975), 36-37.

5245. Moise, L.E. "In Sickness and in Death," *Mental Retardation*, 16 (December, 1978), 397-399.

5246. Monroe, E. "From One Death, Two Lives," *Assistants of Operating Rooms Nurses Journal*, 20 (October, 1974), 613-617.

5247. Montagu, A. "The Illusion of Mortality and Health," *Preventive Medicine*, 5 (December, 1976), 496-507.

5248. Montague, P. "The Mortality of Active and Passive Euthanasia," *Ethics in Science and Medicine*, 5 (1978), 39-45.

5249. Montgomery, H., M. Montgomery. *Beyond Sorrow*. Minneapolis: Winston Press, 1977.

5250. Montgomery, J.W. "Do We Have the Right to Die?," *Chrisianity Today*, 21 (January, 1977), 49-50.

5251. Mood, D.W., B.A. Lakin. "Attitudes of Nursing Personnel Toward Death and Dying: Linguistic Indications of Avoidance," *Research in Nursing and Health*, 2 (June, 1979), 53-60.

5252. Moods, A. *Mr. Death: Four Stories*. New York: Harper & Row, 1975.

5253. Moody, R.A., Jr. "Near Death Experiences: Dilemma for the Clinician," *Virginia Medicine*, 104 (October, 1977), 687-690.

5254. ________. Life After Life. Georgia: Mockingbird Books, 1975. New York: Bantam, 1976.

5255. ________. Life After Life: The Investigation of a Phenomenon. New York: Stackpole Books, 1976.

5256. ________. Reflections on Life After Life. New York: Bantam/ Mockingbird, 1977.

5257. Mooney, G.H. The Valuation of Human Life. London: Macmillan, 1977.

5258. Moore, A. "The Cot Death Syndrome," Midwife Health Visit Community Nurse, 12 (May, 1976), 154-156.

5259. Moore, J.C., Jr. "Sudden Infant Death Syndrome. Progress Report," Journal of the South Carolina Medical Association, 71 (October, 1975), 316-317.

5260. Moore, M. Life After What? Huntsville, Alabama: Southern Publishing, 1977.

5261. Moore, R.J., J.H. Newton. "Attitudes of the Life Threatened Hospitalized Elderly," Essence, 1 (1977), 129-138.

5262. Moos, R.H. Coping With Physical Illness. New York: Plenum, 1977.

5263. Morgan, D.W. "Altered States Variables as Predictors of Death Anxiety," Essence, 1 (1976), 51-61.

5264. Morgan, E. A Manual of Death Education and Simple Burial. Burnsville, North Carolina: Celo Press, 1977.

5265. Morgan, H.G. Death Wishes? The Understanding and Management of Deliberate Self-Harm. New York: Wiley, 1979.

5266. Morgan, J.H. (ed). Death and Dying: A Resource Bibliography for Clergy and Chaplains (1960-1976). Wichita: Institute on Ministry and the Elderly, 1977.

5267. Morgan, L.A. "A Re-examination of Widowhood and Morale," Journal of Gerontology, 31 (November, 1976), 687-695.

5268. Moriarty, J.J. "Death Anxiety in Hysteric and Obsessive Personalities," Dissertation Abstracts International, 36 (February, 1976), 4169.

5269. Moriya, H., Y. Kinoshita. "Life and Death of Patients Over 70 - A Proposal for Organization of Group of Citizens Preferring a Dignified Death Over Meaningless Prolongation of Life. A Discussion," Japan Journal of Nursing, 40 (January, 1976), 66-73.

5270. Morley, J. Death, Heaven and the Victorians. Pittsburg: University of Pittsburg, 1971.

5271. Morris, D. "Parental Reactions to Perinatal Death," Proceedings of the Royal Society of Medicine, 69 (November, 1976), 837-838.

5272. Morris, L.L. "To Die Young, To Die Old," Journal of Geriatric Psychiatry, 8 (1975), 127-135.

5273. Morris, N. "Mattick, Hans and the Death Penalty - Sentimental Notes on 2 Topics," University of Toledo Law Review, 10 (1979), 299-316.

5274. Moss, B.B., M.A. Werckle. "Letter: Not to Die Alone," Modern Health Care, 3 (January, 1975), 16.

5275. Mosse, C.L. "National Cemeteries and National Revival - Cult of the Fallen Soldiers of Germany," Journal of Contemporary History, 14 (1979), 1-20.

5276. Mount, B.M. "Death and Dying: Attitudes in a Teaching Hospital," Urology, 4 (December, 1974), 741-747.

5277. ________. "The Problem of Caring for the Dying in a General Hospital: The Palliative Care Unit as a Possible Solution," Canadian Medical Association Journal, 115 (July, 1976), 119-121.

5278. ________ et al. "Use of the Brompton Mixture in Treating Chronic Pain of Malignant Disease," Canadian Medical Association Journal, 115 (July, 1976), 122-124.

5279. Mueller, J.M., Jr. "I Taught About Death and Dying," Phi Delta Kappan, 60 (October, 1978), 117.

5280. Mueller, M.L. "Fear of Death and Death Education," Notre Dame Journal of Education, 6 (Spring, 1975), 84-91.

5281. ________. "Death Education and Death Fear Reduction," Education, 97 (Winter, 1976), 145-148.

5282. Mullaly, R.W., H. Osmond. "Medical Education and the Dying Patient," *Southern Medical Journal*, 72 (1979), 409-411.

5283. Mulvey, P.M. "Letter: Sudden Death in Infancy," *Medical Journal of Australia*, 2 (November, 1974), 409-411.

5284. Mundhenke, C.A. "Establishing a Grief Center," *Bulletin of the American Protestant Hospital Association*, 40 (March, 1976), 44-48.

5285. Mundy, J. *Learning to Die*. New York: Freedeeds Association, 1976.

5286. Munk, W. *Euthanasia. Or Medical Treatment in Aid of an Easy Death*. New York: Arno Press, 1976. (Orig. Pub. 1887).

5287. Munter, P.K. "Death in the Infirmary: Some Observations About the Dying Patient," *Journal of the American College Health Association*, 23 (December, 1974), 151-153.

5288. Murchison, K.M. "Toward a Perspective on the Death-Penalty Cases," *Emory Law Journal*, 27 (1978), 469-555.

5289. Murphy, C.R. *The Valley of the Shadow*. Wallingford, Pennsylvania: Pendle Hill Publications, 1972.

5290. Murphy, G.K. "Death on the Railway," *Journal of Forensic Science*, 21 (January, 1976), 218-226.

5291. Muslin, H.L. et al. "Separation Experience and Cancer of the Breast," *Annals of New York Academy of Science*, 125 (1966), 802-806.

5292. Myers, G. "Cross-National Trends in Mortality Rates Among the Elderly," *Gerontologist*, 18 (October, 1978), 441-448.

5293. Myers, J. "Werewolves in Literature for Children," *Language Arts*, 53 (May, 1976), 552-556.

5294. Myers, S. "Effects of Death on the Living," *Journal of Practical Nursing*, 25 (January, 1975), 31 & 36.

5295. Myerson, P.G. et al. "To Die Young, To Die Old," *Journal of Geriatric Psychiatry*, 8 (1975), 137-157.

5296. Myska, M.J., R.A. Pasewark. "Death Attitudes of Residential and Non-Residential Rural Aged Persons," *Psychological Reports*, 43 (December, 1978), 1235-1238.

5297. Nadelman, M.S. "Preconscious Awareness of Impending Death: An Addendum," Bulletin of the Menninger Clinic, 40 (November, 1976), 655-659.

5298. Naeye, R.L. et al. "Carotid Body in the Sudden Infant Death Syndrome," Science, 191 (February 13, 1976), 567-569.

5299. ________ et al. "Hypoxemia and the Sudden Infant Death Syndrome," Science, 186 (November 29, 1974), 837-838.

5300. ________ et al. "Sudden Infant Death Syndrome Temperment Before Death," Journal of Pediatrics, 88 (March, 1976), 511-515.

5301. ________ et al. "The Sudden Infant Death Syndrome: A Review of Recent Advances," Archives of Pathology and Laboratory Medicine, 101, (April, 1977), 165-167.

5302. ________ et al. "Sudden Infant Death Syndrome: A Prospective Study," American Journal of Diseases of Children, 130 (November, 1976), 1207-1210.

5303. Nagi, M.H. et al. "Attitudes of Catholic and Protestant Clergy Toward Euthanasia," Omega, 8 (1977-1978), 153-164.

5304. Nagai, M. "Editorial: Death, Be Not Proud," Neurological Surgery (Tokyo), 3 (May 1975), 361-362.

5305. Nagaraja, J. "Child's Reaction to Death," Child's Psychiatry Quarterly, 10 (April, 1977), 24-28.

5306. Nakahara, T. "Fetal Death," Japan Journal Midwife, 30 (October, 1976), 632.

5307. Nakushian, J.M. "The Other Victims of SIDS," Journal of Emergency Nursing, 2 (May-June, 1975), 15-16.

5308. ________. "Restoring Parents' Equilibrium After Sudden Infant Death," American Journal of Nursing, 76 (October, 1976), 1600-1604.

5309. Nash, M.L. et al. "Toward Dignity in Care: An Inservice Model," Death Education, 1 (Spring, 1977), 113-130.

5310. Nathanson, C.A., M.H. Becker. "The Influence of Physician's Attitudes on Abortion Performance, Patient Management and Professional Fees," Family Planning Perspectives, 9 (July-August, 1977), 158-163.

5311. Naylor, D. "Physicians, Patients and Social Psychological Death," Ohio Journal of Science, 79 (1979), 62.

5312. Neale, R.E. The Art of Dying. New York: Harper and Row, 1973.

5313. Nehrke, M.F. et al. "Death Anxiety, Locus of Control & Satisfaction in the Elderly," Omega, 8 (1977-1978), 359-368.

5314. Neimeyer, R.A. "Death Anxiety and the Threat Index: An Addendum," Death Education, 1 (Winter, 1978), 464-467.

5315. ________ et al. "Convergent Validity, Situational Stability and Meaningfulness of the Threat Index," Omega, 8 (1977), 251-265.

5316. Nelson, J. "Live Thoughts on Dying Patients," Nursing Times, 72 (April, 1976), 592-593.

5317. ________. "The Question of Euthanasia," Engage/Social Action, 4 (April, 1976), 17-18.

5318. Nelson, L.J. "Death, Who is thy 'Cause' Letter," Hastings Center Report, 6 (October, 1976), 4.

5319. Nelson, R.C. "Counselors, Teachers and Death Education," School Counselor, 24 (May, 1977), 322-329.

5320. ________, W.D. Peterson. "Challenging the Last Great Taboo: Death," School Counselor, 22 (May, 1975), 353-358.

5321. Nesbitt, B.N. "Life or Death," Journal of Psychiatric Nursing, 15 (September, 1977), 13-17.

5322. Ness, M. "An Appraisal of Abortion Counseling," British Journal of Guidance and Counseling, 4 (January, 1976), 79-87.

5323. Neuringer, C. "Semantic Perception of Life, Death and Suicide," Journal of Clinical Psychology, 35 (1975), 255-258.

5324. Nevins, M. A Bioethical Perspective on Death and Dying. Rockville, Maryland: Information Planning Associates, 1977.

5325. ________ (ed). Annotated Bibliography of Bioethics. Rockville, Maryland: Information Planning Associates, 1977.

5326. Newman, C.J. "Disaster at Buffalo Creek. Children of Disaster: Clinical Observations at Buffalo Creek," American Journal of Psychiatry, 133 (March, 1976), 306-312.

5327. Newell, M. et al (eds). The Role of the Volunteer and Volunteer Director in Caring for the Dying Patient and the Bereaved. New York: MSS Information Company, 1978.

5328. Newton, L.H. "Abortion in the Law: An Essay on Absurdity," Ethics, 87 (April, 1977), 244-250.

5329. Nicholi, A.M. (ed). The Harvard Guide to Modern Psychiatry. Cambridge, Massachusetts: Harvard University Press, 1978.

5330. Nicholi, R.M. "Those Misappreciated and Complex Biotypes Human Burial Places," Omega, 9 (1979), 79-92.

5331. Nichols, M.P., M. Zax. Catharsis in Psychotherapy. New York: Gardner Press, 1977.

5332. Nicholson, P. "Should the Patient Be Allowed To Die," Journal of Medical Ethics, 1 (March, 1975), 5-9.

5333. Niitsu, F. "Refractory Diseases of Home Nursing. Death of an Aged Patient: A Lesson From Peaceful Death of a Patient Nursed by Family Members," Japan Journal of Nursing, 40 (June, 1976), 617-620.

5334. Ninvaggi, F.J., R. Harris. "Attitudes Toward Living and Death in Chronic Cardiovascular Disease," New York State Journal of Medicine, 76 (September, 1976), 1493-1496.

5335. Nixon, J., J. Pearn. "Emotional Sequelae of Parents and Sibs Following the Drowning or Near-Drowning of Child," Australian & New Zealand Journal of Psychiatry, 11 (December, 1977), 265-268.

5336. Nolan-Haley, J.M. "Defective Children, Their Parents and the Death Decision," Journal of Legal Medicine, 4 (January, 1976), 9-14.

5337. Norman, S.M. "Attitudes of Students in Selected Alabama Junior Colleges Related to Death and Dying," Dissertation Abstracts International, 38 (December, 1977), 330.

5338. Nothinger, F. "Experience With Our Disaster Service," Helvetica Chirurgica Acta, 42 (September, 1975), 497-501.

5339. Novak, D. Suicide & Mortality: The Theories of Plato, Acquinas & Kant. New York: Scholars Studies Press, 1975.

5340. Noyes, R., Jr. "The Dying Patient: Establish His Role to Improve Care," *Psychosomatics*, 18 (August, 1977), 42-46.

5341. ________, J. Clancy. "The Dying Role: Its Relevance to Improved Patient Care," *Psychiatry*, 40 (February, 1977), 41-47.

5342. ________, D.J. Slymen. "The Subjective Response to Life-Threatening Danger, *Omega*, 9 (1978-1979), 313-321.

5343. ________, R. Kletti. "Depersonalization in the Face of Life-Threatening Danger, A Description," *Psychiatry*, 39 (February, 1976), 19-27.

5344. ________. "Panoramic Memory: A Response to the Threat of Death," *Omega*, 8 (1977), 181-194.

5345. ________ et al. "The Changing Attitudes of Physicians Toward Prolonging Life," *Journal of the American Geriatrics Society*, 25 (October, 1977), 470-474.

5346. Nuttall, D. "Cruse: The Work of the National Organization for Widows and Their Children," *Nursing Mirror*, 142 (February, 1976), 74.

5347. ________. "Attitudes to Dying and The Bereaved," *Nursing Times*, 73 (October, 1977), 1605-1607.

5348. Oakley, N. "Letter, Sudden Death and Sport," Lancet, 1 (March, 1975), 584.

5349. Oates, W. Pastoral Care and Counselling in Grief and Separation. New York: Fortress Press, 1977.

5350. O'Brien, C.R. "Pastoral Dimensions in Death Education Research," Journal of Religion and Health, 18 (1979), 74-77.

5351. ________ et al. "Death Education, What Students Want and Need," Adolescence, 13 (Winter, 1978), 729-734.

5352. O'Connell, W.E. et al. "Thanatology For Everyone: Developmental Labs and Workshops," Death Education, 1 (Fall, 1977), 305-313.

5353. O'Connor, N.D. "An Exploration of the Effects of Anticipatory Grief Versus Acute Grief on Recovery After Loss of Spouse Among Divorced and Separted Women," Dissertation Abstracts International, 37 (March, 1977), 5708.

5354. O'Donohue, N. "Perinatal Bereavement: The Role of the Health Care Professional," Quality Review Bulletin, 4 (September, 1978), 30-32.

5355. Okura, K.P. "Mobilizing in Response to a Major Disaster," Community Mental Health Journal, 11 (Summer, 1975), 136-144.

5356. Olin, H.S. "When a Child Dies," American Family Physician, 18 (September, 1978), 107-110.

5357. Oliver-Smith, A. "Disaster Rehabilitation and Social Change in Yungay, Peru," Human Organization, 36 (Spring, 1977), 5-13.

5358. Olivier, J.A. "The Moment of Death," South African Medical Journal, 49 (May, 1975), 863-864.

5359. Olmsted, K. "A Time to Die: Thoughts on Comforting the Dying Patient," Journal of The American Health Care Association, 3 (March, 1977), 5-8.

5360. Opie, L.H. "Sudden Death and Sport," Lancet, 1 (February, 1975), 263-266.

5361. ________. "Letter: Sudden Death and Sport," Lancet, 1 (March, 1975), 678.

5362. Oraison, M. Death and Then What? Paramus, New Jersey: Newman Press, 1969.

5363. Orbach, I., H. Glaubman. "Suicidal, Aggressive, and Normal Children's Perceptions of Personal and Impersonal Death," Journal of Clinical Psychology, 34 (October, 1978), 850-856.

5364. Orcutt, B. et al. Social Work and Thanatology. New York: MSS Information Company, 1978.

5365. O'Rourke, K.D. "Active and Passive Euthanasia: The Ethical Distinctions," Hospital Progress, 57 (November, 1976), 68-73, 100.

5366. O'Rourke, W.D. "The Relationship Between Religiousness, Purpose-in-Life and Fear of Death," Dissertation Abstracts International, 37 (May, 1977), 7046-7047.

5367. Ortiz, A. "Infant Mortality in Our Area," Boletin - Asociacion Medica De Puerto Rico, 68 (December, 1976), 326-332.

5368. Osborne, E.G. When You Lose a Loved One. New York: Public Affairs Committee, 1958. Paramus, New Jersey: Newman Press, 1969.

5369. O'Shaughnesay, T. Muhammed's Thoughts on Death. A Thematic Study of the Qur'anic Data. London: Brill, 1969.

5370. Oshman, H.P. "Death Education: An Evaluation of Programs and Techniques," Catalog of Selected Documents in Psychology, 8 (May, 1978), 1680.

5371. ________, M. Manosevitz. "Death Fantasies of Father-Absent and Father-Present Late Adolescents," Journal of Youth and Adolescents, 7 (March, 1978), 41-48.

5372. Osis, K., E. Haraldsson. At the Hour of Death. New York: Avon Books, 1977.

5373. Osler, W. Science and Immortality. New York: Arno Press, 1976. (Orig. Pub. 1904).

5374. Osmond, H., M. Siegler. "The Dying Role--Its Clinical Importance," Alabama Journal of Medical Science, 13 (July, 1976), 313-317.

5375. Ostheimer, N.C., J.M. Ostheimer. Life or Death - Who Controls? New York: Springer Publishing Company, 1976.

5376. O'Suilleabhain, S. Irish Wake Amusements. New York: Irish Book Center, 1976.

5377. Otero, G.G. Death: A Part of Life. An Experimental Unit. Washington, D.C.: Office of Education, 1975.

5378. Owatari, J. "Karen Quinlan Case--Dignified Death and Nursing. Warning Against Hasty Decision for Euthanasia," Japan Journal of Nursing, 40 (August, 1976), 800-802.

5379. Owen, G. "Grief Therapy: A Review and Critical Assessment," The Director, (April, 1977), 12-16.

5380. Owen, G. et al. "Death at a Distance: A Study of Family Survivors," Center Death Education and Research, University of Minnesota, Minneapolis, 1978.

5381. Pacovsky, V. "The Aged, Dying and Death," *Zdravotnicke Aktuality* (Prague), 25 (October, 1977), 83-86.

5382. Padilla, G.V. et al. "Interacting With Dying Patients," *Community Nursing Research*, 8 (March, 1977), 101-114.

5383. Page, B.B. "Socialism, Health Care and Medical Ethics," *Hastings Center Report*, 6 (October, 1976), 20-23.

5384. Paige, R.L., J.F. Looney. "When the Patient is Dying: Hospice Care for the Adult," *American Journal of Nursing*, 77 (November, 1977), 1812-1815.

5385. Palmer, I.Q. "Discussing Death," *Nursing Times*, 72 (February, 1976), 261.

5386. Pandey, R.E. "Factor Analytic Study of Attitudes Toward Death Among College Students," *The International Journal of Social Psychiatry*, 21 (Winter-Spring, 1974-1975), 7-11.

5387. Panton, J.H. "Personality Characteristics of Death-Row Prison Inmates," *Journal of Clinical Psychology*, 32 (April, 1976), 306-309.

5388. Parad, H.J. et al (eds). *Emergency and Disaster Management.* Bowie, Maryland: Charles Press, 1976.

5389. Park, J. *An Existential Understanding of Death*. Minneapolis: Existential Books, 1975.

5390. Parker, M.G. "You Are a Child of the Universe: You Have a Right to be Here," *Manitoba Law Journal*, 7 (1977), 151-182.

5391. Parkes, C.M. "Psycho-Social Transitions: Comparison Between Reactions to Loss of a Limb and Loss of a Spouse," *British Journal of Psychiatry*, 127 (September, 1975), 204-210.

5392. ________. "The Emotional Impact of Cancer on Patients and Their Families," *Journal of Laryngology and Otology*, 89 (December, 1975), 1271-1279.

5393. ________. "Family Reactions to Child Bereavement," *Proceedings of the Royal Society of Medicine*, 70 (January, 1977), 54-55.

5394. Parks, H.W. "The Anatomy of Sudden Death," *Illinois Medical Journal*, 153 (June, 1978), 447-451.

5395. Parks, P. "Hospice Care: Implications for Hospitals," Hospitals, 53 (March, 1979), 58-62.

5396. Parness, E. "Effects of Experiences With Loss and Death Among Preschool Children," Children Today, 4 (November-December, 1975), 2-7.

5397. Parry, S.M. "The Fear of Death and Responses to Others: Concerns About Death," Dissertation Abstracts International, 38 (September, 1977), 1306-1307.

5398. Pascalis, G. et al. "Death and Psychosis," Revista De Neuro-Psiquiatria (Lima), 25 (July, 1977), 383-390.

5399. ________. "Death, Psychosis and Obsession, a Statistical Study," Annales Medico-Psychologiques (Paris), 2 (October, 1976), 453-458.

5400. Patey, E.H. "Matters of Life and Death. To Care or to Kill," Nursing Mirror, 141 (October, 1975), 40-41.

5401. Patten, B.M., W.W. Stump. "Death Related to Informed Consent," Texas Medicine, 74 (December, 1978), 49-50.

5402. Pattison, E.M. "The Fatal Myth of Death in the Family," American Journal of Psychiatry, 133 (June, 1976), 674-678.

5403. ________. The Experience of Dying. Englewood Cliffs, New Jersey: Spectrum/Prentice-Hall, 1977.

5404. Patton, J.F., C.B. Freitag. "Correlational Study of Death Anxiety. General Anxiety and Locus of Control," Psychological Reports, 40 (February, 1977), 51-54.

5405. Paulay, D. "Slow Death: One Survivor's Experience," Omega, 8 (1977-1978), 173-179.

5406. Payne, E.C. et al. "Outcome Following Therapeutic Abortion," Archives of General Psychiatry, 33 (June, 1976), 725-733.

5407. Pearson, L., R.B. Pertilo. Separate Paths: Why People End Their Lives. New York: Harper & Row, 1977.

5408. Pearson, P.W. "The Dying Patient With Oral Malignant Disease," Otolaryngology Clinics of North America, 12 (February, 1979), 241-244.

5409. Pelgrin, M. et al (eds). And a Time to Die. Wheaton, Illinois: Theosophical Publishing House, 1976.

5410. Pelizza, J.J. "Is the Study of Death and Dying Important for Life?" New York State School Nurse-Teachers Association Journal, 9 (Fall, 1977), 25-27.

5411. Penick, E.C. et al. "Mental Health Problems and Natural Disaster: Tornado Victims," Journal of Community Psychology, 4 (January, 1976), 64-67.

5412. Pennington, E.A. "Postmortem Care: More Than Ritual," American Journal of Nursing, 78 (May, 1978), 846-847.

5413. Perkes, A.C. "Classroom Animal Death--Its Learning Potential for Death Education," School Science and Mathematics, 77 (February, 1977), 93-96.

5414. ________. "Teachers' Attitudes Toward Death-Related Issues," School Science and Mathematics, 78 (February, 1978), 135-141.

5415. ________, R. Schlidt. "Death Related Attitudes of Adolescent Males and Females," Death Education, 2 (1979), 359-368.

5416. Perkes, G.S. "Some Thoughts on Death," Nursing Times, 73 (July, 1977), 101-104.

5417. ________. "Some Thoughts on Death," Nursing Times, 73 (August, 1977), 105-107.

5418. Perper, J.A. "Sudden, Unexpected Death in Alcoholics," Legal Medicine Annual, (1974), 101-110.

5419. Peterson, D.R., J.B. Beckwith. "The Sudden Infant Death Syndrome in Hospitalized Babies," Pediatrics, 54 (November, 1974), 644-647.

5420. ________, N.M. Chinn. "Sudden Infant Death Trends in Six Metropolitan Communities," (165-174), Pediatrics, 60 (July, 1977), 75-79.

5421. Peterson, W.D., R.L. Sartore. "Helping Children Cope With Death," Elementary School Guidance and Counseling, 9 (March, 1975), 226-232.

5422. Petrasek, J., J. Drabkova. "Criteria of Death," Zdravotnicke Aktuality (Praha), 26 (July, 1976), 393-395.

5423. Petrie, A. Individuality in Pain and Suffering. Chicago: University of Chicago Press (2nd edition), 1978.

5424. Pett, D. "Care of the Terminal Patient. Grief in the Hospital," Nursing Times, 75 (April, 1979), 709-712.

5425. Pettigrew, C.G., J.G. Dawson. "Death Anxiety: 'State' or 'Trait'," Journal of Clinical Psychology, 35 (January, 1979), 154-158.

5426. Pfefferbaum, B., R.O. Pasnau. "Post Amputation Grief," Nursing Clinics of North America, 11 (December, 1976), 687-690.

5427. Phillips, D.Z. Death and Immortality. New York: Macmillan. London and St. Martin's Press, 1970.

5428. Piemme, J.R. "Death Education: A Different Approach," Oncology Nursing Forum, 6 (January, 1979), 4.

5429. Pierce, C.M. "Capital Punishment. Effects of the Death Penalty: Data and Deliberations From the Social Sciences," American Journal of Orthopsychiatry, 45 (July, 1975), 580.

5430. Piettre, A. "Aspects of Economics, Ethics and Civilization," Intensive Care Medicine, 3 (December, 1977), 253-256.

5431. Pike, D.K. Life is Victorious! How to Grow Through Grief. New York: Simon & Schuster, 1976 . New York: Pocket Books, 1977.

5432. Pilsecker, C. "Help for the Dying," Social Work, 20 (May, 1975), 190-194.

5433. Pincus, L. Death and the Family. The Importance of Mourning. New York: Pantheon Books, 1974.

5434. Pine, V.R. "Institutionalized Communication About Dying and Death," Journal of Thanatology, 3 (1975), 1-12.

5435. ________. "A Socio-Historical Portrait of Death Education," Death Education, 1 (Spring, 1977), 57-80.

5436. ________. Caretaker of the Dead. New York: Irvington Publishers, 1975.

5437. ________ (ed). Acute Grief and the Funeral. Springfield, Illinois: C.C. Thomas Publisher, 1975.

5438. Pinney, J.M. "Largest Preventable Cause of Death in the United States," Public Health Reports, 94 (1979), 107-108.

5439. Pitkin, F.I. "Accidental Death--Fact, Fancy or Fable," Proceedings of The Medical Section of the American LIfe Insurance Association (1973), 23-32.

5440. Place, M. "Dying--The Ultimate Clinical Course," Practitioner, 219 (November, 1977), 693-696.

5441. Plachy, R. "On Death and Leading," Modern Health Care, 3 (March, 1975), 86.

5442. Planansky, K., R. Johnston. "Preoccupation With Death in Schizophrenic Men," Diseases of the Nervous System, 38 (March, 1977), 194-197.

5443. Plank, E.N., R. Plank. "Children and Death: As Seen Through Art and Autobiographies," Psychoanalytic Study of the Child, 33 (1978), 593-620.

5444. Plant, J. "Finding a Home for Hospice Care in the United States," Hospitals JAHA, 51 (July, 1977), 53-67.

5445. Platt, N.V. "What Will Happen to the Flowers When Winter Comes?," Journal of Religion and Health, 16 (October, 1977), 326-332.

5446. Polderman, R.L. "An Experimental Strategy to Reduce Death Anxiety," Dissertation Abstracts International, 37 (February, 1977), 4161-4162.

5447. Poletti, R. "The Child and Death," Zeitschrift Fur Krankenflege (Bern), 68 (May, 1975), 158-161.

5448. Pollak, J.M. "Relationships Between Psychoanalytic Personality Pattern, Death Anxiety and Self-Actualization," Perceptual and Motor Skills, 46 (June, 1978), 846.

5449. Pollitt, E. "The Family Leukemia Association," Essence, 1 (1976), 107-115.

5450. Pollock, G.H. "The Mourning Process and Creative Organizational Change," Journal of the American Psychoanalytic Association, 25 (1977), 3-34.

5451. ________. "Process and Affect: Mourning and Grief," International Journal of Psychoanalysis, 59 (1978), 255-276.

5452. Pollock. W.F. "'Cognitive' and 'Sapient'--Which is the Real Death?," American Journal of Surgery, 136 (July, 1978), 2-7.

5453. Polson, C.J. (ed). The Disposal of the Dead. New York: Philosophical Library, 1953.

5454. ________, T.K. Marshall. The Disposal of the Dead. London: English Universities Press (3rd edition), 1975.

5455. Pontoppidan, H. "Optimum Care for Hopelessly Ill Patients," The New England Journal of Medicine, 295 (August, 1976), 362-364.

5456. Popoff, D., G.R. Funkhouser. "What Are Your Feelings About Death and Dying?," Nursing (Jenkintown), 5 (August, 1975), (part 1) 15-24.

5457. ________. "What Are Your Feelings About Death and Dying?," Nursing (Jenkintown), 5 (September, 1975), (part 2) 55-62.

5458. ________. "What Are Your Feeling About Death and Dying?," Nursing (Jenkintown), 5 (October, 1975), (part 3) 39-50.

5459. Porter, J.V. "A Therapeutic Community for the Dying," Assistant of Operating Rooms Nurses Journal, 21 (April, 1975), 838-839, 842-843.

5460. Porter, W.H., Jr. "The Professional-Commercial Debate: The Funeral Business Trade as a Mirror of Intra-Industry Controversy," Mt. Union College, Alliance, Ohio, 1977.

5461. Posner, J. "Death as a Courtesy Stigma," Essence, 1 (1976), 39-48.

5462. Poteet, G.H. Death and Dying: A Bibliography (1950-1974). Troy, New York: Whitston, 1976.

5463. Pottgen, P., L.M. Hillegass. "Botulism and Sudden Infant Death Letter," Lancet, 1 (January, 1977), 147-148.

5464. ________, E.R. Davis. "Sudden Infant Death Syndrome," Archives of Pathology and Laboratory Medicine, 101 (November, 1977), 615.

5465. Poulshock, S.W., E.S. Cohen. "The Elderly in the Aftermath of a Disaster," Gerontologist, 15 (August, 1975), 357-361.

5466. Powner, D.J. et al. "Brain Death Certification," Critical Care Medicine, 5 (September-October, 1977), 230-233.

5467. Pradeau, J. I Had This Little Cancer. New York: Abelard-Schuman, 1976.

5468. Prado de Monina, M. "The Confrontation With Death," American Journal of Psychoanalysis, 36 (Fall, 1976), 267-271.

5469. Pratt, L.L. "American Attitudes Toward Violent and Nonviolent Death as Reflected in Death Symbols in Still Visual Media: An Exploratory Study," Dissertation Abstracts International, 38 (December, 1977), 2945.

5470. Preger, R. "Euthanasia--A Modern Therapy," Medizinische Monatsschrift Fur Pharmazeuten, 30 (May, 1976), 193-195.

5471. Prescott, J.W. "Abortion or the Unwanted Child: A Choice for a Humanistic Society," Journal of Pediatric Psychology, 1 (Spring, 1976), 62-67.

5472. Presswalla, F.B. "The Philosophy of Classification of Deaths," Medical Legal Bulletin, 26 (March-April, 1977), 1-5.

5473. Pressey, S.L. "Comment: Any Rights as to My Dying," Gerontologist, 17 (August, 1977), 296-302.

5474. Preston, P., R. Smith. "Letter: The Cost of Death," Lancet, 1 (May, 1975), 1186.

5475. Preston, S.H., V.E. Nelson. "Structure and Change in Causes of Death: An International Study," Population Studies, 28 (March, 1974), 19-51.

5476. Price-Bonham, S. et al. "An Analysis of Clergymen's Attitudes Toward Abortion," Review of Religious Research, 17 (Fall, 1975), 15-27.

5477. Price, C.J. et al. "The Patient's Right to Live or Die," Hospital Administration Currents, 20 (September, 1976), 17-22.

5478. Price, K. "Defining Death and Dying - Bibliographic Overview," Law Library Journal, 71 (February, 1978), 49-67.

5479. Price, T., B.J. Bergen. "The Relationship to Death as a Source of Stress for Nurses on a Coronary Care Unit," Omega, 8 (1977), 229-238.

5480. Prilook, M.E. (ed). "When Caring is All That's Left to Give: A Patient Care Roundtable on Dying and Death," Patient Care, 11 (June, 1977), 18-24.

5481. Prouty, D. "Read About Death? Not Me," Language Arts, 53 (September, 1976), 679-682.

5482. Pryke, M.M. "The Child's Concept of Death," Australas. Nurses Journal, 5 (January-February, 1977), 41-42.

5483. Pschingbauer, T.R. et al. "Development of the Texas Inventory of Grief," American Journal of Psychiatry, 134 (June, 1977), 696-698.

5484. Purisman, R., B. Moaz. "Adjustment and War Bereavement--Some Considerations," British Journal of Medical Psychology, 50 (March, 1977), 1-9.

5485. Purtilo, R.B. "Bioethics and Euthanasia," American Journal of Occupational Therapy, 31 (July, 1977), 394-396.

5486. Quarantelli, E.L. (ed). Disasters: Theory and Research. London: Sage Publications, 1978.

5487. ________, R.R. Dumes. "Community Conflict: Its Absence and Its Presence in Natural Disasters," Mass Emergencies, 1 (February, 1976), 139-152.

5488. Quijano, M. "Attitude of the Physician on Impending Death," Gaceta Medica de Mexico, 113 (January, 1977), 3-4.

5489. Qvarnstrom, U. "Patients' Reactions to Impending Death," International Nursing Review, 26 (July-August, 1979), 117-119.

5490. Rabinowicz, H. "Care of the Terminal Patient, The Jewish View of Death," Nursing Times, 75 (May, 1979), 757.

5491. Rabkin, M.T. et al. "Order Not to Resuscitate," New England Journal of Medicine, 295 (August, 1976), 364-366.

5492. Rachels, J. "Medical Ethics and the Rule Against Killing," in: Spicker, S.F. et al (eds). Philosophical Medical Ethics: Its Nature and Significance. Boston: Reidel, 1977, 63-69.

5493. ________. "Killing and Starving to Death," Philosophy, 54 (1979), 159-191.

5494. Raether, H.C. The Funeral Director and His Role as a Counselor. Milwaukee: National Funeral Directors Association, Bulfin, 1975.

5495. Raimbault, G. L'Enfant El La Mort. (Des Enfants Malades Parlent De La Mort). Toulouse: Editions Privat, 1977.

5496. Raines, A.E. "Death With Dignity and Survivor Guilt Letter," American Journal of Psychiatry, 134 (December, 1977), 1449.

5497. Rainey, L.C., F.R. Epting. "Death Threat Constructions in the Student and The Prudent," Omega, 8 (1977), 19-28.

5498. Rakel, R.E. "Care of the Dying Patient," in: his Principles of Family Medicine. Philadelphia: W.B. Saunders, 1977, 367-397.

5499. Ralya, K. "The Hospital Staff and the Dying Patient," Counseling and Values, 21 (April, 1977), 167-171.

5500. Ramsay, R.W. "Behavioral Approaches to Bereavement," Behavior Research and Therapy, 15 (1977), 131-135.

5501. ________, J.A. Happee. "The Stress of Bereavement: Components and Treatment," in: Spielberger, C.D., I.G. Sarason (eds). Stress and Anxiety. Washington, D.C.: Hemisphere, 1977.

5502. Ramsey, P. "'Euthanasia' and Dying Well Enough," Linacre Quarterly, 44 (February, 1977), 37-46.

5503. ________. "The Quinlan Decision: Five Commentaries. Prolonged Dying: Not Medically Indicated," Hastings Center Report, 6 (February, 1976), 14-17.

5504. ________. "Behavioral Approaches to Bereavement," Behavior Research and Therapy, 15 (1977), 131-135.

5505. ________. "The California Natural Death Act," in his: Ethics at the Edges of Life: Medical and Legal Intersections. New Haven: Yale University Press, 1978. 318- 332.

5506. ________. "In the Matter of Quinlan," in his: Ethics at the Edges of Life: Medical Legal Intersections. New Haven: Yale University Press, 1978. 268-299.

5507. ________. "The Benign Neglect of Defective Infants," in his: Ethics at the Edges of Life Medical and Legal Intersections. New Haven: Yale University, 1978. 189-227.

5508. ________. Ethics at the Edges of Life: Medical and Legal Intersections. New Haven: Yale University Press, 1978.

5509. Rangell, L. "Discussion of the Buffalo Creek Disaster: The Course of Psychic Trauma," American Journal of Psychiatry, 133 (March, 1976), 313-316.

5510. Raphael, B. "The Management of Pathological Grief," Australia and New Zealand Journal of Psychiatry, 9 (September, 1975), 173-180.

5511. ________. "The Presentation and Management of Bereavement," Medical Journal of Australia, (December, 1975), 909-911.

5512. ________. "Death, Dying and Patient Care: The Patient and His Family," Australian Hospital, 2 (November, 1976), 10.

5513. ________. "Preventive Intervention With the Recently Bereaved," Archives of General Psychiatry, 34 (December,1977), 1450-1454.

5514. Raudive, K. Break-Through. New York: Zebra Books, 1977.

5515. Raven, C. "Letter: Legislation for Sudden Infant Death Syndrome," Journal of the American Medical Association, 231 (January, 1975), 344.

5516. ________. "Sudden Infant Death Syndrome," Journal of the American Medical Associaton, 235 (January, 1976), 249.

5517. ________. "Crib Deaths, Sudden Unexpected Death in Infancy, or the Sudden Infant Death Syndrome: A Hypersensitive Reaction," Journal of the American Womens' Association, 32 (April, 1977), 148-149.

5518. Raven, R. The Dying Patient. United Kingdom: Pitman Medical, 1975.

5519. Ray, R. "The Mentally Handicapped Child's Reaction to Bereavement," Health Visit, 51 (September, 1978), 333-334.

5520. Rayner, K. "Euthanasia: A Christian Perspective," Australian and New Zealand Journal of Surgery, 46 (November, 1976), 293-294.

5521. Rebele, M.E. "When We Tried to Get Close to Carrie She Pushed Us Away," Nursing (Horsham), 9 (August, 1979), 52-55.

5522. Reck, A.J. "A Contextualist Thanatology: A Pragmatic Approach to Death & Dying," Death Education, 1 (Fall, 1977), 315-323.

5523. Reed, N. "Voluntary Euthanasia Letter," Journal of Medical Ethics, 3 (June, 1977), 102.

5524. ________. "Legislate Euthanasia," Sunday Times (London), (March 7, 1976), 13.

5525. ________"Recent Thinking About Voluntary Euthanasia," New Humanist, 92 (January-February, 1977), 173-174.

5526. Reed, T.M. "The Paneuthanasia Argument," Personalist, 58 (January, 1977), 84-87.

5527. Regan, W.A. "Chemotherapy Withheld From Retarded Patient," Nursing Progress, 59 (May, 1978), 94, 96.

5528. Reich, W.T. "Quality of Life and De ective Newborn Children: An Ethical Analysis," in: Swinyard, C.A. (ed). Decision Making and the Defective Newborn. Springfield, Illinois: C.C. Thomas, 1978. 489-511.

5529. Reik, T. "On the Effect of Unconscious Death Wishes," Internationale Aeitschrift f;ur :rtzliche Psychoanalyse, Bd. 2. Psychoanalytic Review, 65 (Spring, 1978) 38-77. (Translated by Harry Zohn).

5530. Reiser, S.J. et al (eds). Ethics in Medicine: Historical Perspectives and Contemporary Concerns. Cambridge, Massachusetts: MIT Press, 1977.

5531. Reisler, R., Jr. "The Issue of Death Education," School Counselor, 24 (May, 1977), 331-337.

5532. Reite, M. "Towards A Pathophysiology of Grief," Psychosomatic Medicine, 41 (1979), 78.

5533. Resnik, H.L.P., H.S. Ruben. Emergency Psychiatric Care. Bowie, Maryland: Charle Press, 1975.

5534. Reynolds, F.E., E.A. Waugh (ed). Religious Encounters with Death: Insights From the History and Anthropology of Religions. University Park, Pennsylvania: Pennsylvania State University Press, 1977.

5535. Richards, J.G., J.McCallum. "Bereavement in the Elderly," New Zealand Medical Journal, 89 (March, 1979), 201-204.

5536. Richards, V. "Death and Cancer," in: Shneidman, E.S. (ed.). Death: Current Perspectives. Palo Alto, California: Mayfield Publishing Company, 1976.

5537. Richardson, J. "Edwin Stevens Lecture on Dying and Dying Well. Medical Aspects," Proceedings of the Royal Society of Medicine, 70 (February, 1977), 71-73.

5538. Richardson,P. "A Multigravida's Use of a Living Child in Grief and Mourning for a Lost Child," Maternal Child Nursing Journal, 3 (Fall, 1974), 181-217.

5539. Rickarby, G.A. "Four Cases of Mania Associated With Bereavement," Journal of Nervous and Mental Diseases, 165 (October, 1977), 255-262.

5540. Riedel, M. "The Death Penalty and Discretion: Implications of the Furman Decision For Criminal Justice," Journal of Sociology and Social Welfare, 3 (July 1976), 649-655.

5541. Riemer, J. Jewish Reflections on Death. New York: Schocken Books, 1975.

5542. Rievman, E.B. "The Cyronics Society: A Study of Variant Behavior Among the Immortalists," Dissertation Abstracts International, 38 (January, 1978), 4385.

5543. Rinear, E.E. "Helping the Survivors of Expected Death," Nursing (Jenkintown), 5 (March, 1975), 60-65.

5544. Riskey, R.J. "Reflections on Death Education," Forecast for Home Economics, 22 (February, 1977), 70, 72-73.

5545. Rizzo, R.F. "Hospice. Comprehensive Terminal Care," New York State Journal of Medicine, 78 (October, 1978), 1902-1910.

5546. Roberts, C.M. "Doctors to the Dying," South Dakota Journal of Medicine, 29 (November, 1976), 23-28.

5547. Roberts, F.J. "The Doctors' Attitude to the Dying Patient," <u>New Zealand Medical Journal</u>, 87 (March, 1978), 181-184.

5548. Robertson, J.A. "Involuntary Euthanasia of Defective Newborns: A Legal Analysis," <u>Stanford Law Review</u>, 27 (January, 1975), 213-269.

5549. ________, N. Fost. "Passive Euthanasia of Defective Newborn Infants: Legal Considerations," <u>Journal of Pediatrics</u>, 88 (May, 1976), 883-889.

5550. Robertson, S. "Adolescents and Dying (Editorial)," <u>Medical Journal of Australia</u>, 1 (April, 1978), 419-421.

5551. Robinson, C.M. "Developmental Counseling Approach to Death and Dying Education," <u>Elementary School Guidance and Counseling</u>, 12 (February, 1978), 178-187.

5552. Robinson, D.O. "The Medical Student Spouse Syndrome: Grief Reactions to the Clinical Years," <u>American Journal of Psychiatry</u>, 135 (August, 1978), 972-974.

5553. Robinson, R.A. "The Development of a Concept of Death in Selected Groups of Mexican American and Anglo American Children," <u>Dissertation Abstracts International</u>, 38 (March, 1978), 4478.

5554. Robson, K.S. "Clinical Report, Letters to a Dead Husband," <u>Journal of Geriatric Psychiatry</u>, 7 (1974), 208-232.

5555. Rock, J.F.C. <u>The Zhi-Ma Funeral Ceremony of the Na-Khi of Southwest China</u>. (Described and translated from Na-Khi manuscripts). Vienna: St. Gabriel's Press, 1955.

5556. Rodman, F.R. <u>Not Dying</u>. New York: Random House, 1977.

5557. Rodrigues, R.S. "After the Child Dies: Autopsies and Forgotten Parents," <u>Journal of Pedicatrics</u>, 89 (November, 1976), 859-860.

5558. Rogan, J. "Ethics and Nurses," <u>Nursing Mirror</u>, 143 (October, 1976), 75-76.

5559. Rogers, B.L. "Using the Creative Process With the Terminally Ill," <u>Death Education</u>, 2 (Spring-Summer, 1978), 123-126.

5560. Rogers, J., M.L. Vachon. "Nurses Can Help the Bereaved," <u>Canadian Nurse</u>, 71 (June, 1975), 16-19.

5561. Rogers, W.F. <u>The Place of Grief Work in Mental Health</u>. Madison, Wisconsin: Microcard Foundation for the American Theological Library Association, 1956.

5562 Rogness, A.N. Appointment With Death. Nashville: T. Nelson, 1972.

5563. Rogo, D.S. Man Does Survive Death. Secaucus, New Jersey: Citadel Press, 1977.

5564. ________. "Research on Deathbed Experiences: Some Contemporary and Historical Perspectives," Parapsychology Review, 9 (January-February, 1978), 20-27.

5565. Roll, W.G. "Comments on Ian Stevenson's Paper: Some Assumptions Guiding Research on Survival after Death," Journal of Nervous and Mental Disease, 165 (September, 1977), 176-180.

5566. Romero, C. "Children, Death and Literature," Language Arts, 53 (September, 1976), 674-678.

5567. Roos, B.E. "Terminal Care," Lakartidnigen, 74 (January, 1977), 107-108.

5568. Rosel, A. "Toward a Social Theory of Dying," Omega, 9 (1979), 49-55.

5569. Rosen, J. Medicine and Ethics: A Guide to the Issues and the Literature. East Lansing: Michigan State University, Department of Human Development, 1975.

5570. Rosen, R.H. "Sex Role Perceptions and the Abortion Decision," Wayne State University, Detroit, 1978.

5571. ________ et al. "Contraception, Abortion and Self-Concept," Journal of Population, 2 (1979), 118-139.

5572. ________ et al. "Health Professionals Attitudes Toward Abortion," The Public Opinion Quarterly, 38 (Summer, 1974), 159-173.

5573. Rosenblatt, P.C. et al. Grief & Mourning in Cross-Cultural Perspectives. Washington, D.C.: Human Relations Area Files, 1977.

5574. Rosenfield, A. Prolongevity. New York: Alfred A. Knopf, 1976.

5575. Rosenfield, S. The Time of Their Dying. New York: Norton, 1977.

5576. Rosenthal, N.R. "Teaching Educators to Deal With Death," Death Education, 2 (Fall, 1978), 293-306.

5577. ________, C. Terkelson. "Death Education and Counseling: A Survey," Counselor Education and Supervision, 18 (December, 1978), 109-114.

5578. Rosner, F. "The Use and Abuse of Heroic Measures to Prolong Dying," Journal of Religion and Health, 17 (January, 1978), 8-18.

5579. Ross, C.W. "Nurses' Personal Death Concerns and Responses to Dying Patient Statements," Nursing Research, 27 (January-February, 1978), 64-68.

5580. Rossman, P. Hospice: Creating New Models of Care For the Terminally Ill. New York: Association Press, 1977.

5581. Roth, N. "Fear of Death in the Aging," American Journal of Psychotherapy, 32 (October, 1978), 552-560.

5582. Roth, S.M. "Attitudes Toward Death Across the Life Span," Dissertation Abstracts International, 38 (February, 1978), 3858.

5583. Rothman, D.A., N.L. Rothman. "Death," in their: The Professional Nurse and the Law. Boston: Little Brown, 1977.

5584. Rotter, H. "Ethical Considerations of Euthanasia," Osterr Kankenpflegez, 26 (1976), 351-357.

5585. Rovinski, C.A. "Hospice Nursing: Intensive Caring," Cancer Nursing, 2 (February, 1979), 19-26.

5586. Rowe, K.B., L.C. Loesch. "An Affective-Education Experience for Helping Children Reduce Their Anxieties About Death," Humanist Educator, 16 (March, 1978), 103-109.

5587. Rowland, K.F. "Environmental Events Predicting Death for the Elderly," Psychological Bulletin, 84 (March, 1977), 349-372.

5588. Ruben, H.L. "Managing Suicidal Behavior," Journal of the American Medical Association, 241 (1979), 282-284.

5589. Rubin, A. et al. "Issues Related to Death and Dying," Senior Scholastic, 104 (May, 1974), 6-17.

5590. Rubin, C. "The Dying Child," Nursing Care, 8 (October, 1975), 31.

5591. Rubin, S. "Bereavement and Vulnerability: A Study of Mother's of Sudden Infant Death Syndrome Children," Dissertation Abstracts International, 38 (October, 1977), 1902-1903.

5592. Rucker, M. E. et al. "Puppet Life and Death Education," Clearing House, 51 (May, 1978), 458-459.

5593. Rudolph, M. *Should the Children Know? Encounters With Death in the Lives of Children*. New York: Schocken Books, 1978.

5594. ________. "The Saddest Day of My Life," *Death Education*, 2 (Fall, 1978), 281-291.

5595. Rupert, M.K. "Death and its Definitions: Medical, Legal and Theological," *Michigan Academician*, 8 (Winter, 1976), 235-247.

5596. Rushford, N.B. et al. "Violent Death in a Metropolitan County. Changing Patterns in Homicide (1958-1974)," *New England Journal of Medicine*, 297 (September, 1977), 531-538.

5597. Russell, B. "Still a Live Issue," *Philosophy and Public Affairs*, 7 (Spring, 1978), 278-281.

5598. Russell, O.R. "Supplement to the First Edition: Developments From Early 1974 to Late 1976," in her: *Freedom to Die: Moral and Legal Aspects of Euthanasia*. (revised edition). New York: Human Sciences Press, 1977.

5599. Russell, R. "The Choice," *Nursing* (Jenkintown), 5 (June, 1975), 57.

5600. Russell, R.D. "Educating About Death," *Health Education*, 8 (November-December, 1977), 8-10.

5601. Rutherford, W.H. "Surgery of Violence, II. Disaster Procedures," *British Medical Journal*, 1 (February, 1975), 443-445.

5602. Ryan, J.M. et al. "Childhood Mortality in an Urban Area 1969-1976. Some Demographic Correlates of Multiple Causes of Death," *Pediatric Research*, 13 (1979), 394.

5603. Ryder, C.F., D.M. Ross. "Terminal Care: Issues and Alternatives," *Public Health Reports*, 92 (January-February, 1977), 20-29.

5604. Ryerson, M.S. "Death Education and Counseling for Children," *Elementary School Guidance and Counseling*, 11 (February, 1977), 147-173.

5605. Sabom, M.B., S. Kruetziger. "Near Death Experiences," Journal of the Florida Medical Association, 64 (September, 1977), 648-650.

5606. ________. "Near Death Experiences, Letter," New England Journal of Medicine, 297 (November, 1977), 1071.

5607. ________. "The Experience of Near Death," Death Education, 1 (Summer, 1977), 195-203.

5608. Sadker, D. et al. "Death--A Fact of Life in Children's Literature," Instructor, 85 (March, 1976), 75-84.

5609. Sakamoto, K. "Analysis of Seasonal Variation of Perinatal Death," Japan Journal of Hygiene, 30 (April, 1975), 252.

5610. Sakamoto-Momiyama, M. Seasonality in Human Mortality. Tokyo: Univeristy of Tokyo Press, 1977.

5611. Salter, C.A., C.D. Salter. "Attitudes Toward Dying and Behaviors Toward the Elderly Among Young People as a Function of Death Anxiety," Gerontologist, 16 (June, 1976), 232-236.

5612. Salzberger, R.C. "Death: Beliefs, Activities and Reactions of the Bereaved--Some Psychological and Anthropological Observations," The Human Context, 7 (Spring, 1975), 103-116.

5613. Samaniego, L.R. "Parent Loss in Childhood: Ego Functions, Death and Mourning," Dissertation Abstracts International, 38 (May, 1978), 5593.

5614. Samburg, M. "Sudden Infant Death Syndrome: A Parent's Experience," Nursing News (Hartford), 50 (June, 1977), 1-2.

5615. Sampson, W.I. "Letter, Dying at Home," Journal of the American Medical Association, 235 (April, 1976), 1840.

5616. ________. "Dying at Home," Journal of the American Medical Association, 239 (April, 1978), 1612.

5617. Samuel, V.N. "Brain Death," Diseases of the Nervous System, 38 (September, 1977), 691-693.

5618. Sandser, C.M. "Typologies and Symptoms of Adult Bereavement," Dissertation Abstracts International, 38 (January, 1978), 3372.

5619. Sank, L.I. "Community Disasters: Primary Prevention and Treatment in a Health Maintenance Organization," American Psychologist, 34 (1979), 334-338.

5620. Sarda, F. "A French Lawyer's View on Life and Death," Hastings Center Report, 6 (April, 1976), 8-9.

5621. Sarat, A., N.Vidmar. "Public Opinion, the Death Penalty and the Eighth Amendment: Testing the Marshall Hypothesis," Wisconsin Law Review, 1 (1976), 171-206.

5622. Sassone, R.L. "Euthanasia in the Context of the Population Debate," Australas Nurses Journal, 4 (March, 1976), 12.

5623. Saul, S. S. Saul. "Old People Talk About--The Right to Die," Omega, 8 (1977-1978), 129-139.

5624. Saunders, C. "Care of the Dying--Problems of Euthanasia," Nursing Times, 72 (July 1, 1976), 1003-1005.

5625. ________. "Care of the Dying--Problems of Euthanasia, part 2," Nursing Times, 72 (July 8, 1976), 1049-1051.

5626. ________. "Care of the Dying--Should a Patient Know?," Nursing Times, 72 (July 15, 1976), 1089-1091.

5627. ________. "Care of the Dying--Control of Pain in Terminal Cancer," Nursing Times, 72 (July 22, 1976), 1133-1135.

5628. ________. "Care of the Dying--Mental Distress in the Dying," Nursing Times, 72 (July 29, 1976), 1172-1174.

5629. ________. "Care of the Dying--The Nursing of Patients Dying of Cancer," Nursing Times, 72 (August 5, 1976), 1203-1205.

5630. ________. "Care of the Dying--The Last Achievement," Nursing Times, 72 (August 12, 1976), 1247-1249.

5631. ________. "On Dying and Dying Well," Proceedings of the Royal Society of Medicine, 70 (April, 1977), 290-291.

5632. ________. Care of the Dying. Nursing Times Publications Section. (2nd edition) 1976.

5633. ________. "Care of the Dying Patient & His Family," Documentation in Medical Ethics, 5 (1975), 4.

5634. ________. The Management of Malignant Disease. London: Edward Arnold, 1978.

5635. ________. "Hospice Care," American Journal of Medicine, 65 (November, 1978), 726-728.

5636. ________. "A Therapeutic Community: St. Christopher's Hospice," in: Schoenberg, B. et al (eds). Psychosocial Aspects of Terminal Care. New York: Columbia University Press, 1972. 275-289.

5637. ________. "St. Christopher's Hospice," in: S hneidmen, E.S. (ed). Death: Current Perspectives. Palo Alto, Calfornia: Mayfield Publishing Company, 1976.

5638. Savard, C. "Pastoral Care of the Dying," Bulletin Des Infirmieres Catholiques Du Canada (Quebec), 42 (April-June, 1975), 69-73.

5639. Scala, M.E. "A Matter of Grave Importance," Rhode Island Medical Journal, 60 (September, 1977), 427-431.

5640. ________. "Proposal for a Pallitative Care Unit in Rhode Island: The So-Called Hospice Concept," Rhode Island Medical Journal, 62 (February, 1979), 55-57.

5641. Scheff, T.J. "The Distancing of Emotion in Ritual," Current Anthropology, 18 (September, 1977), 483-490.

5642. Schelling, T.C. "Strategic Relationships in Dying," in: McMullin, E. (ed). Death and Decision. Boulder, Colorado: Westview Press, 1978.

5643. Scher, J.M. "The Collapsing Perimeter. A Commentary on Life, Death and Death-In-Life," American Journal of Psychotherapy, 30 (October, 1976), 641-657.

5644. Schiff, H.S. The Bereaved Parent. New York: Crown Publishers, 1977.

5645. Schiffer, R.B. "The Concept of Death: Tradition and Alternative," Journal of Medicine and Philosophy, 3 (March, 1978), 24-37.

5646. Schlesinger, B. "The Crisis of Widowhood in the Family Cycle," Essence, 1 (1977), 147-155.

5647. Schmidt, D.D., E. Messner. "The Management of Ordinary Grief," Journal of Family Practice, 2 (August, 1975), 259-262.

5648. Schmueli, M. "Children Facing Death," Nurse in Israel, 24 (February, 1976), 23-25.

5649. Schnaper, L.A. et al. "Euthanasia. An Overview," Maryland State Medical Journal, 26 (March, 1977), 42-48.

5650. Schnaper, N. et al. "Euthanasia: Is There an Answer," Maryland State Medical Journal, 25 (November, 1976), 25, 66-68.

5651. Schneider, C.D. Shame, Exposure & Privacy. Boston: Beacon Press, 1977.

5652. Schneider, D.H. "Cancer Patient Without Hope," South African Medical Journal, 49 (March, 1975), 297-298.

5653. Schneider, L. "Observations of a Nurse on the Theme of Euthanasia," Krankenpflege, 31 (June, 1977), 195-196.

5654. Schneider, M.A. "Letter: Facts of Life and Death," New England Journal of Medicine, 294 (February, 1976), 449.

5655. Schneider, P.B. "Talking About Cancer - Talking About Death," Summary Proceedings of the International Conference on Public Education About Cancer, (1975), 26-30.

5656. Schneider, S. "Attitudes Toward Death in Adolescent Offspring of Holocaust Survivors," Adolescence, 13 (Winter, 1978), 575-584.

5657. Schneiderman, G. et al. "Family Reactions, Physician Responses and Management Issues in Fatal Lipid Storage Disease," Clinical Pediatrics (Philadelphia), 15 (October, 1976), 887-890.

5658. Schori, T.R., C.B. Thomas. "Precursors of Premature Disease and Death: Rorschach and Figure-Drawing Factors," Psychological Reports, 40 (June, 1977), 1115-1122.

5659. Schorr, T.M. "Editorial: The Right to Die," American Journal of Nursing, 76 (January, 1976), 53.

5660. Schowalter, J.E. "How Do Children and Funerals Mix?," Journal of Pediatrics, 89 (July, 1976), 139-142.

5661. Schpholme, A. "Who Helps? Coping With the Unexpected Outcomes of Pregnancy," Journal of Obstetric, Gynecologic and Neonatal Nursing, 7 (July-August, 1978), 36-39.

5662. Schreibaum, D. "Approaches and Developments in the Study of Attitudes to Death," Israel Annals of Psychiatry and Related Disciplines, 13 (September, 1975), 259-269.

5663. Schrire, C., W.L Steiger. "A Matter of Life and Death: An Investigation into the Practice of Female Infanticide in the Arctic," Man, 9 (June, 1974), 161-184.

5664. Schroeder, J.S. et al. "Detection of the High-Risk Patient for Sudden Death," Advances in Cardiology, 15 (1975), 25-36.

5665. Schulman, J.L. Coping With Tragedy: Successfully Facing the Problem of a Seriously Ill Child. Chicago: Follett Publications Company, 1976.

5666. Schulman, K.R. "Repression and Sensitization as Determinants of Responses to a Message Designed to Arouse Thoughts of One's Own Death," Psychological Reports, 39 (August, 1976), 189-190.

5667. Schultz, C.A. "STAT Developing Foundations for Healing Grief," Journal of Emergency Nursing, 3 (January-February, 1977), 25-34.

5668. ________. "Cultural Aspects of Death and Dying," Journal of Emergency Nursing, 5 (January-February, 1979), 24-27.

5669. ________. "The Dying Person," Journal of Emergency of Nursing, 5 (May-June, 1979), 12-16.

5670. Schultz, R. The Psychology of Death & Dying. Reading, Massachusetts: Addison-Wesley Publication Company, 1978.

5671. Schulz, C.M. "Death Anxiety and the Structuring of a Death Concerns Cognitive Domain," Essence, 1 (1977), 171-187.

5672. Schulz, R. "Some Life and Death Consequences of Perceived Control," in: Carrol, J.S., J.W. Payne (eds). Cognition and Social Behavior. Hilldale, New Jersey; Lawrence Erlbaum, 1976. 135-153.

5673. ________. "Meeting the Three Major Needs of the Dying Patient," Geriatrics, 31 (June, 1976), 132-137.

5674. Schulz, Z.R., D. Aderman. "Physicians Death Anxiety and Patient Outcomes," Omega, 9 (1979), 327-332.

5675. Schwartz, A.M., T.B. Karasu. "Psychotherapy with the Dying Patient," American Journal of Psychotherapy, 31 (January, 1977), 19-35.

5676. Schwartz, J.L., L.H. Schwartz. Vulnerable Infants: A Psychosocial Dilemma. New York: McGraw-Hill, 1977.

5677. Schwartz, P.J. "Near-Miss Sudden Infant Death Letter," Lancet, 2 (October, 1976), 853.

5678. Schweisheimer, W. "The Right to Die," Krankenpflege, 31 (June, 1977), 197-198.

5679. Schweitzer, B. "Miss Pinet Knew?," Nursing (Jenkintown), 5 (April, 1975), 18.

5680. Scott, D.H. Is There Life After Death? New York: Bantam Books, 1977.

5681. Secundy, M.G. "Bereavement: The Role of the Family Physician," Journal of the National Medical Assocaition, 69 (September, 1977), 649-651.

5682. Sederberg, O. The Immortality Factor. New York: Dutton, 1974.

5683. ________. Living With Death. New York: Dutton, 1976.

5684. Selby, J.W. "Situation Correlates of Death Anxiety: Reactions to Funeral Practices," Omega, 9 (1977), 247-250.

5685. Seldon, E. "Why Don't We Let Them Die at Home? Even the Elderly?," RN, 39 (January, 1976), 66-70.

5686. Seligman, M. Helplessness: On Depression, Development and Death. San Francisco: W.H. Freeman, 1975.

5687. Sell, I.L. "Guide to Materials on Death and Dying for Teachers of Nursing," Ann Arbor: University Microfilms International, 175, 213 pages.

5688. ________. Death and Dying: An Annotated Bibliography. New York: Tiresias Press, 1977.

5689. Seskin, J. A Time to Live. Englewood Cliffs, New Jersey: Spectrum (Prentice-Hall), 1977.

5690. Shady, G. "Death Anxiety and Care of the Terminally Ill: A Review of the Clinical Literature," Canadian Psychological Review, 17 (April, 1976), 137-142.

5691. ________. "Coping Styles of Patients With Life-Threatening Illness: A Literature Review," Essence, 2 (1978), 149-154.

5692. ________. "Death Anxiety and AB Therapeutic Styles as Factors in Helping Patients With Different Coping Styles Accept Life-Threatening Illness," Dissertation Abstracts International, 38 (August, 1977), 916-917.

5693. Shaffer, J.W. et al. "Social Adjustment Profiles of Female Drivers Involved in Fatal and Non-Fatal Accidents," American Journal of Psychiatry, 134 (July, 1977), 801-804.

5694. Shannon, T.A. "Caring for the Dying Patient: What Guidance from the Guidelines," Hastings Center Report, 7 (June, 1977), 28-30.

5695. Sharapan, H. "'Mister Rogers' Neighborhood': Dealing With Death on a Children's Television Series," Death Education, 1 (Spring, 1977), 131-136.

5696. Sharpe, G. "Listening for the Death-Bells," Canadian Nurse, 74 (January, 1978), 20-23.

5697. Shaw, E.B. "Remarks on SIDS," in: Bosma, J.R., J. Showacre (eds). Development of Upper Respiratory Anatomy and Function. Washington, D.C.: National Institute of Health, 1975.

5698. ________. "Letter: Another Idea Regarding SIDS," Pediatrics, 56 (October, 1975), 612.

5699. Sheer, B.L. "Help For Parents in a Difficult Job--Broaching the Subject of Death," Maternal Child Nursing Journal, 2 (September-October, 1977), 320-324.

5700. Sheets, P.D. "Maya Recovery From Volcanic Disasters - Ilopango and Ceren," Archaeology, 32 (1979), 32-42.

5701. Shepard, D.A. "Terminal Care: Towards an Ideal," Canadian Medical Association Journal, 115 (July, 1976), 97-98, 100.

5702. ________. "Principles and Practice of Pallitative Care," Canadian Medical Association Journal, 116 (March, 1977), 522-523.

5703. Shepard, M. Someone You Love is Dying. New York: Harmony Books, 1975.

5704. Shepherd, D.M., E.M. Barraclough. "Help For Those Bereaved by Suicide," British Journal of Social Work, 9 (1979), 67-74.

5705. Sherizen, S., L. Paul. "Dying in a Hospital Intensive Care Unit: The Social Significance for the Family of the Patient," Omega, 8 (1977), 29-40.

5706. Sheskin, A., S.E. Wallace. "Differing Bereavements: Suicide, Natural and Accidental Death," Omega, 76 (1976), 229-242.

5707. Shimizu, A. "Karen Quinlan Case--Dignified Death and Nursing. Its Impact on Nursing," Japan Journal of Nursing, 40 (August, 1976), 790-799.

5708. Shinozaki, H. "An Epedemiological Study of Death of Psychiatric Inpatients," Comprehensive Psychiatry, 17 (May-June, 1976), 790-799.

5709. Shippey, L. "Sudden Infant Death: The Survivor's Suffering," Journal of Practical Nursing, 26 (December, 1976), 28-29.

5710. Shirkey, H.C. "Facing the Inevitable: The Physician's Supportive Role in the Death of a Child," Hospital Formulary, 11 (March, 1976), 146-147.

5711. Shivan, J. "The Dark Side of Nursing: What Happened to the Man in Bed 14?," Nursing Mirror, 148 (April, 1979), 14-15.

5712. Shneidman, E.S. (ed). Death: Current Perspectives. Palo Alto, California: Mayfield Company, 1976.

5713. Shubin, S. "Cancer Widows: A Special Challenge," Nursing (Horsham) 8 (April, 1978), 56-60.

5714. Shuman, R. Day by Day. Oakland, California: The Scrimshaw Press, 1977.

5715. Shumiatcher, M.C. "Medical Heroics and the Good Death," Canadian Medical Association Journal, 117 (September, 1977), 520-522.

5716. Shusterman, L.R. "The Psychosocial Factors of the Abortion Experience: A Critical Review," Psychology of Women Quarterly, 1 (Fall, 1976), 79-106.

5717. Siegler, M., H. Osmond. "The Doctor and the Dying Role," Practitioner, 216 (June, 1976), 690-694.

5718. Silverman, L.H. "Psychoanalytic Theory, 'The Reports of My Death Are Greatly Exaggerated," American Psychology, 31 (September, 1976), 621-637.

5719. Silverman, P. et al. If You Will Lift the Load... Gutterman-Musicant-Kreitzman, Inc., 1976.

5720. Silverman, P.R., A. Cooperband. "On Widowhood. Mutual Help and the Elderly Widow," Journal of Geriatric Psychiatry, 8 (1975), 9-27.

5721. Simmons, R.G. et al. Gift of Life: The Social and Psychological Impact of Organ Transplantation. New York: John Wiley & Sons, 1977.

5722. Simms, L.M. "Dignified Death: A Right Not a Privilege," Journal of Geriatric Nursing, 1 (November-December, 1975), 21-25.

5723. Simms, M. "Abortion Law and Medical Freedom," The British Journal of Criminology, 14 (April, 1974), 118-131.

5724. Simon, S.B., J. Goodman. "A Study of Death Through Celebration of Life," Learning, 4 (March, 1976), 70-74.

5725. Simonds, L. "Care of the Terminal Patient--Californian Inspiration," Nursing Times, 75 (May, 1979), 905-906.

5726. Simpson, L.B. "Care of the Dying Patient," Pelican News, 35 (Spring, 1979), 8-9,11-14.

5727. Simpson, M.A. The Facts of Death. New York: Spectrum (Prentice-Hall), 1979.

5728. ________. "Dying on Television," Omega, 9 (1979), 93-95.

5729. ________, B.M. Mount. "Living With the Dying," Canadian Medical Association Journal, 117 (July, 1977), 14-15.

5730. Sims, J.K. "Criteria for Pronouncement of Death and the Human Brain Death Syndrome," Hawaii Medical Journal, 35 (January, 1976), 11-14.

5731. Sinick, D. "Counseling the Dying and Their Survivors," Personnel and Guidance Journal, 55 (November, 1976), 122-123.

5732. ________. Counseling Older Persons: Careers, Retirement, Dying. New York: Human Service Press, 1977.

5733. Sirois, F. "Mourning and Its Vicissitudes," Union Medicale Du Canada, 105 (July, 1976), 1095-1100.

5734. Sister Helen Marie. "Reorienting Staff Attitudes Toward the Dying," Hospital Progress, 59 (August, 1978), 74-76.

5735. Sister Paula. "Care of the Terminal Patient: The Work of the Hospice," Nursing Times, 75 (April, 1979), 667.

5736. Skegg, P.D. "The Case for a Statutory 'Definition of Death'," Journal of Medical Ethics, 2 (December, 1976), 190-192.

5737. Skolnick, V. "The Addictions as Pathological Mourning: An Attempt at Restitution of Early Losses," American Journal of Psychotherapy, 33 (April, 1979), 281-290.

5738. Slater, E. et al. Death With Dignity: A Reply to 'On Dying Well'. London: Voluntary Euthanasia, 1976.

5739. Slavin, M.D. "Oedipal Grief: Mourning or Melancholia," International Journal of Psychoanalysis & Psychotherapy, 7 (1978-1979), 405-436.

5740. Slivkin, S.E. "Psychiatric Day Hospital Treatment of Terminally Ill Patients," International Journal of Psychiatry in Medicine, 7 (1976-1977), 123-131.

5741. ________. "Death and Living: A Family Therapy Approach," American Journal of Psychoanalysis, 37 (Winter, 1977), 317-323.

5742. Small, L. "Pathological Grief," in his (ed): The Briefer Psychotherapies. New York: Brunner/Mazel, 1979.

5743. Smialek, J.E. "Physicians Must Show Compassion for SIDS Victims' Families," Michigan Medicine, 76 (May, 1977), 268-270.

5744. ________. "Letter: Sudden Death in Infants," Canadian Medical Association Journal, 114 (March, 1976), 498.

5745. Smialek, Z. "Observations on Immediate Reactions of Families to Sudden Infant Death," Pediatrics, 62 (August, 1978), 160-165.

5746. Smith, A.A. Rachel. New York: Morehouse-Barlow, 1975.

5747. Smith, A.H. "A Multivariate Study of Factor Analyzed Predictors of Death Anxiety in College students," Dissertation Abstracts International, 36 (January, 1976), 3585.

5748. ________. "A Multivariate Study of Personality, Situational and Demographic Predictors of Death Anxiety in College Students," Essence, 1 (1977), 139-144.

5749. Smith, B.B. "Human Dignity in Living and Dying," Journal of the Medical Association of the State of Alabama, 45 (May, 1976), 24-25.

5750. Smith, C. et al. "Witnessing Death as Nurses," Australas Nursing Journal, 7 (October, 1977), 25-27.

5751. Smith, D.A. "Life and Death Decisions: Editorial," Pennsylvania Medicine, 79 (June, 1976), 28.

5752. Smith, D.H. "Fatal Choices: Recent Discussions of Dying," Hastings Center Report, 7 (April, 1977), 8-10.

5753. ________. (ed). No Rush to Judgement: Essays on Medical Ethics. Bloomington, Indiana: Indiana University Poynter Center, 1977.

5754. Smith, D.W. "Survivors of Serious Illness," American Journal of Nursing, 79 (March, 1979), 440-446.

5755. Smith, G.M. et al. "Pain of First Trimester Abortion - Its Qualifications and Relations With Other Variables," American Journal of Obstetrics and Gynecology, 133 (1979), 489-498.

5756. Smith, K. Help for the Bereaved. London: Duckworth, 1978.

5757. Smith, P.J. et al. "Death Anxiety and Coping Styles - Comparison of the Templer and Alpha-Omega Measurement Scales," Ohio Journal of Science, 79 (1979), 76.

5758. Smith, R.J. et al. "Reactions to Death as a Function of Perceived Similarity to Deceased," Omega, 9 (1979), 125-138.

5759. Smith, W.J. "The Etiology of Depression in a Sample of Elderly Widows," Journal of Geriatric Psychiatry, 11 (1978), 81-83.

5760. Smith, W. "Defining the Basis for Terminating Life Support Under the Right of Privacy," (re: Quinlan) Tulsa Law Journal, 12 (1976), 150-167.

5761. Snowdon, J. et al. "Feigned Bereavement: Twelve Cases," British Journal of Psychiatry, 133 (July, 1978), 15-19.

5762. Sollitto, S., R.M. Veatch. The Hastings Center Bibliography of Society, Ethics and the Life Sciences. New York: Hastings-On-Hudson, 1976-1977.

5763. Solomon, G.F. "Capital Punishment as Suicide and as Murder," American Journal of Orthopsychiatry, 45 (July, 1975), 701-711.

5764. Solomon, H.M. "Grief and Bereavement," International Journal of Social Psychiatry, 23 (Autumn, 1977), 211-222.

5765. Solomon, M.A., L.B. Hersch. "Death in the Family - Implications for Family Development," Journal of Marital and Family Therapy, 5 (1979), 43-49.

5766. Somers, A.R. "Consumer Health Education--To Know or to Die," Hospitals, 50 (May, 1976), 52-56.

5767. Somerville, R.M. "Perspective on Death: A Thematic Teaching Unit," Family Coordinator, 23 (October, 1974), 421.

5768. Sonstegard, L. et al. "Dealing With Death. The Grieving Nurse," American Journal of Nursing, 76 (September, 1976), 1488-1491.

5769. Spanton, J. "Coping With Death," Nursing Times, 72 (May, 1976), 741.

5770. Sparks, R.A. et al. "Maternal Death and the I.U.D. Letter," Lancet, 1 (January, 1977), 98.

5771. Speck, P. "Easing the Pain and Grief of Stillbirth," Nursing Mirror, 146 (June, 1978), 38-41.

5772. ________. Loss and Grief in Medicine. London: Bailliere Tindall, 1978.

5773. Speers, W.F. "Rapid Positive Identification of Fatal Air Disaster Victims," South African Medical Journal, 52 (July, 1977), 150.

5774. Spencer, C.S. "The Effect of Near-Death Experience on Death Anxiety," Journal of Undergraduate Psychological Research, 3 (July, 1976), 21-26.

5775. Spencer, S. "Childhoods End - Hopeless Future Inclines the Young Toward Death," Harpers, 258 (1979), 16-19.

5776. Spicker, S.T. et al (eds). Philosophical Medical Ethics: Its Nature and Significance. Boston: Reidel, 1977.

5777. Spiegel, D., I.D. Yalom. "A Support Group for Dying Patients," International Journal for Group Psychotherapy, 28 (April, 1978), 223-245.

5778. Spiegel, Y. The Grief Process. London: SCM Press, Ltd., 1978.

5779. ________. The Grief Process: Analysis & Counseling. Nashville: Abingdon Press, 1977.

5780. Spilka, B. et al. "Those Who Are About to Fly: Death Concern and Feelings and Behavior About Air Travel," Omega, 8 (1977-1978), 107-116.

5781. ________ et al. "Death and Personal Faith: A Psychometric Investigation," Journal for the Scientific Study of Religion, 16 (June, 1977), 169-178.

5782. Spilane, E.J. "An Analysis of Catholic-Sponsored Hospices," Hospital Progress, 60 (March, 1979), 46-50.

5783. Spinetta, J., J. Maloney. "Death Anxiety in the Outpatient Leukemic Child," Pediatrics, 56 (December, 1975), 1034-1037.

5784. Sporken, P. "Euthanasia in the Care of the Living and Dying," Therapie Der Gegenwart, 115 (April, 1976), 543-569.

5785. Squire, M.B. "Death, Dying and Hard Time Therapy," International Journal of Social Psychiatry, 23 (Spring, 1977), 5-7.

5786. Stalcup, S.A. et al. "Planning for a Pediatric Disaster--Experience Gained From Caring for 1600 Vietnamese Orphans," New England Journal of Medicine, 293 (October, 1975), 691-695.

5787. Stallings, R.A. "Differential Response of Hospital Personnel to a Disaster," Mass Emergencies, 1 (October, 1975), 47-54.

5788. Stamm, W.P. "Must They Die? Letter," British Medical Journal, 1 (May, 1977), 1347.

5789. Stanford, G. "Methods and Materials for Death Education," School Counselor, 24 (May, 1977), 350-360.

5790. ________, D. Perry. Death Out of the Closet: A Curriculum Guide to Living With Dying . New York: Bantam Books, 1976.

5791. Stanley, A.T. "Is it Ethical to Give Hope to a Dying Person?," Nursing Clinics of North America, 14 (March, 1979), 69-80

5792. Stannard, D.E. The Puritan Way of Death: A Study in Religion, Culture and Social Change. New York: Oxford University Press, 1977.

5793. Stanton, A.N. et al. "Terminal Symptoms in Children Dying Suddenly and Unexpectedly at Home," British Medical Journal, 2 (November, 1978), 1249-1251.

5794. Stanton, M.D. "The Addict as Savior: Heroin, Death and the Family," Family Process, 16 (June, 1977), 191-197.

5795. Starenko, R.C. God, Grass and Grace: A Theology of Death. St. Louis: Concordia Publishing House, 1975.

5796. Stark, R.E., S.N. Nathanson. "Unusual Features of Cry in an Infant Dying Suddenly and Unexpectedly," in: Bosma, J.F., J. Showacre (eds). Development of Upper Respiratory Anatomy and Function.

5797. Starr. A. "Auditory Brain Stem Responses in Brain Death," Brain, 99 (September, 1976), 543-554.

5798. Stecchi, J.M. "The Death of a Child. Looking Back From a Parent's Point of View," Journal of Nursing Care, 12 (May, 1979), 13-16, 26.

5799. Steele, R.L. "Dying, Death and Bereavement Among the Maya Indians of Mesoamerica: A Study in Anthropological Psychology," American Psychology, 32 (December, 1977), 1060-1068.

5800. Steele, S. (ed). Nursing Care of the Child With Long-Term Illness. (2nd edition) New York: Appleton-Century-Crofts, 1977.

5801. Stefan, E.S. "Perspective in Death. An Experimental Course on Death Education," Teaching of Psychology, 5 (October, 1978), 142-144.

5802. Stein, S.B. About Dying. New York: Walder and Company, 1974.

5803. Stein, S, "An Earthquake Shakes up a Mental Health System," in: Tulifan, A.B. et al (eds). Beyond Clinic Walls. University: University of Alabama Press, 1974.

5804. Steinbock, B. "The Intentional Termination of Life," Ethics in Science and Medicine, 6 (1979), 59-64.

5805. Steinfels, P. R.M. Veatch. Death Inside Out. New York: Harper Row, 1975.

5806. Steininger, M., S. Colsher. "Correlates of Attitudes About 'The Right to Die' Among 1973 and 1976 High School and College Students," Omega, 9 (1978-1979), 355-368.

5807. Steinschneider, A. Narsopharyngitis and the Sudden Infant Death Syndrome," Pediatrics, 60 (October, 1977), 531-533.

5808. Steinzor, B. "Death and Construction of Reality - Revisit to Literature from 1969," Omega, 9 (1979), 97-124.

5809. Stephansky. P.S. "From War to Quiet Thanatos: Beyond the Pleasure Principle Revisited," Psychological Issues, 10 (1977), 170-189.

5810. __________. "Thanatos and Aggression: The Strained Linkage," Psychological Issues, 10 (1977), 8-24.

5811. Stephan, L.D., M.N. Billings. "The Law and Death- An Overview," Journal of Contemporary Law, 1 (Spring, 1975), 224-233.

5812. Stephens, C.S. Natural Salvation: The Message of Science, Outlining The First Principles of Immortal Life on the Earth. New York: Arno Press, 1976. (Orig. Pub. 1905).

5813. Stern, G.M. "From Chaos to Responsibility," American Journal of Psychiatry, 133 (March, 1976), 300-301.

5814. Sternbach, O. "Aggression, The Death Drive and the Problems of Sadomasochism. A Reinterpretation of Freud's Second Drive Theory," International Journal of Psychoanalysis, 56 (August, 1975), 321-333.

5815. Stevens, C. Stories From a Snowy Meadow. New York: Seabury, 1976.

5816. Stevens, H.A., R.A. Conn. "Right to Life/Involuntary Pediatric Euthanasia," Mental Retardation, 14 (June, 1978), 3-8.

5817. Stevenson, I. "The Belief in Reincarnation and Cases of the Reincarnation Type Among The Haida," Journal of the American Society for Pyschical Research, 71 (April, 1977), 177-189.

5818. Stevenson, I. "Further Observations on the Combination Lock Test for Survival," _Journal of the American Society for Psychical Research_ 70 (April, 1976), 219-229.

5819. _________. "The Explanatory Value of the Idea of Reincarnation," _Journal of Nervous and Mental Disease_, 164 (May, 1977), 305-326.

5820. _________. "Research Into the Evidence of Man's Survival After Death: A Historical and Critical Survey with Summary of Recent Developments," _Journal of Nervous and Mental Disease_, 165 (September, 1977), 152-170.

5821. _________. _Cases of the Reincarnation Type_. Charlottesville, Virginia: University Press of Virginia, 1975.

5822. Stoddart, S. _The Hospice Movement: A Better Way of Caring for the Dying_. New York: Stein & Day, 1978.

5823. Stoneberg, T. "Deaths in a Family: Who's in Charge," _Counseling and Values_, 21 (April, 1977), 160-166.

5824. Storley, C.J. _Beginning at the End: A Study in Death and Life_. Minneapolis: Augsburg Publishing House, 1975.

5825. Stranix, E.L. _The Cemetery: An Outdoor Classroom. A Student Workbook, Project Kare Edition_. Philadelphia, Pennsylvania: Con-Stran Productions, 1977.

5826. Strauss, A.L. _Chronic Illness and the Quality of Life_. St. Louis: C.V. Mosby, 1975.

5827. Strauss, S.A. "Death and the Moment of Death: Several Legal Aspects," _South African Medical Journal_, 49 (June, 1975), 976-980.

5828. Stromberg, R.E. "The Right to Die Controversy: Physician, Not the Courts Should Resolve the Issue," _Hospital Medical Staff_, 6 (February, 1977), 9-14.

5829. Strugnell, C. _Adjustment to Widowhood and Some Related Problems_. New York: Health Sciences Publishing Corporation, 1974.

5830. Stubblefield, K.S. "A Preventive Program for Bereaved Families," _Social Work Health Care_, 2 (Summer, 1977), 379-389.

5831. Stump, J.E. "Deciding: The Problems it Brings and the Problems Brought to It," _Journal of the Medical Society of New Jersey_, 75 (February, 1978), 139-144.

5832. Suckiel, E.K. "Death and Benefit in the Permanently Unconscious Patient: A Justification of Euthanasia," Journal of Medicine and Philosophy, 3 (March, 1978), 139-144.

5833. Sufrin, R. "Everything is in Order, Warden. A Discussion of Death in the Gas Chamber," Suicide, 6 (Spring, 1976), 44-57.

5834. Sullivan, T.D. "Active and Passive Euthanasia: An Impertinent Distinction?," Human Life Review, 3 (Summer, 1977), 40-46.

5835. Summers, D.H. "Care of the Terminal Patient. Staff Support," Nursing Times, 75 (May, 1979), 790.

5836. Suszycki, L.H. "Effective Nursing Home Placement for the Elderly Dying Patient," in: Prichard, E.R. et al (eds). Social Work With the Dying Patient and Family. New York: Columbia University Press, 1977. 185-197.

5837. Swain, J. From My World to Yours. New York: Walker and Company, 1977.

5838. Swift, J.K. "The Chaplains Role in Care for the Dying: Toward a New Understanding,: Canadian Medical Association Journal, 115 (July, 1976), 181-182 & 185.

5839. Swigar, M.E. et al. "Grieving and Unplanned Pregnancy," Psychiatry 39 (February, 1976), 72-80.

5840. Swinton, A. "Grief and Stillbirth (letter)," British Medical Journal, 1 (April, 1977), 971.

5841. Swiss, T. "Death Education in the Language Arts Classroom," Language Arts, 53 (September, 1976), 690-699.

5842. Swyter, J. "When Is Life Without Value - Study of Life-Death Decisions on a Hemodialysis Unit," Omega, 9 (1979), 369-380.

5843. Tbachnic, N. "Death Trend and Adaptation: A Psychoanalytic Theory of Accident," Journal of American Academy of Psychoanalysis, 4 (January, 1976), 49-62.

5844. Tagochi, T. "Karen Quinlan Case--Dignified Death and Nursing. Warning Against Cursory Attitude Toward Human Life," Japan Journal of Nursing, 40 (August, 1976), 806-807.

5845. ________. "Aftermath of Euthanasia Controversy--Nursing Education and the Problem of Death," Japan Journal of Nurses Education, 17 (December, 1976), 762-765.

5846. Tait, B.D. et al. "HLA and the Sudden Infant Death Syndrome," Monographs in Allergy, 11 (1977), 50-59.

5847. Takeshita, H. "Problems of Brain Death. A Reappraisal," Japan Journal of Anesthesiology, 24 (April, 1975), 317-322.

5848. Tamura, M. "Death as an Inevitable Phenomenon in Man's Life," Japan Journal of Nurses Education, 17 (December 1976), 741-745.

5849. Taney, E. "The Lethal State," Michigan Medicine, 75 (February, 1976), 211-212.

5850. Tanner, E.R. "A Time to Die," Nursing Times, 74 (February, 1978), 16.

5851. Tarrow, A.B. "The Philadelphia Airport Disaster Exercise, South African Medical Journal, 52 (July, 1977), 157-158.

5852. Tattah, E.B., M.C. Ekere. "Death Patterns in Sickle Cell Anemia," Journal of the American Medical Association, 233 (August, 1975), 889-890.

5853. Tayback, M. "Death With Dignity," Journal of Gerontological Nursing, 1 (July-August, 1975), 42-44.

5854. Taylor, C.J. "A Grief Experience in Juvenile Diabetes," Journal of Psychiatric Nursing, 15 (January, 1977), 26-29.

5855. Taylor, C. "Death, American Style," Death Education, 1 (Summer, 1977), 177-185.

5856. Taylor, J.R. "Meeting The Many Problems of an Unexpected Infant Death," Michigan Medicine, 75 (April, 1976), 205-207.

5857. Taylor, M.J. The Mystery of Suffering and Death. Staten Island, New York: Alba House, 1973.

5858. Taylor, N.K. Bibliography of Society, Ethics and the Life Sciences: Supplement for 1977-1978. New York: Hastings-On-Hudson, 1977.

5859. Taylor, S. "Confrontation With Death and the Renewal of Life," Suicide and Life-Threatening Behavior, 8 (September, 1978), 89-98.

5860. Teige, K., D. Gerlack. "Apparent Death or Dead Only of the Certificate," Medizinische Welt, 26 (January 24, 1975), 167-169.

5861. Temes, R. Living With An Empty Chair: A Guide Through Grief. Amherst, Massachusetts: Mandala Press, 1977.

5862. Tmekin, O. "The Idea of Respect for Life in the History of Medicine " in: Temkin, O. et al. Respect for Life in Medicine and Philosophy and the Law. Baltimore, Maryland: John Hopkins University, 1976.

5863. Templer, D.I. "Two Factor Theory of Death Anxiety: A Note," Essence, 76 (1976), 91-93.

5864. _______. "The Time of Death of Psychologists," Essence, 1 (1976), 62-64.

5865. _______ et al. "Death Anxiety of Convicted Felons," Corrective and Social Psychiatry and Journal of Behavior Technology Methods and Therapy, 25 (1979), 18-20.

5866. Tenbrinck, M.S., P.W. Brewer. "The Stages of Grief Experience by Parents of Handicapped Children," Arizona Medicine, 33 (September, 1976), 712-714.

5867. Teramoto, M. "Karen Quinlan Case--Dignified Death and Nursing. Importance of Preservation of Natural Life," Japan Journal of Nursing, 40 (August, 1976), 804-805.

5868. _______. "Nursing of Dying Patients--Expectation of Nursing," Cold Spring Harbor, Quantum Biology Symposium, 22 (October, 1976), 89-95.

5869. Terhune, J. "About Aging and Death," Health Education, 8 (November-December, 1977), 13-16.

5870. Terjesen, N.C., L.P. Wilkins. "Proposal for a Model of Sudden Infant Death Syndrome Act - Help for the Other Victims of SIDS," Family Law Quarterly, 12 (1979), 285-308.

5871. Tew, B.J. et al. "Marital Stability Following the Birth of a Child With Spina Bifada," British Journal of Psychiatry, 131 (July, 1977), 79-82.

5872. Thauberger, P.C. et al. "Avoidance of the Ontological Confrontation of Death and a Phenomenological Encounter With a Simulated Death Atmosphere," Perceptual and Motor Skills, 45 (August, 1977), 171-178.

5873. ________, E.M. Thauberger. "A Consideration of Death and a Sociological Perspective in the Quality of the Dying Patient's Care," Social Science Medicine, 8 (August 1974), 437-441.

5874. ________. "Avoidance of the Ontological Confrontation of Death and Psychological Measurements in a Field Setting Simulating Death Atmosphere," Social Science Medicine, 10 (November-December, 1976), 527-533.

5875. ________. "Satiation as a Personality Source Trait in the Avoidance/Confrontation of Death," Psychological Reports, 41 (October, 1977), 483-492.

5876. Thauberger, P.C. "Affective Measurements and a Field Setting Simulating a Death Atmosphere," Essence, 2 (1978), 159-170.

5877. Thielicke, H. The Doctor as Judge of Who Shall Live and Who Shall Die. Philadelphia: Fortress Press, 1976.

5878. Thiroux, J.P. "Euthanasia and Allowing Someone to Die," in his: Ethics: Theory and Practive. Encino, California: Glencoe Press, 1977. 121-144.

5879. Thomas, C.W., S.C. Foster. "A Sociological Perspective on Public Support for Capital Punishment," American Journal of Orthopsychiatry, (July, 1975), 641-657.

5880. Thompson, D.M. "Thoughts on Bereavement," Nursing Times, 73 (August, 1977), 1334-1335.

5881. Thompson, M.L. "'Symbolic Immortality'--A New Approach to the Study of Death," Media and Methods, 13 (February, 1977), 60-64.

5882. Thompson, R. "Thoughts of Death in General Practice," Australian Family Physician, 6 (September, 1977), 1100-1102.

5883. Thompson, W.A. A Dictionary of Medical Ethics and Practice. Bristol: John Wright and Sons, 1977.

5884. Thorson, J.A. "Variations in Death Anxiety Related to College Students' Sex, Major Field of Study and Certain Personality Traits," Psychological Reports, 40 (June, 1977), 857-858.

5885. Thurman, V. "Euthanasia: The Physician's Liability," <u>John Marshall Journal of Practice and Procedure</u>, 10 (Fall, 1976), 148-172.

5886. Tibbles, L. "Is He Dead? Should He Be Allowed to Die? Who Decides?" <u>Connecticut Medicine</u>, 39 (November, 1975), 731-732.

5887. Tierney, E.A. "Accepting Disfigurement When Death is the Alternative," <u>American Journal of Nursing</u>, 75 (December, 1975), 2149-2150.

5888. Tietz, W. et al. "Family Sequelae After a Child's Death Due to Cancer," <u>American Journal of Psychotherapy</u>, 31 (July 1977), 417-425.

5889. Titchener, J.L., F.T. Kapp. "Family and Character Change at Buffalo Creek," <u>American Journal of Psychiatry</u>, 133 (March, 1976), 295-299.

5890. Tobin, C. "A Statement on Legislation Concerning Death and Dying," <u>Catholic Mind</u>, 75 (April, 1977), 7-10.

5891. Tolentino, A.S. "Is There a Right to Die? A Study of the Law of Euthanasia," <u>Philippine Law Journal</u>, 49 (September, 1974), 444-461.

5892. Tooley, K. "The Choice of a Surviving Sibling as 'Scapegoat' in Some Cases of Maternal Bereavement," <u>Journal of Child Psychology and Psychiatry</u>, 16 (October, 1975), 331-339.

5893. Tooley, W.H. "Editorial: Sudden Infant Death Syndrome," <u>American Review of Respiratory Disease</u>, 112 (August 1975), 157-158.

5894. Tonkin, S. "Sudden Infant Death Syndrome: Hypothesis of Causation," <u>Pediatrics</u>, 55 (May, 1975), 650-651.

5895. Tordella, M.A., J.J. Neutens. "Instrument to Appriase Attitudes of College Students Toward Euthanasia," <u>Journal of School Health</u>, 49 (1979), 351-352.

5896. Towers, B. "The Impact of the California Natural Death Act," <u>Journal of Medical Ethics</u>, 4 (June, 1978), 96-98.

5897. Toynbee, A. et al. <u>Life After Death</u>, London: Weidenfeld & Nocolson, 1976.

5898. Trachtenberg, S. "When Medical Technology Fails," <u>Rhode Island Medical Journal</u>, 58 (December, 1975), 504-505 & 511.

5899. Trammell, R.L. "The Presumption Against Taking Life," <u>Journal of Medicine and Philosophy</u>, 3 (March, 1978), 53-67.

5900. Travis, G. Chronic Illness in Children: In Impact on Child and Family. Stanford: Stanford University Press, 1976.

5901. Triche, C.W. III. The Euthanasia Controversy (1812-1974). Troy, New York: Whitston, 1975.

5902. Troyer, J. "Euthnasia, The Right to Life and Moral Structures," in: Spicker, S,F,, H.T. Engelhardt (eds) Philosophical Medical Ethics: Its Nature and Significance. Boston: Reidel, 1977.

5903. Trube-Becker, E. "The Death of Children Following Negligence: Social Aspects," Forensic Science, 9 (March-April, 1977), 111-115.

5904. Tsuang, M.T., R.F. Woolson. "Mortality in Patients With Schizophrenia, Mania, Depression and Surgical Considerations," British Journal of Psychiatry, 130 (February, 1977), 162-166.

5905. Turnage, A.S. More Than You Dare Ask. Atlanta: John Knox Press, 1976.

5906. Turner, A.W. Houses for the Dead. New York: David McKay, 1976.

5907. Turner, B.A. "The Development of Disasters--A Sequence Model for the Analysis of the Origins of Disasters," The Sociological Review, 24 (November, 1976), 753-774.

5908. Turner, J., D. Helms. Contemporary Adulthood. Philadelphia: W.B. Saunders, 1978.

5909. Turner, R.E., C. Edgley. "Death as Theater: A Dramaturgical Analysis of the American Funeral," Sociology and Social Research, 60 (July, 1976), 337-392.

5910. Tursky, S.P., F.M. Lewistohn. "Perceived Aversiveness of Death Related Events in Depressed and Non-Depressed Individuals," Omega, 9 (1979), 333-336.

5911. Twycross, R,G, The Dying Patient. London: Christian Medical Fellowship, 1975.

5912. Uchida, Y. *The Birthday Visitor*. New York: Scribners, 1975

5913. Ufema, E.V. "Dare To Care for the Dying," *American Journal of Nursing*, 76 (January, 1976), 88-90.

5914. Ulin, R.O. *Death and Dying Education*. Washington, D.C.: National Education Association, 1977.

5915. Ullman, M. "Discussion of Dr. Stevenson's Paper: 'The Evidence of Man's Survival After Death'," *Journal of Nervous and Mental Diseases*, 165 (September, 1977), 174-175.

5916. Uroda, S.F. "Counseling the Bereaved," *Counseling and Values*, 21 (April, 1977), 185-191.

5917. Uta, K. "Karen Quinlan Case--Dignified Death and Nursing. Discussion: The Right to Die and the Legal Decidion. The Relationship between the Law and Medicine seen in the Karen Quinlan Case," *Japan Journal of Nursing*, 40 (August, 1976), 776-788.

5918. Vaccarino, J.M. "If Your Patient is Hopelessly Ill, Must You Go to Court," Legal Aspects of Medical Practice, 6 (July, 1978), 50-51.

5919. Vachon, M.L. "Grief and Bereavement Following the Death of a Spouse," Canadian Psychiatric Association Journal, 21 (February, 1976), 35-44.

5920. _______. "Motivation And Stress Experienced by Staff Working With the Terminally Ill," Death Education, 2 (Spring-Summer 1978), 113-122.

5921. _______ et al. "The Final Illness in Cancer: The Widow's Perspective," Canadian Medical Association Journal, 117 (November 19, 1977), 1151-1154.

5922. _______ et al. "Stress Reactions to Bereavement," Essence, 76 (1976), 23-33.

5923. _______ et al. "Measurement and Management of Stress in Health Professionals Working With Advanced Cancer Patients," Death Education, 1 (Winter, 1978), 365-375.

5924. Vaile, I.R. "Hospice or Rehabilitation Hospital? Alternatives For the Terminally Ill," Canadian Medical Association Journal, 120 (May 19, 1979), 1291-1292.

5925. Vasirub, S. "Editorial: Sudden Death and Lingering Hope," Journal of the American Medical Association, 235 (April 19, 1976), 1726.

5926. _______. "Afterthoughts on Afterlife (Editorial)," Archives of Internal Medicine, 137 (February, 1977), 150.

5927. Valdes-Depena, M.A., M.M. Billane, et al. "Brown Fat Retention in the Sudden Infant Death Syndrome," Archives of Pathology and Laboratory Medicine, 100 (October, 1976), 547-549.

5928. Valdes-Depena, M.A. "Sudden Unexplained Infant Death, 1970 Through 1975, An Evolution in Understanding," Pathology Annual, 12 (1977), 117-145.

5929. Vale, J.A. (ed). Medicine and the Christian Mind. London: Christian Medical Fellowship Publications, 1975.

5930. Valent, P. "Issues With Dying Patients," Medical Journal of Psychiatry, 1 (April, 1978), 433-437.

5931. Vallin, J. "World Trends in Infant Mortality Since 1950," World Health Statistics Report, 29 (1976), 646-647.

5932. Van Dell, R.A. "The Role of Death Romanticization in the Dynamics of Suicide," Suicide and Life Threatening Behavior, 7 (Spring, 1977), 45-56.

5933. Van den Berg, J.H. Medical Power and Medical Ethics. New York: W.W. Norton, 1978.

5934. Vandevelde, P. "Social Anthropology of a Neolithic Cemetery in the Netherlands," Current Anthropology, 20 (1979), 37-58.

5935. Van Till-d'Auinis de Bourouill, H.A. "How Dead Can You Be?" Medicine, Science and the Law, 15 (April, 1975), 133-147.

5936. ________. "Diagnosis of Death in Comatose Patients Under Resuscitation Treatment: A Critican Review of the Harvard Report," American Journal of Law and Medicine, 2 (Summer, 1976), 1-40.

5937. Veatch, R.M. Death, Dying and the Biological Revolution: Our Last Quest for Responsibility. New Haven, Connecticut: Yale University Press, 1976.

5938. ________. "Death and Dying: Legislative Options," Hastings Center Report, 7 (October, 1977), 5-8.

5939. ________. Case Studies in Medical Ethics. Cambridge, Massachusetts: Harvard University Press, 1977.

5940. ________. "Caring for the Dying Person--Ethical Issues at Stake," in: Barton, D. (ed) Dying and Death: A Clinical Guide for Caregivers. Baltimore: Williams and Wilkins, 1977. 150-169.

5941. Veith, F.J., J.M. Fein, et al. "Brain Death. A Status Report of Medical and Ethical Considerations," Journal of the American Medical Association, 238 (October 10, 1977), 1651-1655.

5942. Velcek, F.T., A. Weiss, et al. "Traumatic Death in Urban Children," Journal of Pediatric Surgery, 12 (June, 1977), 375-384.

5943. Venes, J.L. et al. "Severely Deformed Infants," New England Journal of Medicine, 295 (July 8, 1976), 115-116.

5944. Vere, D. "Euthanasia," in: Vale, J.A. (ed) Medicine and the Christian Mind. London: Christian Medical Fellowship Publications, 1975. 75-82.

5945. Vernon, G.M. "Myth Conceptions Concerning Death Related Behavior," Journal of Religion and Health, 16 (April, 1977), 144-152.

5946. ________. "Perceived Mortality of Euthanasia," Journal of Contemporary Law, 1 (Spring, 1975), 286-291.

5947. Videbech, T. "A Study of Genetic Factors, Childhood Bereavement and Premorbid Personality Traits in Patients With Anacastic Endogenous Depression," Acta Psychiatrica Scandinavica, 52 (September, 1975), 178-222.

5948. Vincent, R.H. "The Right to Die in Georgia- Maybe Next Year," Journal of the Medical Association of Georgia, 67 (April, 1978), 309-310.

5949. Vogel, H.P., E.G. Knox. "Reproductive Patterns After Stillbirth and Early Infant Death," Journal of Biosocial Science, 7 (April, 1975), 103-111.

5950. Vogel, L.J. Helping a Child Understand Death. Philadelphia: Fortress Press, 1975.

5951. Volkan, V.D. "Mourning and Adptation After a War," American Journal of Psychotherapy, 31 (October, 1977), 561-569.

5952. Voysey, M. A Constant Burden. London & Boston: Routledge & Kegan Paul, 1975.

5953. Waddell, R.W. "The Third Leading Cause of Death: How Virginia Physicians Can Fight It," Virginia Medicine, 104 (September, 1977), 609-610.

5954. Waern, U., H. Hedstrand. "What Middle-Aged Men Know of Their Parents' Cause of Death and Age at Death. A Comparison Between History and Death Certificate," Scandinavian Journal of Social Medicine, 4 (1976), 123-129.

5955. Wagenaar, T.C., I.W. Knol. "Attitudes Toward Abortion: A Comparative Analysis of Correlates for 1973-1975," Journal of Sociology and Social Welfare, 4 (July, 1977), 927-944.

5956. Wagner, J. (ed). Reforming the Rights of Death. New York: Paulist Press, 1968.

5957. Wagner, J., E. Goldstein. "Pharmicist's Role in Loss and Grief," American Journal of Hospital Pharmacy, 34 (May, 1977), 490-492.

5958. Wakin, E. "Is The Right-To Die Wrong?" U.S. Catholic, 43 (March, 1978), 6-12.

5959. Wald, F.S. "Hospice Movement Must Recognize Human Needs Editorial," American Nursing, 11 (March 20, 1979), 4-5.

5960. Waldron, I., J. Eyer. "Socioeconomic Causes of the Recent Rise in Death Rates for 15-24 Year Olds," Social Science Medicine, 9 (July, 1975), 383-396.

5961. ________, S. Johnston. "Why Do Women Live Longer Than Men? Accidents, Alcohol and Cirrosis," Journal of Human Stress, 2 (June, 1976), 19-30.

5962. Walker, A.E., G.F. Molinari. "Criteria of Cerebral Death," American Neurological Association. Transactions. Annual Meeting. 100, (1975) 29-35.

5963. Walker, C. "Effect of Group Psychotherapy on Bereavement With Spouses of Dying Cancer Patients," Dissertation Abstracts International, 38 (April, 1978), 5049.

5964. Walker, G.A. Gatherings From Graveyards. New York: Arno Press, 1976. (Orig. Pub. 1839).

5965. Walker, K.N., A. MacBride. "Social Support Networks and the Crisis of Bereavement," Social Science Medicine, 11 (January, 1977), 35-41.

5966. Walker, L. "My Fight for Life," Canadian Nurse, 74 (November, 1978), 28-29.

5967. Walker, M. "Last Rites for Young Readers," Children's Literature in Education, 9 (Winter, 1978), 188-197.

5968. Wallace, E.R. "Thanatos--A Re-evaluation," Psychiatry, 39 (November, 1976), 386-393.

5969. ________. "Freud's Anniversary Reactions and Their Fantasy and Reality Elements," Psychiatric Forum, 7 (Fall, 1977), 12-18.

5970. Wallace, S.H. "Attitudes of College Students Toward Death," Dissertation Abstracts International, 37 (July, 1976), 208-209.

5971. Wallis, C.L. The Funeral Encyclopedia, A Source Book. Grand Rapids, Michigan: Baker Books, 1953.

5972. Walsh, F.W. "Concurrent Grandparent Death and Birth of Schizophrenic Offspring: An Intriguing Finding," Family Process, 17 (December, 1978), 457-463.

5973. Walter, N.T. "Continuing Care of the Cancer Patient as a Social Engineering Problem," Cancer Research, 39 (July, 1979), 2859-2862.

5974. Walters, L. (ed). Bibliography of Bioethics. Detroit: Gale Research Company. Volume I, 1975. Volume II, 1976. Volume III, 1977.

5975. Walton, D.N. "On Logic and Methodology in the Study of Death," Ethics in Science and Medicine, 3 (September, 1976), 135-147.

5976. ________. "Active and Passive Euthanasia," Ethics, 86 (July, 1976), 343-349.

5977. Ward, A.W.M. "Terminal Care in Malignant Disease," Social Science and Medicine, 7 (July, 1974), 413-420.

5978. ________. "The Impact of a Special Unit for Terminal Care," Social Science and Medicine, 10 (1976), 373-376.

5979. ________. "Mortality of Bereavement," British Medical Journal, 1 (March 20, 1976), 700-702.

5980. Ward, B.J. "Hospice Home Care Program," <u>Nursing Outlook</u>, 26 (October, 1978), 646-649.

5981. Warheit, G.J. "A Note on Natural Disasters and Civil Disturbances: Similarities and Differences," <u>Mass Emergencies</u>, 1 (February, 1976), 131-137.

5982. Warr, D. "On Pain of Death," <u>New Zealand Journal</u>, 68 (October, 1974), 21-24.

5983. Warren, J.V. "Editorial: Recurrent 'Sudden Death'," <u>New England Journal of Medicine</u>, 293 (August 7, 1975), 298-299.

5984. Warren, W., P. Chopra. "Physicians and Death: Some Australian Data," <u>Medical Journal of Australia,</u> (March 10, 1979), 191-193.

5985. ________. "Australian Survey of Attitudes to Death," <u>Australian Journal of Social Issues</u>, 14 (1979), 134-142.

5986. ________. "Some Reliability and Validity Considerations on Australian Data From Death Anxiety Scale," <u>Omega</u>, 9 (1979), 293-299.

5987. Warthin, A.S. <u>The Physician and the Dance of Death</u>. New York: Arno Press, 1976. (Orig. Pub. 1931).

5988. Wass, H., J. Shaak. "Helping Children Understand Death Through Literature," <u>Childhood Education</u>, 53 (November-December, 1976), 80-85.

5989. Wass, H. "Views and Opinions of Elderly Persons Concerning Death," <u>Educational Gerontology</u>, 2 (January-March, 1977), 15-26.

5990. ________. <u>Dying: Facing the Facts</u>. New York: McGraw-Hill, 1979.

5991. Wass, H., Z.C. Guenther, et al. "United States and Brazilian Childrens Concepts of Death," <u>Death Education</u>, 3 (1979), 41-55.

5992. Wass, H., M. Christian, et al. "Similarities and Dissimilarities in Attitudes Toward Death in a Population of Older Persons," <u>Omega</u>, 9 (1979), 337-354.

5993. Watkin, B. "Should Doctors Kill?," <u>Nursing Mirror</u>, 141 (December, 1975), 39.

5994. Watson, C.G., H.R. Buerkle. "Involuntary Transfer as a Cause of Death and of Medical Hospitalization in Geriatric Neuropsychiatric Patients," Journal of the American Geriatrics Society, 24 (June, 1976), 278-282.

5995. Watson, E. "A Two Year Study of Sudden Death in Infants in Inner North London," Public Health, 89 (May, 1975), 153-155.

5996. ________. "Two Clustered Cases of 'Cot Death' with Identical Physical and Social Pathology," Medicine, Science and the Law, 17 (July, 1977), 183-186.

5997. Watson, W. "The Aging Sick and the Near Dead: A Study of Some Distinguishing Characteristics and Social Effects," Omega, 76 (1976), 115-123.

5998. Watts, P.R. "Evaluation of Death Attitude Change Resulting From a Death Education Instructional Unit," Death Education, 1 (Summer, 1977), 187-193.

5999. Weaver, J.L. "Policy Responses to Complex Issues: The Case of Black Infant Mortality," Journal of Health Policy Law, 1 (Winter, 1977), 433-443.

6000. Webber, D.L. "Darwin Cyclone: An Exploration of Disaster Behavior," Australian Journal of Social Issues, 11 (February, 1976), 54-63.

6001. Weber, L.J. Who Shall Live? The Dilemma of Severely Handicapped Children and Its Meaning for Other Moral Questions. New York: Paulist Press, 1976.

6002. Wehrley, M. "Sudden Death," Canadian Nurse, 72 (November, 1976), 28-29.

6003. Weingarten, V. Imitations of Mortality. New York: Alfred A Knopf, 1978.

6004. Weiniger, C. "Young Children's Concepts of Dying and Death," Psychological Reports, 44 (1979), 395-407.

6005. Weinstock, E., C. Tietze, et al. "Abortion Need and Services in the United States 1974-1975," Family Planning Perspectives, 9 (March-April, 1976), 58-69.

6006. Weir, R.F. (ed). Ethical Issues in Death and Dying. New York: Columbia University Press, 1977.

6007. Weisman, A.D. "On Death and Dying. Decisions and Destiny in Growing Older," Journal of Geriatric Psychiatry, 7 (1974), 84-93.

6008. ________. "Common Fallacies About Dying Patients," in: Shneidman, E.S. (ed) Death: Curent Perspectives. Palo Alto, California: Mayfield Publishing Company, 1976.

6009. Weist, V.A. "St. Christopher's Hospice," International Nursing Review, 14 (1967), 38.

6010. Weisskopf, S., J.L. Einder. "Grieving Medical Students: Educational and Clinical Considerations," Comprehensive Psychiatry, 17 (September-October, 1976), 623-630.

6011. Weller, M.F. "Bereavement," Health Visit, 48 (May, 1975), 155-156. Also, Australas Nurses Journal, 4 (August, 1975), 5.

6012. Wennberg, R. "Euthanasia: A Sympathetic Appraisal," Christian Scholar's Review, 6 (1977), 281-302.

6013. Wentzel, K.B. "The Dying are the Living," American Journal of Nursing, 76 (June, 1976), 956-957.

6014. Werner, P.T., T.E. Zerberl. "Physicians Need to Understand Role of Hospice, Integrate It In Community," Michigan Medicine, 78 (June, 1979), 305-306.

6015. Werner, R. "Abortion: The Moral Status of the Unborn," Social Theory and Practice, 3 (Fall, 1974), 201-222.

6016. Wessel, M.A. "A Death in the Family, The Impact on Children," Journal of the American Medical Association, 234 (November 24, 1975), 865-866.

6017. ________"Letter: The Role of the Pediatrician 'After a Child Dies'," Journal of Pediatrics, 88 (June, 1976), 1065.

6018. ________. "The Grieving Child," Clinical Pediatrics (Philadelphia), 17 (July, 1978), 559-568.

6019. West, J. The Woman Said Yes: Encounters With Life and Death. New York: Janovich, 1976.

6020. West, L.J. "Psychiatric Reflections on the Death Penalty," American Journal of Orthopsychiatry, 45 (July, 1975), 869-700.

6021. West, N.D. "Child's Response to Death Loss," Nebraska Medical Journal, 60 (July, 1975), 228-233.

6022. West, T.S. "Symposium: Care of the Dying: Approach to Death," Nursing Mirror, 139 (October, 1974), 56-59.

6023. Wetli, C.V. "Death Caused by Recreational Cocaine Use," Journal of the American Medical Association, 241 (1979), 2519-2522.

6024. Whipple. D.W. "A Premonitory Association of a Patient About to Die," Psychoanalytic Review, 66 (Spring, 1979), 31-34.

6025. Whisman, S. "Four Distinctive Views of the Dying Patient. (Turn the Respirator Off and Let Danny Die)," RN, 38 (April, 1975), 34-35.

6026. White, E.A. "A Description of Kindergarten Through Fourth Grade Students' Conceptions of Death," Dissertation Abstracts International, 37 (March, 1977), 5721.

6027. ________, et al. "Children's Conceptions of Death," Child Development, 49 (June, 1978), 307-310.

6028. White, R.B., H.T. Engelhardt, Jr. "Case Studies in Bioethics. Case No. 228. A Demand to Die," Hastings Center Report, 5 (June, 1975), 9-10.

6029. Whiter, W. Dissertation of the Disorder of Death: Or That State of the Frame Under the Signs of Death Called Suspended Animation. New York: Arno Press, 1976. (Orig. Pub. 1819)

6030. Whitley, E. "Grandma--She Died," Childhood Education, 53 (November -December, 1976), 77-79.

6031. Whyte, F. The Dance of Death in Spain and Catalonia. New York: Arno Press, 1976. (Orig. Pub. 1931)

6032. Wigglesworth, E.C. "Sudden Infant Cot Death: Accident or Disease," Medical Journal of Australia, 2 (September 4, 1976), 389.

6033. Wilcox, S.G., M. Sutton (eds). Understanding Death and Dying. Sherman Oaks, California: Alfred Publishers, 1977.

6034. Wilkerson, R. Beyond and Back: Those Who Died--And Lived to Tell About It. Anaheim, California: Melodyland Productions, 1977.

6035. Wilkes, E. "Quality of Life: Effects of the Knowledge of Diagnosis in Terminal Illness," Nursing Times, 73 (September, 1977), 1506-1507.

6036. Wilkes, J.R. "Don't Forget the Children," Canadian Medical Association Journal, 115 (September, 1976), 528-529.

6037. Wilkins, L.P. "Wrongful Death of McCord, Willie, or, Beware of Public Parks--Ghosts of Immunity and the Ohio Guest Statute Still Roam," American Journal of Physical Anthropology, 47 (1979), 591-611.

6038. Will, G.F. "A Good Death," Journal of the Indiana State Medical Association, 71 (August, 1978), 734-735.

6039. Williams, A.L. "Sudden Death in Infancy Syndrome Letter," Medical Journal of Australia, 2 (July 31, 1976), 188.

6040. ________. "Cot Death," Australian Journal of Early Childhood," 3 (March, 1978), 32-33.

6041. Williams, J.C. "Understanding the Feelings of the Dying," Nursing (Jenkintown), 6 (March, 1976), 52-56.

6042. Williams, P.C. "Rights and the Alleged Right of Innocents to be Killed," Ethics, 87 (July, 1977), 383-394.

6043. Williams, P.W. When a Loved One Dies. Minneapolis: Augsburg Publishing House, 1976.

6044. Williams, W.D. "Dealing With Death," History and Social Science Teacher, 11 (Winter, 1975), 43-45.

6045. Williams, W.V. et al. "Crisis Intervention: Effects of Crisis Intervention on Family Survivors of Sudden Death Situations," Community Mental Health Journal, 12 (Summer, 1976), 128-136.

6046. Williams, W.V., P.R. Polak. "Follow-up Research in Primary Prevention - Model of Adjustment in Acute Grief," Journal of Clinical Psychology, 35 (1979), 35-45.

6047. Willmer, W.K. "The Implications of a Death in the Family for Student Development," National Association of Student Personnel Administrators Journal, 16 (Fall, 1978), 2-8.

6048. Wilson, D.C. et al. "Models of Care," Death Education, 2 (Spring-Summer, 1978), 3-95.

6049. Wilson, J.L. "Anticipatory Grief in Response to Threatened Amputation," Maternal Child Nursing Journal, 6 (Fall, 1977), 177-186.

6050. Wilson, J.M. "Communicating With the Dying," Journal of Medical Ethics, 1 (April, 1975), 18-22.

6051. Wilson, S.M. et al. "Teaching About Technological Death and Dying and Euthanasia," American Biology Teacher, 41 (1979), 226.

6052. Winget, C. et al. "Attitudes Toward Euthanasia," Journal of Medical Ethics, 3 (March, 1977), 18-25.

6053. Wise, D.J. "Learning About Death," Comprehensive Nursing Quarterly, 10 (August, 1975), 69-74.

6054. Wittkower, E., H. Warner (eds). Psychosomatic Medicine - Its Clinical Applications. New York: Harper & Row, 1977.

6055. Witzel, L. "Behavior of the Dying Patient," British Medical Journal, 2 (April 12, 1975), 81-82.

6056. Wokcik, J. Muted Consent: A Casebook in Modern Medical Ethics. West Lafayette, Indiana: Purdue University, 1978.

6057. Wolfstein, M. Disaster. New York: Arno Press, 1976. (Orig. Publ 1957).

6058. Wolitzer, H. Ending. New York: Macmillan, 1977.

6059. Wood, W.B., A.M.C. Murphy. "Broadbeach Aboriginal Burial Site, Woutheast Queensland - Metrical Features of the Tibiae," Journal of Anatomy, 128 (May, 1979), 663.

6060. Woods, D.J., T. Royder. "Determination of Death: Perspectives from a Psychological Assessment," Psychological Reports, 42 (June, 1978), 851-857.

6061. Woodward, K.L. et al. "Living With Dying," Newsweek, 91 (May 1, 1978), 52-56.

6062. Woolsey, R.M. "Death of the Brain," Missouri Medicine, 74 (September, 1977), 540-543.

6063. Wooton, B. "The Right Way to Die," Sunday Times (London), (March 12, 1978), 16.

6064. Worcester, A. The Care of the Aged, Dying and Dead. New York: Arno Press (Orig. Pub. 1950)

6065. Worden, J.W., W. Proctor. PDA (Personal Death Awareness). Breaking Free of Fear to Live a Better Life Now. New York: Prentice-Hall, 1976.

6066. Worpole, K. "Death in Southall," New Society, 48 (1979), 458-459.

6067. Wren, C.G. "Caring for Others When They Need You Most," Humanist Educator, 17 (March, 1979), 98-102.

6068. Wright, D.G. "Season of Birth and Death in Early and Recent Connecticut," American Journal of Physical Anthropology, 50 (1979), 494.

6069. Wright, H.T. The Matthew Tree. New York: Pantheon Books, 1975.

6070. Wright, I.S. "Guidelines Concerning Euthanasia. Dying Patient," New York State Journal of Medicine, 78 (January, 1978), 61-63.

6071. Wulf, V.C. "Parent Death in Childhood and Later Psychological Adjustment," Dissertation Abstracts International, 37 (June, 1977), 6357-6358.

6072. Wylie, B.J. Beginnings: A Book For Widows. Toronto: McClelland & Stewart, 1977.

6073. Yakulis, I.M. "Changing Concepts of Death in a Child with Sickle Cell Disease," Maternal Child Nursing Journal, 4 (Summer, 1975), 117-120.

6074. Yalom, I.D., C. Greaves. "Group Therapy With the Terminally Ill," American Journal of Psychiatry, 134 (April, 1977), 396-400.

6075. Yamaguchi, N., Y. Miura. "Nursing of a Dying Child Separated from Her Mother and Cared for in a Pediatric Ward," Kango Tenbo, 2 (August, 1977), 15-18.

6076. Yarber, W.L. "Death Education: A Living Issue," Science Teacher, 43 (October, 1976), 21-23.

6077. ________. "'Where's Johnny Today?' Explaining The Death of a Classmate," Health Education, 8 (January-February, 1977), 25-26.

6078. Yates, M. Coping: A Survival Manual For Women Alone. New York: Spectrum/Prentice Hall, 1976.

6079. Yazu, M. "Causes of Death Among Dentists and Their Prevention," Journal of Japan Dental Association, 29 (June, 1976), 281-289.

6080. Young, E.S. "Care of the Dying--A Country Doctor Speaks Out," Journal of the Maine Medical Association, 69 (May, 1978), 144-145.

6081. Young, E.W. "Reflections on Life and Death," in: Garfield, C.A. (ed) Psychosocial Care of the Dying Patient. New York: McGraw Hill, 1978.

6082. Young, J. "A Mother's Grief Work Following the Death of Her Deformed Child," Maternal Child Nursing Journal, 4 (Spring, 1975), 57-62.

6083. Young, R.K. "Chronic Sorrow: Parent's Response to the Birth of a Child With a Defect," Maternal Child Nursing Journal, 2 (January-February, 1977), 38-42

6084. Zahn, M.A., M. Bencivengo. "Violent Death: A Comparison Between Drug Users and Non-Drug Users," Addict Disease, 1 (1974), 283-295.

6085. Zammuner, V.L. "Attitudes Toward Abortion: A Pilot Cross-Cultural Comparison," Ciornale Intaliano Di Psicologia, 3 (April, 1976), 75-116.

6086. Zandee, J. Death as an Enemy According to Ancient Egyptian Conceptions. New York: Arno Press, 1976. (Orig. Pub. 1960).

6087. Zarit, S.H. (ed). Readings in Aging and Death. New York: Harper & Row, 1977.

6088. Zeitlin, S.J. "The Effect of Recent Father Death on Adolescent Identity Formation," Dissertation Abstracts International, 36 (March, 1976), 4716.

6089. Zelizer, V.V. "Human Values and the Market: The Case of Life Insurance and Death in 19th Century America," American Journal of Sociology, 84 (November, 1978), 591-610.

6090. Zim, H.S., S. Bleeker. Life and Death. New York: Morrow, 1970.

6091. Zisook, S., R.A. deVaul. "Grief-Related Facsimile Illness," International Journal of Psychiatry and Medicine, 7 (1976-1977), 329-336.

6092. Zucker, K.W. "Legislaturer Provide For Death With Dignity," Journal of Legal Medicine, 5 (August, 1977), 21-24.

6093. ________. "Premature Infant's Death Leads to Suit," Legal Aspects of Medical Practice, 6 (June, 1978), 13-14.

6094. Zuehlke, T.E., J.T. Watkins. "The Use of Psychotherapy With Dying Patients: An Exploratory Study," Journal of Clinical Psychology, 31 (October, 1975), 729-732.

6095. ________. "Psychotherapy With Terminally Ill Patients," Dissertation Abstracts International, 36 (February, 1976), 4188-4189.

6096. Zung, W.W.K. "Suicide Prevention by Suicide Detection," Psychosomatics, 20 (1979), 1-2.

6097. Zweig, A.R. "Children's Attitudes Toward Death," Dissertation Abstracts International, 37 (January, 1977), 4249-4250.

6098. Zweig, J.P., J.Z. Csank. "Mortality Fluctuations Among Chronically Ill Medical Geriatric Patients as an Indicator of Stress Before and After Relocation," Journal of the American Geriatrics Society, 24 (June, 1976), 264-277.

INDEX

Note: The numbers following each entry correspond to the items as numbered in the bibliography.

References greater than 6098 are cited in the _Addendum_, following the Index.

ADDENDUM

numbers 6099 through 6164

6099. Agatstein, F. "Attitude Change and Death Education: A Consideration of Goals," Death Education, 3 (1980), 323-332.

6100. Ames, R.P. et al. "Mercy Hospice: A Hospital Based Program," Hospital Progress, 60 (March, 1979), 63-67.

6101. Anonymous. "Hospice Leaders Hear Promises of Federal Help and Words of Caution," Hospital Progress, 59 (November, 1978), 20-21.

6102. Atchley, R.C. "Death, Dying, Bereavement and Widowhood," in his: The Social Forces in Later Life (3rd ed). Belmond, California: Wadsworth Publishing, 1980. 198-216.

6103. Ayalon, O. "Community Oriented Preparation for Emergency Care," Death Education, 3 (1979), 227-244.

6104. Barrett, C.J. "The Advantages of Non-Credit Gerontology Courses: Widowhood as an Illustration," Death Education, 3 (1980), 333-345.

6105. Bertman, S.L. "Workshops in Caring: A First Module," Death Education, 3 (1979), 271-281.

6106. Bremer, M.S. ...And Send the Sun Tomorrow. Minneapolis, Minnesota: Winston Publicity, 1979.

6107. Butler, R.N. "The Need for Quality Hospice Care," Death Education, 3 (1979), 215-225.

6108. __________. "A Humanistic Approach to our Last Days," Death Education, 3 (1980), 359-361.

6109. Cairns, N.U., S.B. Lansky. "MMPI Indicators of Stress and Marital Discord Among Parents of Children With Chronic Illness," Death Education, 4 (1980), 29-42.

6110. Carson, U. "A Child Loses a Pet," Death Education, 3 (1980), 399-404.

6111. Chafetz, P.K. "Jewish Practices in Death and Mourning," Death Education, 3 (1980), 363-369.

6112. Dharmaz, K. The Social Reality of Death. Reading, Massachusetts: Addison-Wesley Publishing Company, 1980.

6113. Decker, D.L. "Religion, Death and Dying," in his: Social Gerontology. Boston: Little, Brown & Company, 1980. 248-261.

6114. deVries, A., A. Carmi. The Dying Human. Ramat Gan, Israel: Turtledove Publishers, 1979.

6115. Dyak, M. Dying. Lebanon, New Hampshire: New Victoria Publishers, Inc., 1978.

6116. Feigenberg, L. Terminal Care: Friendship Contracts With Dying Patients. New York: Brunner/Mazel, 1980.

6117. Frigenberg, L., E. Shneidman. "Clinical Thanatology and Psychotherapy: Some Reflections on Caring for the Dying Person," Omega, 10 (1979).

6118. Gadow, S. "Caring for the Dying: Advocacy or Paternalism," Death Education, 3 (1980), 387-390.

6119. Goddard, H.L., D. Leviton. "Intimacy-Sexuality Needs of the Bereaved: An Exploratory Study," Death Education, 3 (1980), 347-358.

6120. Grollman, E.A. When Your Loved One is Dying. Boston: Beacon Press, 1980.

6121. Harrah, B., D. Harrah. Funeral Service: A Bibliography of Literature on Its Past, Present and Future. Metuchen, New Jersey: Scarecrow, 1976.

6122. Harris, A.P. "Content and Method in a Thanatology Training Program for Paraprofessionals," Death Education, 4 (1980), 21-27.

6123. La Grande, L.E. "Reducing Burnout in the Hospice and Death Education Movement," Death Education, 4 (1980), 61-75.

6124. Maicinek, M.A. "The Right to Die: In Support of Passive Euthanasia," Weather Vane, 48 (February, 1979), 15-18.

6125. Manning, D. Disaster Technology: An Annotated Bibliography. New York: Pergamon Press, 1976.

6126. Marshall, V.M. "Socialization for Impending Death in a Retirement Village," in: J.S. Quadagno. Aging, the Individual and Society. New York: St. Martin's Press, 1980. 554-568.

6127. ____________. Last Chapters: A Sociology of Aging and Dying. Belmont, California: Wadsworth Incorporated, 1980.

6128. McAleer, C.A. et al. "Counseling Needs and Approaches for Working With a Cancer Patient," Rehabilitation Bulletin, 21 (March, 1978), 238-245.

6129. McBride, M.M. "Children's Literature on Death and Dying," Pediatric Nurse, 5 (May-June, 1979), 31-33.

6130. Miller, A. M. Acri. Death: A Bibliographic Guide. Meutchen, New Jersey: Scarecrow, 1977.

6131. Miller, M. "A Review of the Research on Geriatric Suicide," Death Education, 3 (1979), 283-296.

6132. Norland, M. et al. "The Systematic Development and Efficacy of a Death Education Unit for Ninth Grade Girls," Death Education, 4 (1980), 283-296.

6133. Pattison, E.M. "Attitudes Toward Death," in: J.S. Quadagno (ed). Aging, the Individual and Society. New York: St. Martin's Press, 1980. 537-568.

6134. Pearson, L. (ed) Death and Dying: Current Issues in the Treatment of the Dying Person. New York: University Press Book Service, 1977.

6135. Pincus, L. Death and the Family (The Importance of Mourning). Jaronto, New York: Random House, 1976.

6136. Polslusny, Mary, et al. (eds). Nursing and Thanatology. Edison, New Jersey: Mss Information Corporation, 1978.

6137. Poteet, G.H. Death and Dying: A Bibliography 1950-1974. Troy, New York: Whitson, 1976.

6138. Priemme, J.A. "Death Education: A Different Approach," Oncology Nursing Forum, 6 (January, 1979), 4.

6139. Redding, R. "Doctors, Dyscommunication and Death," Death Education, 3 (1980), 371-385.

6140. Rigdon, M.A. et al. "The Threat Index: A Research Report," Death Education, 3 (1979), 245-270.

6141. Riley, M.O. Set Your House in Order: A Practical Way to Prepare for Death. Garden City, New Jersey: Doubleday, 1980.

6142. Rodabough, T. "Alternatives to the Stages Model of the Dying Process," Death Education, 4 (1980), 1-19.

6143. Roberts, J. The Afterdeath Journal of an American Philosopher. Englewood Cliffs, New Jersey: Mss Information Corporation, 1978.

6144. Ross, E.K. On Death and Dying. New York: Macmillan Information, 1969.

6145. Ruane, G.P. Birth to Birth: The Life-Death. Staten Island, New York: Alba House, 1976.

6146. Sartin, B. "Continuing Care Unit," Cancer Nursing, 1 (August, 1978), 291-295.

6147. Saunders, C. "Dying They Live: St. Christophers Hospice," in: J.S. Quadagno (ed). Aging, The Individual and Society. New York: St. Martin's Press, 1980. 554-568.

6148. Seagraves, K.L. When You're Dead, You're Dead. San Diego, California: Beta Books Company, 1975.

6149. Shecter, B. Across the Meadow. Garden City, New Jersey: Doubleday, 1973.

6150. Shneidman, E.S. "Some Aspects of Psychotherapy With Dying Persons," in: C.A. Garfield (ed). Psychosocial Aspects of Terminal Patient Care. New York: McGraw Hill, 1978.

6151. ____________. Voices of Death. New York: Harper and Row, 1980.

6152. Spurgeon, C.H. Death. Phillipsburg, New Jersey: Pilgrim Publishing Company, 1978.

6153. Thorson, J.A. "Lifeboat: Social Values and Decision Making," Death Education, 1 (Winter, 1978), 459-464.

6154. Wass, H., B.J. Towry. "Children's Death Concepts and Ethnicity," Death Education, 4 (1980), 83-87.

6155. Wass, H. et al. Death Education: An Annotated Resource Guide. Washington, D.C.: Hemisphere Publishing Company, 1980.

6156. Watson, W.H., R.J. Maxwell. Human Aging and Dying: A Study in Sociocultural Gerontology. New York: St. Martin's Press, 1977.

6157. Wilcox, S.G., M. Sulton. Understanding Death and Dying. Port Washington, New York: Alfred Publishing Company, 1977.

6158. Williamson, J.B. et al (eds). "Dying and Death", in his: Aging and Society. New York: Holt, Reinhart, Winston, 1980. 310-335.

6159. ________. "Grief, Mourning and Widowhood," in his: Aging and Society. New York: Holt, Reinhart & Winston, 1980. 341-359.

6160. ________. "Causes of Death", in his: Aging and Society. New York: Holt, Reinhart & Winston, 1980. 392-406.

6161. ________. "Euthanasia and the Hospice Alternative," in his: Aging and Society. New York: Holt, Reinhart & Winston, 1980. 410-424.

6162. Wilson, D. Terminal Candor. Lititz, Pennsylvania: Sutter House, 1978.

6163. Wright, L.L. After Death What? San Diego, California: Point Loma Productions, 1974.

6164. Zarit, S,H. (ed) Readings in Aging and Death: Contemporary Perspectives. New York: Harper and Row, 1977.

SPECIAL FEATURE

GUIDE TO DOCTORAL DISSERTATIONS ON DEATH AND DYING 1970-1978

by

Joseph C. Santora

Assistant Professor
Essex County College
Newark, New Jersey

I would like to thank Dr. Hannelore Wass, editor, "Death Education" for permission to reprint Dr. Santora's bibliography which originally appeared in Winter and Spring, 1980 issues of the quarterly.

9000. Abraham, Y. Patterns of communication and rejection in families of suicidal adolescents (Doctoral dissertation, The Ohio State University, 1977). _Dissertation Abstracts International_, 1978, 38, 4669A. (University Microfilms No. 77-31, 810)

9001. Amberg, W.F. A cross indexed study of suicidal intervention programs and analysis of current models (Doctoral dissertation, Brigham Young University, 1970). _Dissertation Abstracts International_, 1971, 31, 6887B. (University Microfilms No. 71-12, 102)

9002. Andress, L.R. An epidemiological study of the psycho-social characteristics of suicidal behavior in Riverside County between 1960 and 1974 (Doctoral dissertation, United States International University, 1976). _Dissertation Abstracts International_, 1976, 37, 1481B. (University Microfilms No. 76-20, 945)

9003. Angelica, D.M. A comparative study of attitudes toward and denial of their own death of Episcopal clergymen and laymen in Connecticut (Doctoral dissertation, New York University, 1976). _Dissertation Abstracts International_, 1977, 37, 4661B. (University Microfilms No. 77-5, 284)

9004. Ansel, E.L. Correlates of volunteer performance in a suicide prevention/ crisis intervention service (Doctoral dissertation, The University of Florida, 1972). _Dissertation Abstracts International_, 1973 34, 402B. (Univeristy Microfilms No. 73-15, 561)

9005. Arrowsmith, F.L. Pastoral counseling with the dying and the bereaved (Doctoral dissertation, School of Theology at Claremont, 1975). _Dissertation Abstracts International_, 1975, 36, 2993B. (University Microfilms No. 75-28, 866)

9006. Baider, A.L. Family structure and the process of dying: a study of cancer patients and their family interaction (Doctoral dissertation, Brandeis University, 1973). _Dissertation Abstracts International_, 1973, 34, 421A. (University Microfilms No. 73-15, 427)

9007. Bailey, M.L. Attitudes toward death and dying in nursing students (Doctoral dissertation, University of Houston, 1976). _Dissertation Abstracts International_, 1977, 38, 139B. (University Microfilms No. 77-13, 961)

9008. Baird, C.F. Death fantasy in male and female college students (Doctoral dissertation, Boston University Graduate School, 1972). _Dissertation Abstracts International_, 1972, 33, 1778B. (University Microfilms No. 72-25, 241)

9009. Bangert, S.E. An inservice educational model, contextually designed, to promote attitude and behavior change of medical and health personnel (Doctoral dissertation, University of Pittsburgh, 1976). Dissertation Abstracts International, 1976, 37, 1396A. (University Microfilms No. 76-20, 175)

9010. Barnes, T. Time perception and time orientation as assessment devices of suicide potential (Doctoral dissertation, De Paul University, 1977), Dissertation Abstracts International, 1977, 38, 343-344B (University Microfilms No. 77-13, 719)

9011. Bartman, E.R. Assertive training with hospitalized suicide attempters (Doctoral dissertation, The Catholic University of America, 1976). Dissertation Abstracts International, 1976, 37, 1425B. (University Microfilms No. 76-19, 363)

9012. Bascue, L.O. A study of the relationship of time orientation and time attitude to death anxiety in elderly people (Doctoral dissertation, University of Maryland, 1972). Dissertation Abstracts International, 1972, 34, 866-867B. (University Microfilms No. 73-18, 234)

9013. Beauchamp, N.R. The young child's perception of death (Doctoral dissertation, Purdue University, 1974). Dissertation Abstracts International, 1974, 35, 3288-3289A. (University Microfilms No. 74-26, 684)

9014. Beckman, C.W. Aging: Attitudes of social work students as predicted by selected socio-demographic variables, life and educational experiences (Doctoral dissertation, University of Utah, 1974). Dissertation Abstracts International, 1974, 35, 2395A. (University Microfilms No. 74-21, 099)

9015. Behrens, E.M. The use of the computer averaged visual evoked response as a technique for assessing cerebral death (Doctoral dissertation, University of Utah, 1973). Dissertation Abstracts International, 1974, 34, 3979A. (University Microfilms No. 74-185.

9016. Beineke, J.A. An analysis of attitudes toward death of secondary school students (Doctoral dissertation, Ball State University, 1977). Dissertation Abstracts International, 1978, 38, 6048A. (University Microfilms No. 78-3, 911)

9017. Belanger, R.R. CPI predictors of clinical effectiveness of volunteers in a suicide and crisis intervention service: I. factor measures of stability and extraversion: II. a clinical effectiveness scale (Doctoral dissertation, The University of Florida, 1972). Dissertation Abstracts International, 1973, 33, 3297-3298B. (University Microfilms No. 73-545)

9018. Bell, D. Sex and chronicity as variables affecting attitudes of undergraduates towards peers with suicidal behavior (Doctoral dissertation, University of Georgia, 1977). Dissertation Abstracts International, 1978, 38, 3380B. (University Microfilms No. 77-29, 742)

9019. Bendiksen, R.A. Death and the child: an anterospective test of the childhood bereavement and later behavior disorder hypothesis (Doctoral dissertation, University of Minnesota, 1974). Dissertation Abstracts International, 1975, 35, 5549A. (University Microfilms No. 75-2, 086)

9020. Bloom, M.H. An analysis of responses to the "cry for help" (Doctoral dissertation, University of California, Los Angeles, 1971). Dissertation Abstracts International, 1972, 32, 6042-6043B. (University Microfilms No. 72-11, 876)

9021. Blum, A.H. Children's conception of death and an after-life (Doctoral dissertation, State University of New York at Buffalo, 1975). Dissertation Abstracts International, 1976, 36, 5248B. (University Microfilsm No. 76-9, 9032)

9022. Bohart, J.S. The impact of death and dying counseling groups on death anxiety for college student volunteers (Doctoral dissertation, University of Colorado at Boulder, 1976). Dissertation Abstracts International, 1977, 37, 4853-4854A. (University Microfilms No. 77-3, 167)

9023. Bolduc, J. A developmental study of the relationship between experiences of death and age and development of the concept of death (Doctoral dissertation, Columbia University, 1972). Dissertation Abstracts International, 1972, 33, 2758A. (University Microfilms No. 72-30, 311)

9024. Brace, S.M. A psychological study of the aged in the last stages of terminal illness (Doctoral dissertation, University of California, Berkeley, 1977). Dissertation Abstracts International, 1978, 38, 4671A. (University Microfilms No. 77-31, 298)

9025. Bradshaw, A.D. The social construction of suicide rates (Doctoral dissertation, Syracuse University, 1973). Dissertation Abstracts International, 1974, 34, 6775A. (University Microfilms No. 74-8, 228)

9026. Brown, D.J. The fear of death and the western-protestant ethic personality identity (Doctoral dissertation, The Ohio State University, 1971). Dissertation Abstracts International, 1972, 32, 7302-7303B. (University Microfilms No. 72-15, 179)

9027. Brown, I.R. Attempted suicide: a value-added analysis (Doctoral dissertation, University of Missouri, Columbia, 1976). Dissertation Abstracts International, 1977, 37, 6102-6103A. (University Microfilm No. 77-4, 891)

9028. Brown, T.R. The judgment of suicide lethality: a comparison of judgmental models obtained under contrived versus natural conditions (Doctoral dissertation, University of Oregon, 1970). Dissertation Abstracts International, 1970, 31, 2978B. (University Microfilms No. 70-21, 558)

9029. Buch, L.C. Death scales: a factor analytic study (Doctoral dissertation, Kent State University, 1975). Dissertation Abstracts International, 1976, 36, 6371-6372B. (University Microfilms No. 76-14, 355)

9030. Burrows, A.B. Fear of death and attitudes toward death as a function of religion (Doctoral dissertation, State University of New York at Buffalo, 1971). Dissertation Abstracts International, 1971, 32, 3630B. (University Microfilms No. 72-212)

9031. Cabiles, P. Impulsivity and depression as factors in suicidal males (Doctoral dissertation, Long Island University, The Brooklyn Center, 1976). Dissertation Abstracts International, 1976, 37, 1890-1981B. (University Microfilms No. 76-23, 714)

9032. Callas, M.A. The effect of an experience of death education on death attitudes and concepts and on self perception (Doctoral dissertation, The Catholic University of America, 1976. Dissertation Abstracts International, 1976, 37, 1400B. (University Microfilms No. 76-21,489)

9033. Campagna, J.L. Implementation and evaluation of a suicidal prevention program in Quebec (Doctoral dissertation, California School of Professional Psychology, Los Angeles, 1976). Dissertation Abstracts International, 1977, 37, 4666-4667B. (University Microfilms No. 77-6, 290)

9034. Campbell, J.B. Attitudes towards death: a comparison of associate degree nursing students and graduate nurses (Doctoral dissertation, Florida Atlantic University, 1976). Dissertation Abstracts International, 1976, 37, 1622-1623B. (University Microfilms No. 76-22, 968)

9035. Cantor, P.C. Personality and status characteristics of the female youthful suicide attempter (Doctoral dissertation, Columbia University, 1972). Dissertation Abstracts International, 1976, 37, 452B. (University Microfilms No. 76-15, 532)

9036. Carhart, R.L. Death-angst: a synthesis in developmental perspective (Doctoral dissertation, Northern Illinois University, 1977). Dissertation Abstracts International, 1977, 38, 1885A. (University Microfilms No. 77-20, 868)

9037. Carson, L.G. Zen meditation in the elderly (Doctoral dissertation, University of Nevada, Reno, 1974). Dissertation Abstracts International, 1975, 36, 903-904B. (University Microfilms No. 75-5, 310)

9038. Carson, W.J. Modes of coping with death concern (Doctoral dissertation, University of Missouri-Columbia, 1973). Dissertation Abstracts International, 1974, 35, 815A. (University Microfilms No. 74-18, 489)

9039. Cerny, L.J. Death perspectives and religious orientation as a function of christian faith with specific reference to being "born again" (Doctoral dissertation, Rosemead Graduate School of Psychology, 1977). Dissertation Abstracts International, 1977, 38, 1872B. (University Microfilms No. 77-21, 524.

9040. Claton, E.M. Changes in the level of depression and self-concept of suicidal clients following nursing intervention in a small group setting (Doctoral dissertation, The Catholic University of America, 1975). Dissertation Abstracts International, 1976, 36, 4942-4943B. (University Microfilms No. 76-8, 944)

9041. Cogwell, V. Responding to suicidal communications (Doctoral dissertation, Duke University, 1974). Dissertation Abstracts International, 1974, 35, 1043B. (University Microfilms No . 74-16, 584.

9042. Collette, C.L. Attitudinal predictors of devaluation of old age in a young, middle aged, and older adult sample (Doctoral dissertation, University of Oregon, 1974). Dissertation Abstracts International, 1975, 35, 4252B. (University Microfilms No. 75-3, 867.

9043. Coyne, A.B. A conceptual framework for death education for nurses (Doctoral dissertation, University of Pittsburgh, 1977). Dissertation Abstracts International, 1977, 38, 1916A. (University Microfilms No. 77-21, 215.

9044. Cox, G.R. An analysis of factors influencing attitudes toward death (Doctoral dissertation, Ball State University, 1975). Dissertation Abstracts International, 1976, 37, 638A. (University Microfilms No. 76-15, 185).

9045. Curran, M.C. Personality in relation to attitudes toward prolonging life (Doctoral dissertation, The University of Nebraska-Lincoln, 1976). Dissertation Abstracts International, 1976, 37, 2568B. (University Microfilms No. 76-25, 864)

9046. Davis, T.M. The effect of the death education film 'in my memory' on elementary school students in the La Crosse, Wisconsin public schools (Doctoral dissertation, Indiana University, 1975). Dissertation Abstracts International, 1976, 36, 7945-7946A. (University Microfilms No. 76-13, 758)

9047. Diamond, H. Suicide by women professionals (Doctoral dissertation, California School of Professional Psychology, Los Angeles, 1977). Dissertation Abstracts International, 1978, 38, 5009-5010B. (University Microfilms No. 78-2, 823)

9048. Duke, E.H. Meaning in life and acceptance in terminally ill patients (Doctoral dissertation, Northwestern University, 1977). Dissertation Abstracts International, 1978, 38, 3874-3875B. (University Microfilms No. 77-32, 297)

9049. Dunten, D.D. A study of wrist cutting (Doctoral dissertation, The University of Tennessee, 1977). Dissertation Abstracts International, 1977, 38, 893B. (University Microfilms No. 77-16, 580)

9050. Durham, T. A Probability approach to the assessment of suicidal risk among mental hospital patients (Doctoral dissertation, The Florida State University, 1977). Dissertation Abstracts International, 1978, 38, 3875B. (University Microfilms No. 77-31, 028)

9051. Elenewski, J.J. A study of insomnia: the relationship of psychopathology to sleep disturbance (Doctoral dissertation, University of Miami, 1971). Dissertation Abstracts International, 1971, 32, 3631-3632B. (University Microfilms No. 72-2, 176)

9052. Elliott, T.B. Conceptual styles of suicidal psychiatric patients (Doctoral dissertation, University of Missouri-Columbia, 1972). Dissertation Abstracts International, 1973, 34, 1273-1274B. (University Microfilms No. 73-21, 413)

9053. Epstein, G.M. Evaluating the bereavement process as it is affected by variation in the time of intervention (Doctoral dissertation, George Peabody College for Teachers, 1977). Dissertation Abstracts International, 1977, 38, 2362B. (University Microfilms No. 77-25, 096)

9054. Erp, S.H. A study of reactions to the film 'confrontation of death' (Doctoral dissertation, University of Oregon, 1973). Dissertation Abstracts International, 1973, 34, 1075-1076A. (University Microfilms No. 73-20, 201)

9055. Evans, J.C. Impact of theological orientation on pastors' grief work therapy with grieving church members (Doctoral dissertation, California School of Professional Psychology, San Francisco, 1975). Dissertation Abstracts International, 1975, 36, 3032-3033B. (University Microfilms No. 75-26, 134)

9056. Fairchild, D.J. Student nurses' avoidance of dying patients: death anxiety versus statement emotionality (Doctoral dissertation, University of Miami, 1977). Dissertation Abstracts International, 1978, 38, 3391B. (University Microfilms No. 77-28, 933)

9057. Fallon, M.T. Fear of death in young adolescents: a study of the relationship between fear of death and selected anxiety, personality, and intelligence variables (Doctoral dissertation, University of Notre Dame, 1976). Dissertation Abstracts International, 1976, 36, 5941-5942A. (University Microfilms No. 76-6, 624)

9058. Farley, G.A. An investigation of death anxiety and the sense of competence (Docotral dissertation, Duke University, 1970). Dissertation Abstracts International, 1971, 31, 7595B. (University Microfilms No. 71-10, 371)

9059. Ferguson, C.G. Social factors in suicidal behavior (Doctoral dissertation, Boston University Graduate School, 1975). Dissertation Abstracts International, 1975, 36, 1825-1826A. (University Microfilms No. 75-20, 988)

9060. Fink, R.M. Death as conceptualized by adolescents (Doctoral dissertation, University of Maryland, 1976). Dissertation Abstracts International, 1976, 37, 3046B. (University Microfilms No. 76-27, 380.

9061. Fisher, S.A. Suicide prevention and/or crises services: a national survey (Doctoral dissertation, Case Western Reserve University, 1972). Dissertation Abstracts International, 1973, 33, 1835A. (University Microfilms No. 72-26, 153)

9062. Fleming, S.J. Nurses' death anxiety and clinical geriatric training (Docotral dissertation, York University (Canada), 1974). Dissertation Abstracts International, 1976, 36, 5254B. (University Microfilms No. N/A)

9063. Fortier, M.K. Dreams and preparation for death (Doctoral dissertation, California School of Professional Psychology, San Francisco, 1972). Dissertation Abstracts International, 1973, 33, 3300-3301B. (University Microfilms No. 73-988)

9064. Fox, R.A. Guidelines for the cognitive domain of education for death and dying for criminal justice majors at John Jay College of Criminal Justice (Doctoral dissertation, Columbia Univesity Teachers College, 1976). Dissertation Abstracts International, 1977, 37, 5619A. (University Microfilms No. 77-4, 185)

9065. Francis, C.R. Adolescent suicide attempts, experienced rejection and personal constructs (Doctoral dissertation, California School of Professional Psychology, San Diego, 1976). Dissertation Abstracts International, 1978, 38, 4453B. (University Microfilms No. 77-32, 474)

9066. Furlong, P.T. Psychological assessment of potentially suicidal patients at community mental health center, Salt Lake City, Utah (Doctoral dissertation, University of Utah, 1970). Dissertation Abstracts Internaitonal, 1971, 31, 6899-6900B. (University Microfilms No. 71-3, 012)

9067. Furth, G.M. Impromptu painting by terminally ill, hospitalized and healthy children: what can we learn from them (Doctoral dissertation, The Ohio State University, 1973). Dissertation Abstracts International, 1974, 34, 4739-4740A. (University Microfilms No. 74-3, 170)

9068. Goff, J.R. Death anxiety, violence, and psychopathology (Doctoral dissertation, Memphis State University, 1976). Dissertation Abstracts International, 1976, 37, 3073B. (University Microfilms No. 76-29, 245)

9069. Galbaugh, J.J. A study of relationships between personality categories and death concern in a selected group of nurses (Doctoral dissertation, The University of Tennessee, 1975). Dissertation Abstracts International, 1976, 36, 5069A. (University Microfilms No. 76-1, 941)

9070. Gallager, J.T. The impact of community mental health programs in Southwestern Michigan on social indicators: a demonstration and evaluation of the time series method (Doctoral dissertation, Western Michigan University, 1976). Dissertation Abstracts International, 1977, 37, 4677B. (University Microfilms No. 76-28, 430)

9071. Gamble, J.W. The relationship of self-actualization and authenticity to the experience of mortality (Docotral dissertation, Georgia State University-School of Arts & Science, 1974). Dissertation Abstracts International, 1975, 35, 3578B. (University Microfilms No. 74-29, 536)

9072. Geller, A.M. Cognitive and personality factors in suicidal behavior (Doctoral dissertation, Yeshiva University, 1976). Dissertation Abstracts International, 1977, 37, 4678-4579B. (University Microfilms No. 77-5, 004)

9073. Gibson, G.S. The relationship between certain problem areas and suicidal thoughts of adolescents (Doctoral dissertation, George Peabody College for Teachers, 1974). Dissertation Abstracts International, 1975, 35, 6511-6512A. (Univeristy Microfilms No. 74-29, 170)

9074. Glick, M.A. The will to live, the will to die: an existential analysis of self-destruction (Doctoral dissertation, East Texas State University, 1974). Dissertation Abstracts International, 1975, 35, 4156-4157A. (University Microfilms No. 75-1, 581)

9075. Goldsmith, L. Adaptive regression, humor, and suicide (Doctoral dissertation, The City University of New York, 1973). Dissertation Abstracts International, 1973, 34, 1275-1276B. (University Microfilms No. 73-21, 907)

9076. Gortmaker, S.L. Stratification, Health care, and infant mortality in the United States (Doctoral dissertation, The Univesity of Wisconsin, Madision, 1977). Dissertation Abstracts International, 1977, 38, 3765A. (University Microfilms No. 77-17, 829)

9077. Grady, F.P. A case study approach to the Kubler-Ross theory of the five stages of dying (Doctoral dissertation, University of Northern Colorado, 1976). Dissertation Abstracts International, 1977, 37, 3579-3580B. (University Microfilms No. 76-29, 748)

9078. Greth, D.L. Anomie, suicidal ideation and student ecology in a college population (Doctoral dissertation, The Ohio State University, 1972). Dissertation Abstracts International, 1973, 33, 3305B. (University Microfilms No. 72-27, 015)

9079. Gullo, S.V. A study of selected psychological, psychosomatic, and somatic reactions in women anticipating the death of a husband (Doctoral dissertation, Columbia University, 1974). Dissertation Abstracts International, 1975, 35, 5113-5114B. (University Microfilms No. 75-9, 285)

9080. Handal, P.J. Individual and group problem solving and type of orientation as a function repression-sensitization of death anxiety (Doctoral dissertation, St. Louis University, 1970). Dissertation Abstracts International, 1970, 31, 2986B. (University Microfilms No. 70-20, 394)

9081. Hamera, E.K. Positive and negative effects of life threatening illness (Doctoral dissertation, University of Kansas, 1977). Dissertation Abstracts International, 1978, 38, 3469-3470B. (University Microfilms No. 77-28, 874)

9082. Hansen, Y. Development of the concept of death: cognitive aspects (Doctoral dissertation, California School of Professional Psychology, Los Angeles, 1972). Dissertation Abstracts International, 1973, 34, 853B. (University Microfilms No. 73-19, 640)

9083. Hardt, D.V. Development of an investigating instrument to measure attitudes toward death (Doctoral dissertation, Southern Illinois University, 1974). Dissertation Abstracts International, 1975, 36, 646-647B. (University Microfilms No. 75-16, 268)

9084. Hartman, J.H. Community unemployment conditions in relation to four psycho-social indices: mental hospitalization, suicides, homicides, and motor vehicle accidents (Doctoral dissertation, The Florida State University, 1976). Dissertation Abstracts International, 1976, 37, 3076B. (University Microfilms No. 76-28, 616)

9085. Harlow, J.L. The relationship between nurse behavior and attitudes toward terminal patients and nurse exposure to three desensitization experimental conditions (Doctoral dissertation, The Florida State University, 1976). Dissertation Abstracts International, 1976, 37, 3518-3519A. (University Microfilms No. 76-28, 614)

9086. Haun, D.L. Perceptions of the bereaved, clergy, and funeral directors concerning bereavement (Doctoral dissertation, Oklahoma State University, 1976). Dissertation Abstracts International, 1977, 37, 6791A. (University Microfilms No. 77-5, 091)

9087. Hawener, R.M. Teaching about death: an exploration study of teacher candidates' attitudes toward death and behavior in situations involving death (Doctoral dissertation, The University of Texas at Austin, 1974). Dissertation Abstracts International, 1974, 35, 167-168A. (University Microfilms No. 74-14, 705)

9088. Haws, B.F. A study of personality characteristics of students having a suicidal history with other groups (Doctoral dissertation, Brigham Young University, 1972). Dissertation Abstracts International, 1972, 33, 2103A. (University Microfilms No. 72-28, 929)

9089. Hays, D.R. Perceived needs for support of women who participate in a red cross widows program (Doctoral dissertation, Columbia University Teachers College, 1977). Dissertation Abstracts International, 1978, 38, 3129B. (University Microfilms No. 77-27, 887)

9090. Henderson, J.T. Competence, Threat, Hope and self-destruction behavior: suicide (Doctoral dissertation, University of Maryland, 1972). Dissertation Abstracts International, 1972, 33, 439B. (University Microfilms No. 72-20, 493)

9091. Hineman, J.H. Counseling with the terminally ill: a clinical study (Doctoral dissertation, University of Utah, 1971). Dissertation Abstracts International, 1971, 32, 3091A. (University Microfilms No. 71-31, 123)

9092. Hoblit, P.R. An investigation of changes in anxiety level following consideration of death in four groups (Doctoral dissertation, The Louisiana State University and Agricultural and Mechanical College, 1972). Dissertation Abstracts International, 1972, 2346B. (University Microfilms No. 72-28, 353)

9093. Hoey, H.P. The interpersonal behavior of suicidal individuals (Doctoral dissertation, Ohio University, 1970). Dissertation Abstracts International, 1971, 31, 7598B. (University Microfilms No. 71-14, 497.

9094. Holmes, C. An ethnographic look at black upward mobility as it relates to internalization factors in the increase of black suicide (Doctoral dissertation, California School of Professional Psychology, Los Angeles, 1976). Dissertation Abstracts International, 1977, 38, 902B. (University Microfilms No. 77-17, 177)

9095. Howard, M.S. The effectiveness of an action training model (using role playing, doubling, and role reversal) in improving the facilitative interpersonal function (empathy, respect, and genuineness) of nursing students with dying patients (Doctoral dissertation, University of Maryland, 1975). Dissertation Abstracts International, 1975, 36, 3005-3006B. (University Microfilms No. 75-28, 744)

9096. Howell, W. Attitudes toward death and toward the future in aged and young adults (Doctoral dissertation, Michigan State University, 1976). Dissertation Abstracts International, 1977, 37, 4685B. (University Microfilms No. 77-5, 824)

9097. Hughes, J.H. Attitudes toward life and death as affected by confrontation with death, the environment, and personal locus of control (Doctoral dissertation, The Catholic University of America, 1976). Dissertation Abstracts International, 1976, 37, 1036-1037B. (Univeristy Microfilms No. 76-18, 300)

9098. Humphrey, J.A. Homicide, suicide, and role relationships in New Hampshire (Doctoral dissertation, University of New Hampshire, 1973). Dissertation Abstracts International, 1973, 34, 2789-2790A. (Univeristy Microfilms No. 73-25, 783)

9099. Hurley, B.A. Problems of interaction between nurses and dying patients (Doctoral dissertation, University of Washington, 1974). Dissertation Abstracts International, 1975, 36, 3123B. (University Microfilms No. 75-28, 367)

9100. Hynes, J.J. An exploratory study of the affective future time perspective of adolescent suicide attempters: its characteristics, relationship to clinical identification and lethality, and its implicaitons for postvention (Doctoral dissertation, The Catholic University of America, 1976). Dissertation Abstracts International, 1976, 37, 1404-1405A. (University Microfilms No. 76-19, 973)

9101. Jacobson, H.M. An investigation of the relationship between risk taking characteristics, belief in internal-external control, emotional reactivity, and the lethality of the suicide plan in women who have attempted suicide (Doctoral dissertation, New York University, 1973. Dissertation Abstracts Internaitonal, 1973, 34, 2738-2739B. (University Microfilms No. 73-30, 077)

9102. Jennings, B.A. Fear of death in relation to psychopathology, religiosity, and demographic variables in a psychiatric population (Doctoral dissertation, University of Southern Mississippi, 1976). Dissertation Abstracts International, 1976, 37, 1904B. (University Microfilms No. 76-23,01 2.

9103. Johnson, R.F. The effects of encounter groups on selected age related variables in a volunteer geriatric population (Doctoral dissertation, University of Miami, 1970). Dissertation Abstracts International, 1971, 32, 739A. (University Microfilms No. 71-19, 869)

9104. Johnston, L.C. Terminal illness: a psychosocial approach to the experience (Doctoral dissertation, Boston University Graduate School, 1976). Dissertation Abstracts International, 1976, 36, 4163-4164B. (University Microfilms No. 76-2, 377)

9105. Kaller, D.M. An evaluation of self-instructional program designed to reduce anxiety and fear about death and of the relation of that program to sixteen personal history variables (Doctoral dissertation, Memphis State University, 1974). Dissertation Abstracts International, 1975, 35, 7125-7126A. (University Microfilms No. 75-10, 064)

9106. Kane, B. Children's concepts of death (Doctoral dissertation, University of Cincinnati, 1975). Dissertation Abstracts International, 1975, 36, 782A. (University Microfilms No. 75-16, 803)

9107. Kaplan, D.G. The relationship of death concern and ego strength, security-insecurity, and repression-sensitization (Doctoral dissertation, Southern Illinois University, 1976). Dissertation Abstracts International, 1977, 37, 4686B. (University Microfilms No. 77-6, 230)

9108. Karcher, C.J. Normative integration and self-destruction: an examination of the industrial setting (Doctoral dissertation, University of Georgia, 1977). Dissertation Abstracts International, 1978, 38, 4384A. (University Microfilms No. 77-29, 772)

9109. Kelly, P.W. Preparing nursing students to interact with terminal patients (Doctoral dissertation, Fuller theological Seminary, Graudate School of Psychology, 1972). Dissertation Abstracts International, 1973, 33, 3945B. (University Microfilms No. 72-31, 655)

9110. Kendra, J.M. Predicting suicide from the Rorschach inkblot test: a multiple discriminant analysis approach (Doctoral dissertation, Temple University, 1974). Dissertation Abstracts International, 1975, 36, 3049B. (University Microfilms No. 75-28, 179)

9111. Kinsinger, J.R. The relationship between lethality of suicidal intentions and assertive, aggressive, and hostile traits (Doctoral dissertation, The University of Texas, Southern Medical School, Dallas, 1971). Dissertation Abstracts International, 1971, 31, 7600B. (University Microfilms No. 71-16, 177)

9112. Kilpatrick, D.C. Tendencies toward suicide among college students (Doctoral dissertation, University of Illinois at Urbana-Champaign, 1976). Dissertation Abstracts International, 1976, 2160B. (University Microfilms No. 76-24, 114)

9113. Kirk, A.R. Socio-psychological factors in attempted suicide among urban black males (Doctoral dissertation, Michigan State University, 1976). Dissertation Abstracts International, 1977, 37, 4757B. (University Microfilms No. 77-5, 839)

9114. Kochansky, G.E. Risk-taking and hedonic mood stimulation in suicide attempters (Doctoral dissertation, Boston University Graduate School, 1970). Dissertation Abstracts International, 1970, 31, 3709B. (University Microfilms No. 70-22, 395)

9115. Koocher, G.P. Childhood, death, and cognitive development (Doctoral dissertation, University of Missouri-Columbia, 1972). Dissertation Abstracts International, 1973, 33, 4512B. (University Microfilms No. 73-7, 050)

9116. Korella, K. Teen-age suicide gestures: a study of suicidal behavior among high school students (Doctoral dissertation, University of Oregon, 1971). Dissertation Abstracts International, 1972, 32, 5039A. (University Microfilms No. 72-8, 561)

9117. Kovach-Shand, N. Psycho-cultural integration: a cross-cultural study of continuities in artistic expression, contact modalities throughout the life cycle and institutionalized responses to death (Doctoral dissertation, University of Kansas, 1972). Dissertation Abstracts International, 1973, 33, 5106-5107B. (University Microfilms No. 73-11, 907)

9118. Krieger, S.R. Death orientation and the specialty choice and training of physicians (Doctoral dissertation, The University of Florida, 1975) Dissertation Abstracts International, 1977, 37, 3616B. (University Microfilms No. 77-95)

9119. Kurlychek, R.T. The evaluation and comparison of the effects of two methods of death education on participants' attidudes toward life and death (Doctoral dissertation, University of Oregon, 1977). Dissertation Abstracts International, 1978, 38, 3368B. (Univeristy Microfilms No. 77-26, 501)

9120. Langer, L. The fear of death: an exploratory study (Doctoral dissertation, Michigan State University, 1975). Dissertation Abstracts International, 1976, 36, 4694-4695B. (University Microfilms No. 76-5, 593)

9121. Lee, J.M. The nurse and the terminally ill patients: an experimental study (Doctoral dissertation, Texas Tech University, 1972). Dissertation Abstracts International, 1973, 33, 3948-3949B. (University Microfilms No. 73-4, 049)

9122. Lemerond, J.N. Suicide prediction for psychiatric: a comparison of the mmpi and clinical judgments (Doctoral dissertation, Marquette University, 1977). Dissertation Abstracts International, 1978, 38, 5926-5927A. (University Microfilms No. 78-1, 922)

9123. Leming, M.R. The relationship between religiosity and the fear of death (Doctoral dissertation, University of Utah, 1975). Dissertation Abstracts International, 1976, 36, 7674A. (University Microfilms No. 76-11, 304)

9124. Leshem, A., Y. Leshem. Attitudes of college students toward men and women who commit suicidal acts (Doctoral dissertation, University of Northern Colorado, 1976). Dissertation Abstracts International, 1977, 37, 7042A. (University Microfilms No. 77-11, 070)

9125. Levenson, M. Cognitive and perceptual factors in suicidal individuals (Doctoral dissertation, University of Kansas, 1972). Dissertation Abstracts International, 1973, 33, 5521B. (University Microfilms No. 76-11, 914)

9126. Levy, M.D. Psychological factors affecting the treatment and hospitalization of chronically ill children (Doctoral dissertation, California School of Professional Psychology, Los Angeles, 1975). Dissertation Abstracts International, 1976, 36, 5802-5803B. (University Microfilms No. 76-10, 424)

9127. Lewis, G.W. Differences in concerns about death and dying in medical and law students at different levels of training (Doctoral dissertation, The George Washington University, 1977). Dissertation Abstracts International, 1977, 38, 2372-2373B. (University Microfilms No. 77-23, 821)

9128. Lewis, R.L. The effects of type of death and preparation time on bereavement (Doctoral dissertation, St. Louis University, 1977). Dissertation Abstracts International, 1978, 38, 4466-4467B. (University Microfilms No. 77-23, 821)

9129. Lindenberg, S.P. The effects of an existential-type of group psychotherapy on a time-limited group of members for whom the imminence of death is a pressing reality (Doctoral dissertation, University of Georgia, 1977). Dissertation Abstracts International, 1978, 38, 3404B. (University Microfilms No. 77-29, 782)

9130. Linehan, M. Sex differences in suicide and attempted suicides: a study of differential social acceptability and expectations (Doctoral dissertation, Loyola University of Chicago, 1971). Dissertation Abstracts International, 1971, 3036B. (University Microfilms No. 71-28, 130)

9131. Lucas, R.A. A comparative study of measures of general anxiety: and death anxiety among three medical groups including patient and wife (Doctoral dissertation, University of North Carolina at Chapel Hill, 1972). Dissertation Abstracts International, 1972, 1290B. (University Microfilms No. 72-24, 815)

9132. Lynch, J.H. The contexts of death imagery: an investigation of suggested categorical distinctions among twenty death-associated images (Doctoral dissertation, University of Oregon, 1976). Dissertation Abstracts International, 1976, 37, 3049B. (University Microfilms No. 76-27, 661)

9133. Lynch, S.N. A study of role strain in nurses working with dying patients (Doctoral dissertation, Case Western Reserve University, 1977). Dissertation Abstracts International, 1978, 38, 3894B. (University Microfilms No. 77-31, 001)

9134. McCarthy, J.B. Death anxiety, intrinsicness of religion and purpose of life among nuns and roman catholic female undergraduates (Doctoral dissertation, St. John's University, 1973). Dissertation Abstracts International, 1975, 35, 5646B. (University Microfilms No. 75-3259)

9135. McCarthy, M.L. Life issues and group psychotherapy with terminal cancer patients (Doctoral dissertation, California School of Professional Psychology, San Francisco, 1975). Dissertation Abstracts International, 1976, 36, 3615-3616B. (University Microfilms No. 76-383)

9136. McCorkle, M.R. Human attachments and intended goals during terminal illness (Doctoral dissertation, The University of Iowa, 1975). Dissertation Abstracts International, 1976, 36, 3866-3867B. (University Microfilms No. 76-2150)

9137. McDonough, J.L. A descriptive study of the insitutional adjustment of adult male prisoners in Minnesota (1959-1974) (Doctoral dissertation, University of Minnesota, 1974). Dissertation Abstracts International, 1975, 36, 3055-3056B. (University Microfilms No. 75-27, 175)

9138. McGurn, W.M. The will to live, the will to die: correlates of disengagement in hospitalized cancer patients (Doctoral dissertation, University of Pennsylvania, 1976). Dissertation Abstracts International, 1977, 37, 4648A. (University Microfilms No. 77-860)

9139. Malcolm, T.J. The effects of ease of denial on perceiving and adapting to ideas about personal death (Doctoral dissertation, Fuller Theological Seminary Graduate School of Psychology, 1972). Dissertation ABstracts International, 1973, 33, 3351B. (University Microfilms No. 72-31, 652)

9140. Mackinnon, D. Suicide, the community, and the coroners' office: an exploration in reliability and validity (Doctoral dissertation, University of Southern California, 1977). Dissertation Abstracts International, 1978, 38, 6340A. (University Microfilms No. N/A)

9141. Marshall, V.W. Continued living and dying as problematic aspects of old age (Doctoral dissertation, Princeton University, 1973). *Dissertation Abstracts International*, 1973, 34, 873-874A. (University Microfilms No. 73-18, 768)

9142. Martocchio, B.C. The social processes surrounding the dying patient (Doctoral dissertation, Case Western Reserve University, 1975). *Dissertation Abstracts International*, 1976, 37, 1239A. (University Microfilms No. 76-16, 005)

9143. Marty, H.H. The effect of micro-training sessions on the attiude and behavior of freshman student nurses toward the terminally ill (Doctoral dissertation, University of South Dakota, 1973). *Dissertation Abstracts International*, 1973, 34, 2306-2307A. (University Microfilms No. 73-27, 533)

9144. Mednick, R.A. Content and frequency of sexual fantasy as a function of the frequency and content of death fantasy and death anxiety (Doctoral dissertation, United States International University, 1975). *Dissertation Abstracts International*, 1975, 36, 1924-1925B. (University Microfilms No. 75-22, 655)

9145. Michaels, F. The effects of discussing grief, loss, death, and dying on depression levels in a geriatric outpatient therapy group (Doctoral dissertation, Auburn University, 1977). *Dissertation Abstracts International*, 1977, 38, 910B. (University Microfilms No. 77-16, 828)

9146. Miles, M.S. The effects of a small group education/counseling experience on the attitudes of nurses toward dying patients (Doctoral dissertation, University of Missouri, Kansas City, 1976). *Dissertation Abstracts International*, 1977, 38, 636A. (University Microfilms No. 77-16, 872)

9147. Miller, J.M. The effects of aggressive stimulation upon young adults who have experienced death of a parent during childhood and adolescence (Doctoral dissertation, New York University, 1973). *Dissertation Abstracts International*, 1974, 35, 1055-1056B. (University Microfilms No. 74-16, 847)

9148. Miller, M. Suicide among older men (Doctoral dissertation, The University of Michigan, 1976). *Dissertation Abstracts International*, 1976, 37, 3156B. (University Microfilms No. 76-27, 546)

9149. Moriarty, J.J. Death anxiety in hysteric and obsessive personalities (Doctoral dissertation, University of Detroit, 1974). Dissertation Abstracts International, 1976, 36, 4169B. (University Microfilms No. 75-15, 807)

9150. Morrison, R.H. The effect of terminal illness and fantasy of terminal illness on social self-concept (Doctoral dissertation, University of Maine, 1975). Dissertation Abstracts International, 1975, 36, 1447B. (University Microfilms No. 75-20, 269)

9151. Moses, M. Considering death and dying: affective correlates (Doctoral dissertation, State University of New York at Buffalo, 1973). Dissertation Abstracts International, 1973, 34, 877-878B. (University Microfilms No. 73-19, 221)

9152. Motanky, C.S. The role of acting-out and identification in adolescent suicidal behavior (Doctoral dissertation, Illinois Institute of Technology, 1970). Dissertation Abstracts International, 1971, 31, 7606B. (University Microfilms No. 71-14, 051)

9153. Mueller, M.L. Reducing the fear of death in early adolescents through religious education (Doctoral dissertation, University of Notre Dame, 1975). Dissertation Abstracts International, 1975, 36, 1408A. (University Microfilms No. 75-19, 945)

9154. Mullaly, R.W. Death-dying fears and psycho-pathology in psychiatric patients (Doctoral dissertation, The University of Tennessee, 1975). Dissertation Abstracts International, 1975, 36, 1448-1449B. (University Microfilms No. 75-18, 977)

9155. Nelson, J.R. A retrospective survey of survivors of 100 cancer deaths in south central Connecticut, 1975: with special reference to the impact of health care services on the survivor and patient (Doctoral dissertation, New York University, 1977). Dissertation Abstracts International, 1977, 38, 1642-1643B. (University Microfilms No. 77-21, 306)

9156. Nichol, D.S. Factors affecting the negativity of attitudes toward suicide (Doctoral dissertation, York University (Canada), 1973). Dissertation Abstracts International, 1976, 36, 5235-5236B. (University Microfilms No. N/A)

9157. Nightingale, J.A. The relationship of jugian type to death concern and time perspective (Doctoral dissertation, University of South Carolina, 1972). Dissertation Abstracts International, 1973, 33, 3956B. (University Microfilms No. 73-3, 609)

9158. Norman, S.M. Attitudes of students in selected Alabama junior colleges related to death and dying (Doctoral dissertation, University of Alabama, 1977). Dissertation Abstracts International, 1977, 38, 3305A. (University Microfilms No. 77-25, 875)

9159. Odell, J.L. The psychodynamics observed in a stratified-cultural study of death: a phenomenological approach (Doctoral dissertation, United States International University, 1975). Dissertation Abstracts International, 1975, 35, 5623B. (University Mciro-films No. 75-10, 080)

9160. Parkin, J.M. Assignment of responsibility for deaths perceived as unintentioned, subintentioned, or intentioned (Doctoral dissertation, Purdue University, 1971). Dissertation Abstracts International, 1972, 32, 4867B. (University Microfilms No. 72-8, 007)

9161. Parry, S.M. The fear of death and responses to others' concerns about death (Doctoral dissertation, Michigan State University, 1977). Dissertation Abstracts International, 1977, 38, 1306-1307A. (University Microfilms No. 77-18, 531)

9162. Patterson, J.E. Suicide lethality form: a guide to determining the potential lethality of university students' suicide threats (Doctoral dissertation, Kent State University, 1974). Dissertation Abstracts International, 1975, 35, 6465-6466A. (University Microfilms No. 75-7, 463)

9163. Pearson, N.S. Identification of psychological variables distinguishing suicide-attempters from non-suicide-attempters within a sample of depressive individuals (Doctoral dissertation, Rutgers University, The State University of New Jersey, 1972). Dissertation Abstracts International, 1972, 33, 1803B. (University Microfilms No. 72-27, 582)

9164. Peck, D.L. Social integration, goal commitment, and fatalistic suicide (Doctoral dissertation, Washington State University, 1976). Dissertation Abstracts International, 1977, 37, 5394A. (University Microfilms No. 77-2, 877)

9165. Pepitone-Rockwell, F.M. Death anxiety of psychologists, psychiatrists, funeral directors, and suicidologists (Doctoral dissertation, California School of Professional Psychology, San Francisco, 1974). Dissertation Abstracts International, 1974, 35, 3030B. (University Microfilms No. 74-26, 957)

9166. Perlman, B. Suicide taxonomy and behavior: an interpersonal perspective (Doctroal dissertation, Michigan State University, 1974). Dissertation Abstracts International, 1975, 35, 4660B. (University Microfilms No. 75-7, 232)

9167. Polderman, R.L. An experimental strategy to reduce death anxiety (Doctoral dissertation, The University of North Carolina at Chapel Hill, 1976). Dissertation Abstracts International, 1977, 37, 4161-4162B. (University Microfilms No. 77-2, 083)

9168. Pomerance, R.N. Sibling loss in young adult women: a retrospective study (Doctoral dissertation, Boston University Graduate School, 1973). Dissertation Abstracts Iternational 1973, 34, 1757B. (University Microfilms No. 73-23, 509)

9169. Pratt, E.W. A death education laboratory as a medium for influencing feelings toward death (Doctoral dissertation, United States International University, 1974). Dissertation Abstracts International, 1974, 34, 4026B. (University Microfilms No. 74-1115)

9170. Pratt, L.L. American attitudes toward violent and nonviolent death as reflected in death symbols in still visual media: An exploratory study (Doctoral dissertation, California School of Professional Psychology, San Francisco, 1977). Dissertation Abstracts International, 1977, 38, 2945B. (University Microfilms No. 77-27, 607)

9171. Praul, E.J. The role of college counselor with regard to the problem of suicide among students: an exploratory study (Doctoral dissertation, The University of Toledo, 1971). Dissertation Abstracts International, 1972, 32, 6136-6137A.

9172. Rawnsley, M.M. Relationship between the perception of the speed of time and the process of dying: an empirical investigation of the holistic theory of nursing proposed by Marta Rogers (Doctoral dissertation, Boston University School of Nursing, 1977). Dissertation Abstracts International, 1977, 38, 1652B. (University Microfilms No. 77-21, 692)

9173. Redick, R.J. Behavioral group counseling and death anxiety in student nurses (Doctoral dissertation, University of Pittsburgh, 1974). Dissertation Abstracts International, 1974, 35, 1989A. (University Microfilms No. 74-20, 809)

9174. Reinhart, G.R. Social structure and self-destructive behavior (Doctoral dissertation, University of Georgia, 1977). Dissertation Abstracts International, 1978, 38, 4390A. (University Microfilms No. 77-29, 799)

9175. Reubin, R.H. A study of the factors involved in the decision to treat suicidal clients (Doctoral dissertation, University of California, Los Angeles, 1973). Dissertation Abstracts International, 1973, 34, 296-297B. (University Microfilms No. 73-16, 096)

9176. Richards, W.A. Counseling, peak experiences and the human encounter with death: an empirical study of the efficacy of dpt-assisted counseling in enhancing the quality of life of persons with terminal cancer and their closest family members (Doctoral dissertation, The Catholic University of America, 1975). Dissertation Abstracts International, 1975, 36, 1314A. (University Microfilms No. 75-18, 531)

9177. Rievman, E.B. The cryonics society: a study of variant behavior among immortalists (Doctoral dissertation, Florida Atlantic University, 1976). Dissertation Abstracts International, 1978, 38, 4385A. (University Microfilms No. 77-28, 783)

9178. Robinson, R.A. The development of a concept of death in selected groups of Mexican-American and Anglo-American children (Doctoral dissertation, California School of Professional Psychology, San Diego, 1976). Dissertation Abstracts International, 1978, 38, 4478B. (University Microfilms No. 77-32, 510)

9179. Ross, C.W. Death concerns and response to dying patient statements (Doctoral dissertation, University of Missouri-Columbia, 1975). Dissertation Abstracts International, 1976), 37, 1624-1625B. (University Microfilms No. 76-21, 969)

9180. Roth, S.M. Attitudes toward death across the life span (Doctoral dissertation, West Virginia University, 1977). Dissertation Abstracts International, 1978, 38, 3858B. (University Microfilms No. 77-32, 097)

9181. Rubin, S. Bereavement and vulnerability: a study of mothers of sudden infant death syndrome children (Doctoral dissertation, Boston University Graduate School, 1977). Dissertation Abstracts International, 1977, 38, 1902-1903B. (University Microfilms No. 77-21, 614)

9182. Ruby, T. Ridigity in a risk-taking task among serious suicide attempters and non-suicidal psychiatric patients (Doctoral dissertation, University of Missouri-Columbia, 1973). Dissertation Abstracts International, 1974, 35, 1062B. (University Microfilms No. 74-18, 627)

9183. Rutstein, E.H. The effects of aggressive stimulation on suicidal patients: an experimental study of the psychoanalytic theory of suicide (Doctoral dissertation, New York University, 1970). Dissertation Abstracts International, 1971, 31, 7611B. (University Microfilms No. 71-15, 424)

9184. Salter, D. Personality differences between suicidal and non-suicidal blacks: an exploratory study (Doctoral dissertation, Adelphi University, 1977). Dissertation Abstracts International, 1978, 38, 3473B. (University Microfilms No. 77-30, 034)

9185. Salzberg, N. The development of a composite criminal suicide attempt scale (Doctoral dissertation, Utah State University, 1976). Dissertation Abstracts International, 1976, 37, 2527B. (University Microfilms No. 76-25, 630)

9186. Sanders, C.M. Typologies and symptoms of adult bereavement (Doctoral dissertation, University of Southern Florida, 1977). Dissertation Abstracts International, 1978, 38, 3372B. (University Microfilms No. 21, 930)

9187. Schor, A.G. Acute grief in adulthood: toward a cognitive model of normal pathological mourning (Doctoral dissertation, University of Rhode Island, 1974). Dissertation Abstracts International, 1974, 35, 2447B. (University Microfilms No. 74-24, 698)

9188. Schwartzburd, L. Reliability and validity of the timed multiple response method of administering the Rosenzweig picture-frustration study (Doctoral dissertation, The University of Oklahoma, 1971). Dissertation Abstracts International, 1972, 32, 4228B. (University Microfilms No. 72-3, 4345)

9189. Selvey, C.L. Concerns about death in relation to sex, dependency, guilt about hostility, and feelings of powerlessness (Doctoral dissertation, Columbia University, 1970). Dissertation Abstracts International, 1971, 31, 5641B. (University Microfilms No. 71-6, 254)

9190. Shady, G.A. Death anxiety and ab therapeutic styles as factors in helping patients with different coping styles accept life-threatening illness (Doctoral dissertation, The University of Manitoba (Canada), 1977). Dissertation Abstracts International, 1977, 38, 916-917B. (University Microfilms No. N/A)

9191. Sharon, I. A study of self-concept among suicide attempters (Doctoral dissertation, United States International University, 1975). Dissertation Abstracts International, 1975, 36, 2453-2454B. (University Microfilms No. 75-25, 973)

9192. Shearer, R.E. Religious belief and attitudes toward death (Doctoral dissertation, Fuller Theological Seminary Graduate School of Psychology, 1972). Dissertation Abstracts International, 1973, 33, 3292-3293B. (University Microfilms No. 72-31, 653)

9193. Sheehy, D.P. Rules for dying: a study of alienation and patient-spouse role expectations during terminal illness (Doctoral dissertation, Yale University, 1972). Dissertation Abstracts International, 1973, 33, 3777A. (University Microfilms No. 73-11)

9194. Shephard, C.S. The effect of group counseling on death anxiety in children with cancer (Doctoral dissertation, University of Miami, 1975). Dissertation Abstracts International, 1975, 36, 2723-2724A. (University Microfilms No. 75-25, 426)

9195. Sirvis, B. Death and dying: an instructional module for special educators (Doctoral dissertation, Columbia University Teachers College, 1976). Dissertation Abstracts International, 1976, 37, 1501A. (University Microfilms No. 76-21, 039)

9196. Slaikeu, K.A. Telephone referral calls to a suicide prevention and crisis service: an investigation of caller-therapist interaction in the initial call and follow-up of callers (Doctoral dissertation, State University of New York at Buffalo, 1973). Dissertation Abstracts International, 1974, 34, 4677B. (University Microfilms No. 74-4, 448)

9197. Skidmore, S.L. Case studies of personality characteristics of young adult terminal cancer patients (Doctoral dissertation, United States International University, 1975). Dissertation Abstracts International, 1975, 36, 3072B. (University Microfilms No. 75-29, 415)

9198. Smith, V.A. Perceived value deprivation as a predictor of self-destructive behavior (Doctoral dissertation, United States International University, 1975). Dissertation Abstracts International, 1975, 36, 1419B. (University Microfilms No. 75-19, 137)

9199. Smith, W.J. The desolation of Dido: patterns of depression and death anxiety in the adjustment and adaptation behaviors of a sample of variably-aged widows (Doctoral dissertation, Boston University Graduate School, 1975). Dissertation Abstracts International, 1975, 36, 1933B. (Universtiy Microfilms No. 75-21, 16)

9200. Spinetta, J.J. Death anxiety in lukemic children (Doctoral dissertation, University of Southern California, 1972). Dissertation Abstracts International, 1972, 33, 1807-1808B. (University Microfilms No. 72-26, 056)

9201. Steele, D.W. Effects of death affect communication training (Doctoral dissertation, The University of Wisconsin-Madison, 1976). Dissertation Abstracts International, 1977, 37, 3868B. (University Microfilms No. 76-25, 585)

9202. Steinkerchner, R.E. Empirical analysis of suicidal potential among dialysis patients (Doctoral dissertation, George Peabody College for Teachers, 1974). Dissertation Abstracts International, 1975, 36, 1934B. (University Microfilms No. 75-21, 276)

9203. Stewart-Hyerstay, B.J. An exploratory study of the expressed and inferred concerns of persons facing a life-threatening illness, particularly cancer (Doctoral dissertation, University of Oregon, 1974). Dissertation Abstracts International, 1975, 35, 6082-6083B. (University Microfilms No. 75-12, 539)

9204. Stiefel, A.D. Relationships between level of maturity and projected patterns of bereavement ministry (Doctoral dissertation, Boston University Graduate School, 1975). Dissertation Abstracts International, 1975, 35, 4197-4198B. (University Microfilms No. 75-19)

9205. Sutton, W.D. Affiliative behavior in the interpersonal relationships of persons prone to suicide (Doctoral dissertation, California School of Professional Psychology, Los Angeles, 1973). Dissertation Abstracts International, 1974, 34, 5212B. (University Microfilms No. 74-7, 942)

9206. Swain, H.L. The concept of death in children (Doctoral dissertation, Marquette University, 1975). Dissertation Abstracts International, 1976, 37, 898-899A. (University Microfilms No. 76-16, 880)

9207. Tapper, B.J. A behavioral assessment of the reinforcement contingencies associated with the occurrence of suicidal behaviors (Doctoral dissertation, University of Southern California, 1975). Dissertation Abstracts International, 1975, 36, 1462B. (University Microfilms No. 19, 040).

9208. Taylor, D.A. An exploration of the adaptive and defensive functions served by the adult conception of death and their relation to early object loss (Doctoral dissertation, Rutgers University, The State University of New Jersey, 1976). Dissertation Abstracts International, 1977, 37, 5382B. (University Microfilms No. 77-7, 287)

9209. Thauberger, P.C. The avoidance of ontological confrontation: an empirical exploration of the avoidance/confrontation of non-being (Doctoral dissertation, The University of Regina (Canada), 1974). Dissertation Abstracts International, 1975, 35, 5654B. (University Microfilms No. N/A)

9210. Thomas, J.M. An examination of psychological differences among groups of critically ill hospitalized patients (Doctoral dissertation, Oklahoma State University, 1973). Dissertation Abstracts International, 1974, 34, 5212-5213B. (University Microfilms No. 74-8, 131)

9211. Vigderhous, G. Socio-demographic determinants of suicide and homicide: a multivariate cross-cultural investigation (Doctoral dissertation, University of Illinois at Urbana-Champaign, 1975). _Dissertation Abstracts International_, 1975, 36, 3154-3155A. (University Microfilms No. 75-24, 424)

9212. Walker, C. Effect of group psychotherapy on bereavement with spouses of dying cancer patients (Doctoral dissertation, California School of Professional Psychology, Los Angeles, 1977). _Dissertation Abstracts International_, 1978, 38, 5049B. (University Microfilms No. 78-2, 849)

9213. Walker, D.R. A study of the characteristics of individuals treated for attempted suicide in six Utah hospital emergency rooms during 1975 (Doctoral dissertation, Brigham Young University, 1976). _Dissertation Abstracts International_, 1977, 37, 4710B. (University Microfilms No. 77-4, 858)

9214. Wallace, S.H. Attitudes of college students toward death (Doctoral dissertation, Claremont Graduate School, 1976). _Dissertation Abstracts International_, 1976, 37, 208-209A. (University Microfilms No. 76-16, 641)

9215. Walch, S.M. Adolescent attempted suicide: analysis of the differences in male and female suicidal behavior (Doctoral dissertation, California School of Professional Psychology, San Francisco, 1977). _Dissertation Abstracts International_, 1977, 38, 2892-2893B. (University Microfilms No. 77-27, 616)

9216. Walworth, J.H. Conceptions of death and dying in personal poetry (Doctoral dissertation, California School of Professional Psychology, San Francisco, 1972). _Dissertation Abstracts International_, 1973, 33, 3327B. (University Microfilms No. 72-33, 289)

9217. Wells, J.C. An experimental study of the assignment of responsibility for unintentioned, subintentioned, and intentioned death. (Doctoral dissertation, The George Washington University, 1970). _Dissertation Abstracts International_, 1970, 31, 2294-2295B. (University Microfilms No. 70-19, 582)

9218. Welu, T.C. Evaluation of a special program for suicide attempters (Doctoral dissertation, University of PIttsburgh, 1973). _Dissertation Abstracts International_, 1973, 34, 1171B. (University Microfilms No. 73-21, 341)

9219. Wesch, J.E. Self-actualization and the fear of death (Doctoral dissertation, University of Tennessee, 1970). _Dissertation Abstracts International_, 1971, 31, 6270-6271B. (University Microfilms No. 71-7, 692)

9220. Wetzel, R.D. Suicide intent, affect and cognitive style (Doctoral dissertation, St. Louis University, 1974). Dissertation Abstracts International, 1975, 36, 3080B. (University Microfilms No. 75-26, 341)

9221. Wheeler, A.L. The dying person: a deviant in the medical subculture (Doctoral dissertation, Mississippi State University, 1972). Dissertation Abstracts International, 1973, 33, 7051A. (University Microfilms No. 73-13, 620)

9222. White, E.A. A description of kindergarten through fourth grade students' conception of death (Doctoral dissertation, Oklahoma State University, 1972). Dissertation Abstracts International, 1977, 37, 5721A. (University Microfilms No. 77-5, 208)

9223. White, R.S. The effects of specialized group techniques upon the social isolation and depression of suicidal persons (Doctoral dissertation, California School of Professional Psychology, Los Angeles, 1976). Dissertation Abstracts International, 1977, 37, 4714-4715B. (University Microfilms No. 77-6, 317)

9224. Whittemore, K. Role failure and suicide: a sociological analysis of completed and attempted suicides in Los Angeles (Doctoral dissertation, Emory University, 1971). Dissertation Abstracts International, 1972, 32, 4135A. (University Microfilms No. 72-3, 046)

9225. Wilson, K.E. Suicide risk, self-injury risk, and expected intentionality for a population and its component sub-populations (Doctoral dissertaion, The University of Florida, 1976). Dissertation Abstracts International, 1977, 37, 5387B. (University Microfilms No. 77-6, 915)

9226. Windsor, J.C. An analysis of child rearing attitudes of the parents of a group of adolescents who attempted suicide (Doctoral dissertation, University of Virginia, 1972). Dissertation Abstracts International, 1972, 1032A. (University Microfilms No. 72-23, 455)

9227. Wulf, V.C. Parent death in childhood and later psychological adjustment (Doctoral dissertation, Michigan State University, 1976). Dissertation Abstracts International, 1977, 37, 6357-6358B. (University Microfilms No. 77-11, 738)

9228. Zeitlin, S.J. The effect of recent father death on adolescent identity formation (Doctoral dissertation, Harvard University, 1975). Dissertation Abstracts International, 1976, 36, 4716B. (University Microfilms No. 76-6, 596)

9229. Zuehlke, T.E. Psychotherapy with terminally ill patients (Doctoral dissertation, University of South Dakota, 1975). Dissertation Abstracts International, 1976, 36, 4188-4189B. (University Microfilms No. 76-2, 395)

9230. Zweig, A.R. Children's attitudes toward death (Doctoral dissertation, Northwestern University, 1976). Dissertation Abstracts International, 1977, 37, 4249-4250A. (University Microfilms No. 77-1, 393)

INDEX

The numbers following each entry correspond to the items numbered in the 9000 series immediately preceeding this index.